WHAT PEOPLE ARE SAYING ABOUT

DISCOVERING THE LIFE PLAN

A fascinating, informative and inspiring book, drawn from rich personal experience as well as from experience as a past-life regression therapist. It offers the welcome perspective of past lives and how these may impact our lives in the present, shedding light on issues that people find difficult and perplexing and offering insights and exercises to orient them on their present life path with trust and confidence. An outstanding synthesis.

Anne Baring, Jungian analyst, co-author of *The Myth of the Goddess* and author of the *Dream of the Cosmos: who are we and why are we here?* (2012). website: www.annebaring.com

A very interesting look at the karmic patterns influencing each stage of our life cycle. Teeming with cases, quotes and fascinating information. Highly recommended.

Roger J. Woolger, Ph.D, Jungian Psychoanalyst, renowned author and founder of Deep Memory Process therapy. Author of *Other Lives, Other Selves*.

Discovering the Life Plan is overflowing with keen insight and inspiring wisdom. With great compassion, Ann Merivale has probed deeply into and beautifully illuminated this mysterious thing we call "life." If you have questions – and who among us does not? – there are answers within these pages.

Robert Schwartz, author of *Your Soul's Plan: Discovering the Real Meaning of the Life You Planned Before You Were Born* (www.yoursoulsplan.com)

T03Ø6784

Discovering the Life Plan

Eleven Steps to Your Destiny

Discovering the Life Plan

Eleven Steps to Your Destiny

Ann Merivale

BOOKS

Winchester, UK
Washington, USA

First published by Sixth Books, 2012
Sixth Books is an imprint of John Hunt Publishing Ltd., Laurel House, Station Approach,
Alresford, Hants, SO24 9JH, UK
office1@jhpbooks.net
www.johnhuntpublishing.com
www.6th-books.com

For distributor details and how to order please visit the 'Ordering' section on our website.

Text copyright: Ann Merivale 2010

ISBN: 978 1 84694 821 3

A CIP catalogue record for this book is available from the British Library.

Design: Stuart Davies

Printed and bound by CPI Group (UK) Ltd., Croydon, CR0 4YY
Printed in the USA by Edwards Brothers Malloy

We operate a distinctive and ethical publishing philosophy in all
areas of our business, from our global network of authors to
production and worldwide distribution.

CONTENTS

INTRODUCTION – 2012 and All That!   1

CHAPTER ONE - Preparation of the Life Plan   8

CHAPTER TWO – The Coming Down   36

CHAPTER THREE – The First Seven Years   64

CHAPTER FOUR – Seven to Eighteen – The Age of
    Temptation   88

CHAPTER FIVE – Eighteen to Twenty-Seven – Karmic
    Relationships   116

CHAPTER SIX – Twenty-Seven to Thirty-Six –
    Making our Mark   145

CHAPTER SEVEN – Thirty-Six to Forty-Eight –
    The Mid-Life Crisis   173

CHAPTER EIGHT – Forty-Eight to Fifty Six –
    The Search for Spiritual Maturity   203

CHAPTER NINE – The Last Lap   231

CHAPTER TEN – Death   271

CHAPTER ELEVEN – The Afterlife   306

BIBLIOGRAPHY   340

COVER ILLUSTRATION = The Author's 'Life Seal' given her in a past life reading made by Aron Abrahamsen in 1992. It was Aron who told Ann that she had come this time "partly as a writer, to disseminate information on the spiritual life". The stained glass artist is Frans Wesselman of Church Stretton, Shropshire.

The Ankh (which according to Aron Abrahamsen should be at the top, but the artist had to have some free rein) is the Egyptian Symbol of Life and Ann (like most of us!) has had many lives in Egypt.

The silver chalice filled with a variety of different flowers represents what the author has inside herself to give to the world.

The golden key represents the Love of God, which is the key to all difficulties.

The well-worn, three-volume work entitled 'Practice and Wisdom' represents Ann's knowledge accumulated over very many lifetimes.

The word 'Commitment' on the bottom of the seven steps was given to Ann by Aron, who told her to find the other six in meditation. Seven is the spiritual number, and the other six words are 'Truth', 'Perseverance', 'Patience', 'Sacrifice', 'Generosity' and 'Faith' – all very important when we are trying to fulfil our Life Plan.

DEDICATION

To my grandchildren and all their generation – for their part in
bringing into being the Better World for which we are all
yearning.

ACKNOWLEDGEMENTS

My debts for this book are so large and so many that I find it difficult to single out the most important people to whom thanks are owed. I must begin, however, by explaining that it would not have happened without the well-known clairvoyant Lilla Bek. She and I got together for a day way back in 1995 in order to plan a book written by myself but consisting partly of her input. The plan that emerged from that day was largely Lilla's, but she then found herself unable to give any more time to it. I held on to this plan for a long time while waiting for an alternative clairvoyant to appear. Eventually friends persuaded me that, since it was clearly a book that needed to be written, I had no alternative but to write it myself. So thank you, Lilla, and I hope that you are not too disapproving of my efforts! A lot can happen in fifteen or more years, and so I have done my best to update our original plan accordingly.

It goes without saying that I am grateful to all the contributors – not only for providing their stories but also for vetting what I wrote and making useful and important corrections (they know who they are and their names or pseudonyms are all in the book).

A huge THANK YOU to my daughter Alice, who made use of her professional expertise as an editor to offer help at an early stage, and also to my husband David, who read through large sections and gave me further editorial advice.

It is also important in such a work to express appreciation of my spirit guides – particularly Maria, my main guide for this lifetime and also my general writing guide, and Elahim, who has recently shown himself as my guide for this particular book. And as always, last but not least, I offer thanks to my beloved 'guru', the avatar of our age, Sathya Sai Baba.

INTRODUCTION

2012 AND ALL THAT!

For every human there is a quest to find to find the answer to why I am here, who am I, where did I come from, where am I going. For me that became the most important thing in my life. Everything else is secondary.
George Harrison of The Beatles

Is this promised 'Golden Age' **really** imminent, are you wondering? 2010 saw – to mention but a few – the worst oil spills in history (the one in China has been given very little press coverage!), unprecedented flooding in Pakistan, continuing tension in the Middle East, more or less daily killings in Afghanistan, an American pastor who considers himself a Christian threatening to burn copies of the Koran, five per cent of Americans accusing their President of being a Muslim (as though that were a crime even if it were true!), and the formation of a coalition government in Britain that thinks the best way to deal with the deficit is by increasing hardship to the poor. As I write December 21st, 2012 – a particularly important date on account of being (as Diana Cooper explains in *2012 and BEYOND*[1]) the end of both a 26,000 year astronomical period as well as a 260,000 year one – is only twenty-seven months away and things in the world look like getting even worse before they can begin to get better.*

For yes, prophets of the New Age, channels and clairvoyants have for long predicted, and are continuing to predict, massive improvements as our beautiful Earth evolves into the fifth dimension, but for 'more ordinary' people such as myself, these improvements often appear to be elusive. The fact that yet more

I

change is inevitable may seem undeniable, but perhaps the biggest question is: "What can I, a fairly ordinary person, do about it? How are we and our families to survive any further upheavals that may be on their way?"

Personally I have no reason to doubt that the Mayans, who were great astronomers with many other talents besides, had good reasons for naming December 21st, 2012, as the end of an era, but whether the change will be a sudden, overnight one, instantly visible to all, is another matter. I prefer to leave that to the experts and to wait and see (Diana Cooper names 2032 as the first year of noticeable improvement.) What does concern me, and is one of my reasons for writing this book, is how we can best react to and cope with the changes to our world from which none of us can escape.

Firstly, one very simple thing, and one that I try (if not always successfully!) to do all the time is to focus on the positive rather than being forever caught up in the negativity that our media so love to foster or even exaggerate. *Positive News*, the only newspaper that I really like reading, is unfortunately only a quarterly, but it is spreading rapidly into more and more countries and I always find its Youth section particularly encouraging. Some of the achievements of really young people are truly amazing and do a lot to make it easier to believe that a better world is truly on the way.

Secondly, if we really want to 'heal the world', there is surely no better place to start than with ourselves. In fact I think that most therapists and healers would go further than that by saying that the only person one really <u>can</u> heal is oneself. And when I use the word 'healing' I am talking more of spiritual than physical healing (some physical ailments or disabilities are part of our karma or learning), and for me 'spiritual healing' must inevitably include care for others and the planet. So obviously, if everyone were to heal him or herself, then the entire world would be healed too.

Many answers to the question "How can I heal myself?" could well be given, and my years of working as a Deep Memory Process therapist have given me the privilege of witnessing many varying solutions that people have found. I am not proposing any sort of 'foolproof path', but rather simply offering one suggestion – a suggestion that I myself happen to have found to be invaluable. That is, as the title of this book suggests, discovering your own place in the world, precisely what you have come for this time round, and hanging on to that even through times of adversity or sadness. For yes, as a Deep Memory Process therapist who has been able to help both myself and others by finding the root of present-day problems in previous lives, I am of the belief that we all have countless numbers of lives and that each time we incarnate it is with a different purpose (or purposes) and with the aim of learning different things, until we are finally able to achieve a fully rounded personality that can continue its evolution on higher planes.

For me karma, which is the Sanskrit word for "action" and simply means the law of cause and effect, is the only possible answer to the question as to why some should be born into favorable circumstances while others have to spend their entire lives in dire poverty. Following on from that, I would suggest that it was hunger for power that caused the Council of Constantinople in 553 to suppress the doctrine of reincarnation. (Theodora, the wife of the Emperor Justinian of Constantinople, did not like the idea of returning to Earth as anything other than an Empress!) Authors such as the Americans Dr. Ian Stevenson and Carol Bowman[2] have shown that many young children express memories of previous lives; and is it by pure chance that people in so many different cultures all over the world have for so many millennia believed that just one life was insufficient for completing all our learning?

Many years of study and reflection on these sorts of questions have led me to the firm conviction that nothing happens without good reason, and that a broad outline of our life is indeed planned beforehand. My work as a Deep Memory Process (DMP) therapist not only confirms this all the time, but also often brings fascinating answers to both my own and my clients' questions, as well as solutions to our problems. However, it was only some time after first thinking that I had begun to get to grips with the intricate workings of the concept of karma that I gradually realized how easy it was for some people to discover their Life Plan, how very, very difficult for others. From that realization it seemed a logical step to look at life in phases. All cultures make divisions in this way, even though their dividing lines are not all identical.

So, in order to look at life in the most comprehensive way possible, I have gone through it in the stages suggested by Lilla Bek, using illustrations from my personal experience or that of my clients, friends, or acquaintances. For many of the problems and issues that have been faced by my characters may also be familiar to many of my readers in their own lives. Equally, ways that emerge in the pages of this book for tackling some of these problems could also be of help to others.

These stages of life, which include most importantly both the pre-incarnation planning stage and – since death is by no means the end – a description of possible post-death scenarios, have been made to fall neatly into the number Eleven. In mathematics Eleven is a prime number, and in the form of astrology known as numerology it is regarded as a Master Number. According to Dee Feeny[3], Number Eleven possesses "the qualities of intuition, patience, honesty, sensitivity, and spirituality, and is idealistic". She also says that one can turn to people whose numerological number is Eleven for teaching and inspiration, and "be uplifted by the experience".

So you will see that my eleven chapters go through life stage by stage, sometimes touching on the psychological aspects of each stage and sometimes on the astrological. (I am neither a psychologist nor an astrologer, but my seventy years on this Earth have given me the privilege of having been able to cover a certain amount of reading and also to make the acquaintance of many wonderful and knowledgeable people.) Each stage of life has many aspects besides the two just mentioned, and under-standing these, and the reasons for them, can help us all on our 'Eleven Step Journey'.

Many readers of my first book[4], the aim of which was to demonstrate how Deep Memory Process therapy works in practice, have commented that they found the exercises at the end of each section particularly useful. So I have decided to include a few exercises at the end of each of the chapters in this book. You might ask "how can one do an exercise for a stage of life that is now past?", but firstly many of you may be parents who naturally want to do the best for your children, and secondly it is often useful to look back and think about what you have learned from past events. Pain is frequently our greatest teacher! In any case the exercises are not compulsory; this book is not part of an examination course and I leave it up to you to decide which if any of them may be useful to you personally.

Where this book may differ from any other study of the different phases of existence is in my aim of looking at life from a spiritual perspective. So, if you deny the existence of the spirit, you might as well put it straight back on to the shelf and save your money! To me it is crystal clear, firstly that we need numerous incarnations for our learning, and secondly that we come in each time with a certain purpose. Could Nelson Mandela have survived twenty-seven years of imprisonment under a horrendously cruel regime if he were not a highly evolved soul who had developed immense strength of character over countless incarnations and chosen to come to Earth this time with a blueprint destined to have a huge impact on the whole world?

When, many years ago, I was first seeking a publisher for a book on twin-soul relationships[5], a publisher in Australia wanted it if and only if I cut out the personal stories and gave simply the theory. This I could not do! I would not have bothered to train as a therapist if it were not for the fact that I find people endlessly fascinating; and abstraction and generalization are surely enhanced by illustrations from real life. So I am grateful to my clients and friends who have so willingly permitted me to share with you their, often extremely painful, experiences. But others' experiences are most useful when related to our own. If reading this book encourages you to look for or at your own purpose in life, its aim will have been achieved.

Notes

1   *2012 AND BEYOND – An invitation to meet the challenges and opportunities ahead*, Diana Cooper, Findhorn Press, Scotland, 2009.

2   See *Twenty Cases Suggestive of Reincarnation*, Ian Stevenson, 1988, and *CHILDREN'S PAST LIVES – An intriguing account of children's past life memories*, Carol Bowman, Bantam, USA, 1997.

3   www.greatdreams.com/eleven/num11.htm

4   *KARMIC RELEASE – Journeying Back to the Self*, Ann Merivale, Sai Towers Publications, India, 2006.

5   This book was ultimately published in 2009 by Llewellyn Worldwide, USA, as *SOULS UNITED – The Power of Divine Connection*, Ann Merivale.

*Now, as we go to press in 2011, we all have in our minds the unprecedented flooding in Australia followed by the cyclone in Queensland, uprisings in the Middle East, and the terrible earthquake in Christchurch, almost immediately superseded by the even worse one in Japan which is also causing a nuclear disaster. On a recent round-the-world trip with my husband, I flew over the flooded parts of Queensland, having left Cairns shortly before it was hit by the cyclone, and a couple of weeks later we changed planes in Christchurch. Then, on the way home, I had a wonderful swim at Waikiki Beach, where not long after people were stricken with fear by the massive wave that reached there in the wake of the Japanese tsunami. All these 'narrow escapes' reinforce my belief in the Life Plan and that there are super-natural forces guiding us to where we need to be at any given moment. I know that my work here is not yet complete and that my angels are consequently keeping me safe, at least for the time being. So thank you!

CHAPTER ONE

PREPARATION OF THE LIFE PLAN

You do not see the foundations of a multi-storeyed skyscraper. Can you, therefore, argue that it simply sits on the ground? The foundations of this life are laid deep in the past, in lives already lived by you. This structure has been shaped by the ground plan of those lives. The unseen decides the bends and the ends, the number of floors, the height and weight.
Sathya Sai Speaks, Vol. 9[1]

I should like to begin by elaborating a little on my own position on questions of religion and spirituality. I am not going to attempt to argue with the great scientist Stephen Hawking, because if you agreed with his thesis that the universe could well have been started without a Creator, it seems unlikely that you would have bothered to pick up this book.

I was brought up Catholic and have always believed in God, but my concept of God has changed radically over the years. As a child who was given little love and was consequently unable to see myself as lovable, I suppose my first image was something akin to the Old Testament one of a vengeful masculine figure who instilled fear and demanded obedience. Later, during my very actively anti-racist days, I flouted a badge which proclaimed "I saw God and She was black". I am still somewhat attached both to that badge and to the Christian teaching that God dwells inside all of us, but more recently, following a great deal of reading around the subject, my view has changed from the notion of God being the indweller of everything to that of everything being God, i.e. that there is nothing that is not God.

To most Westerners this notion may still seem difficult and

new, but in India it was already being taught thousands of years before the birth of Christianity. If you have not already done so, I strongly recommend you to read Neale Donald Walsch's *Conversations with God*[2] and also some or all of the many writings on the great twentieth-century American prophet Edgar Cayce[3]. Books such as these are an excellent introduction to the Indian concept of *advaita* (non-duality) – the above statement that everything is God – and they also help enormously to make this crazy world seem less illogical.

The first idea to grasp is that in the very beginning, when there was only God, God decided to divide Him/Herself into countless parts, firstly for companionship and secondly for experience. Speaking to Neale Donald Walsch, God puts it thus: "My divine purpose in dividing Me was to create sufficient parts of Me that I could **know Myself experientially**. There is only one way for the Creator to know Itself experientially as the Creator, and that is to create. And so I gave to each of the countless parts of Me (to all of My spirit children) the same power to create which I have as the whole." (Stephen Hawking will be in for something of a shock when he eventually discovers not only that he can never die but also that he himself is just as much God as anyone else!)

Walsch's paragraph continues "So each of us is part of that original whole, just as is each animal, each bird, each tree or plant and even each stone. The only difference is in our stages of evolution from the stone, because some of us have lingered along the way more than others have." This ties in with the Hindu view that we have all evolved through every form of life: mineral to vegetable, to animal to human. Reincarnationists differ in opinion as to whether, once having become human, we ever return to the animal kingdom, but in any case animals such as dogs or dolphins are often regarded as being in some ways superior to many human beings!

This huge journey involves firstly learning and adventure,

and secondly, now that we have come such a long way, the rediscovery of our destination. Is it surprising that over so many eons we have got lost and forgotten what that is? Continuing with my theme of Hindu philosophy, we are at present coming to the end of the *Kali Yuga*, which is the Age when all the negativity in the world is surfacing in order for the cleansing that is necessary for the dawning of the Aquarian, or Golden, Age to take place. And Hindu philosophy maintains too that, whenever humanity has got itself into a particularly bad mess, an *avatar* (divine incarnation) descends to help us back on to the right track. In the West the term 'divine incarnation' is generally used only for Jesus, but is it logical to say that God could only ever incarnate once? Long before Jesus, Rama came, Krishna came, Buddha and others came and, now that the world is in such very great need, we are privileged to have living among us several avatars as well as many enlightened beings and teachers. Readers of my previous two books[4] will appreciate that I myself am now a follower of the Indian avatar Sathya Sai Baba (whom millions believe to be the most powerful divine incarnation ever), but many of you will also be aware of other Indian avatars, such as Mother Meera in Germany and Amma (the hugging one!), whose main ashram is in India but who also travels widely. The purpose of avatars, divine incarnations or other enlightened beings such as Jesus, is to remind us where we have come from and that we are supposed to be heading back there. Unlike most of us, Jesus knew that he was God. Many Christians believe his statement that "I and the Father are one", but ignore the fact that he also said "Ye are gods".

When the baby is first born, it makes no distinction between itself and its mother; it is unable to recognize any difference between itself and the rest of the world. In other words, 'ego' has to be learnt. And I am sure you will agree that, over the many eons during which we human beings have been incarnating, ego has been learnt much too well. So basically what the Great

Masters have always taught is that actually the tiny baby has got it right! Our task, our purpose during our lifetimes on Earth (and how could a single lifetime be sufficient for learning all that we would like and need?) is to re-remember that all is one, that nothing is separate from God. Sai Baba puts it thus: "A bubble is born on water, from water and merges in water. Man is born in God and merges in God. This is the lesson India has been teaching her children as well as all men everywhere for centuries. She gave the message of Divinity to humanity[5]." So, once we have again got this clear in our minds, we shall at last be able to attain *Moksha* or Liberation – that final re-merging with the Source which is the only true bliss, known in Buddhism as *Nirvana*.

When you study the question of reincarnation, you soon discover the widespread belief that for most of us our first human life on Earth was a very long time ago, and that since then we have got trapped in the perpetual cycle of *samsara*. *Samsara*, variously translated as 'passage' or 'worldly life', is the word used in Buddhism for the whole cycle of lives – in all realms, not just those on Earth – and it is symbolized by the picture of the wheel. It is the wheel that turns relentlessly, bringing us back to Earth again over and over, giving us the opportunity to pay some of the debts we have incurred in previous lives, but forcing us through our intransigence simultaneously to create new ones; allowing us to learn new lessons, but at the same time leaving us all too frequently repeating the same mistakes. For me the evidence for all this is so great[6] that I make no apology for basing this book on these assumptions.

One of the books that has touched me the most since I embarked on my present path of learning is Dolores Cannon's *Jesus and the Essenes*[7]. Dolores Cannon is not so much a regression <u>therapist</u> as a researcher who makes use of regression for obtaining her material, and, as a result of her activities in this field, she has a number of very interesting books to her name.

The hypnotic subject of this particular book was a young girl who turned out to have had a past life as a teacher of Jesus when he was young and living with the Essene community. I personally find the story not only totally convincing but extremely informative, and the picture of Jesus that the book describes adds greatly to the one given by the New Testament. Suddi – the name of this teacher that came through in the numerous sessions – portrays Jesus (hardly surprisingly!) as a young man of exceptional wisdom and knowledge, and one who, like Suddi himself, takes reincarnation for granted. Dolores Cannon taped all the regressions she did, and one of the parts of this book that I enjoyed the most was towards the end, when Suddi quotes what Jesus said about our cycle of lives. He describes how Jesus observed nature and drew parallels from that – for instance a plant that puts down roots from which new offspring plants can grow – but I would like to make one quotation in full:

"Another example he came by from watching the water. He pointed out how a wave could come in from the sea and lap up on the shore, and pick up a bit of debris. And when this bit of debris is put back down it's almost at the same place as it was before, but moved over slightly. And so the piece of debris will gradually travel down the shore being picked up and placed back down by the waves. He said that this is like your cycle of lives. You go through your cycle of life, starting at one point and then when you die, it's like being picked up by the wave and then re-deposited in a life. Your spirit is re-deposited and it's a little bit further along the way of where you're meaning to go." In reply Dolores made the comment that this shows how slowly it happens, to which Suddi replied "Yes, it is a very slow process. And one must have patience and work on it diligently." So we need not despair if our own progress seems to be slow: we are each no different from anyone else, and there is still plenty of time left – eternity in fact!

I think I have already made clear that my view is that a

particular life starts not in the womb, nor even immediately prior to conception, but some time before that, when a Plan is made for it in the realms of spirit. And as a Deep Memory Process (or regresssion) therapist, I see the 'end' not as the moment when the soul leaves the body, but after that, in higher realms, when the Life Review has been completed, the lessons understood, and a decision made about what was achieved and what still remains to be worked on. The section of the cycle that lies between any one ending and another beginning – known to the Tibetans as the *Bardo* – could equally well be discussed in either the first chapter of this book or the last, but I have decided to leave most of it until the final one, not only because of my personal preference for books which have happy endings, but also because in our society we tend to speak of the 'Afterlife' rather than the 'Beforelife', even though the latter would be equally logical.

No life is ever planned in very minute detail, but the evidence is that a broad outline is always made beforehand in the world of spirit. My research suggests that there is a great deal of variation in the extent of the planning that is done in advance, but that the cast of 'main characters' is normally decided upon prior to the soul's entry, as are its chief lessons, its personal target and, in the case of the more advanced, its global target. Unless we are very advanced indeed, the teachers and Masters help us with the major decisions, while we make the lesser ones ourselves. Negative and positive karma are both always important factors in the planning. Here it is important to note that karma has nothing at all to do with 'revenge' or any such concept; it is, as I stated above, simply the law of cause and effect. If you throw a stone into a pool, there will inevitably be ripples.

In the words of the poet John Donne, "No man is an island" and so, in planning each new lifetime, many factors must be taken into consideration besides the working out of individual karma. Let us begin by imagining the cosmos as an immense –

unutterably beautiful – jigsaw over which God – that is the main bit of God, which remains discarnate – has a great deal of control, but for pieces of which God requires our assistance. The chief difference between God's jigsaw and the much smaller ones that we might give our children for Christmas is that the former is never constant; it is ever growing in richness and complexity. The vast whole that God oversees has to contain, among other things, the blueprint of each planet, each one of which is under the direction of its own Masters, who are in turn answerable to God, from whom, like us, they originally came. For God, to quote the well-known English clairvoyant Edwin Courtenay, "knows everything but has experienced nothing", and that was His/Her reason for sending us off on our long journeys so many eons ago. Changing the jigsaw metaphor slightly, every experience we have adds to the richness of the Great Artist's tapestry.

A book such as this one will inevitably pose more questions than it can answer. Anyone who had all the answers would not still need to be here! So my question at this point concerns the extent of God's control. I used to think of God as something like a mother who bought her child a difficult jigsaw, which she left her to do on her own, but could complete for her if she were to get really stuck. One day, however, my friend and homeopath, Lawrence, asked me "if God were making a jigsaw with us all helping a bit, would God really bother to get involved in it if God knew exactly how it should be done?" In other words, just as life would be boring for us if we had all the answers, would not helping us through life be boring for God if God knew exactly what was going to happen?

Here we have the perennial problem of reconciling the concept of the omnipotence of God with the fact of His having given us free will. Is it blasphemous to suggest that perhaps our desire to believe in an omnipotent God is akin to a young child's belief in the omnipotence of his parents? Since our return to the Source is necessary for God to be completely whole once more, could it be that not only is everybody's contribution to the jigsaw equally important, but also that it **cannot** be completed until everyone's contribution has been finished? The consequence of this would surely be that in the meantime the 'main bit of God' was not actually completely omniscient about the end product.

One difficulty in attempting to look from the Earthly perspective at a procedure which is being carried out mainly on a higher level, is that as soon as we leave the Earth's plane we are outside both time and space. In fact, even my use of the word 'higher' is strictly speaking a misnomer. However, like all of us, I am at present trapped 'down here' (all be it of my own volition, though I sometimes find that hard to remember!), and am consequently also trapped in time. We must remember that Einstein showed that the time of an event is dependent upon the motion of the observer, and that time is also affected by matter and gravitational fields. People who have near-death or out-of-body experiences sometimes live what seems like hours, or even days, while only a few minutes pass on Earth.

When we set off on the Great Adventure into matter we realized that, for the experience to be as complete as possible, we each had to cover every aspect of it – male and female, rich and poor, black and white, saint and sinner...God is all Good, but how could we appreciate goodness if we had no experience of evil? Would pleasure have any real meaning if we did not know pain? (As The Prophet says, "The deeper that sorrow carves into your being, the more joy you can contain"[8].) The Great Tapestry is made up of countless individual tapestries, representing each individual life, and the beautiful silver and gold threads of joy show up best on a dark background of sorrow. We evolve initially through suffering, but the really good news is that we can learn eventually to evolve through joy. The Dalai Lama's statement that the purpose of life is to be happy is regarded by many people as rather amazing, yet he is echoing some of humanity's oldest scriptures. The Taittiriya Upanishad, for instance, says in III.6 "Beings here are born from bliss, when born they live by bliss, and into bliss, when departing, they enter."

The world would no doubt be more peaceful, but would probably be less interesting if we were all at the same level of evolution. The presence in society of souls who are old, young and in between adds to its diversity and helps us all to learn the lessons we need. In Peter Richelieu's book *A Soul's Journey*[9], his guide explains that during the first couple of hundred or so lifetimes that we had on Earth, most of us created more bad karma than good, and as we progress, this large 'overdraft' is paid off gradually. Occasionally we are permitted 'resting incarnations', in which we pay off few debts or none at all, but at the same time do not accrue any new ones. Then, as we evolve gradually to a state where we are able to create more good karma than bad, we select life circumstances which will enable us to pay off large chunks at a time. It is good to be able to appreciate this point when we meet people who appear to have the scales tipped very heavily against them. And karma is surely also the only way to explain how God can be totally just, which has been such a big problem for the Christian Churches ever since the suppression of belief in reincarnation.

Anyone who has studied spiritual matters at all may already be familiar with the notion that we are all not one but three, but there can nevertheless be no harm in recapping. One problem that I have come up against in my research is variations in vocabulary, and so I have had to decide upon my own use of words, with apologies to anyone who is accustomed to using them differently. In the beginning, after God had first split Herself into many parts for companionship, we were all just spirits. When the 'Great Adventure' had been decided upon, each spirit sent out two souls[10] (or, as some put it, one soul split in half), which clothed themselves repeatedly, firstly in subtle bodies, and secondly in physical bodies. At the end of each lifetime, when the physical body perishes, the soul sheds its subtle bodies in turn and then returns to its own spirit, which always remains in the highest realm, so that the new experiences the soul has gained can be absorbed into the spirit. Alternative terms for 'soul' and 'spirit' are 'lower self' and 'higher self', or in Sanskrit, *jiva* and *atma*. The words 'soul' and 'spirit' are sometimes used in reverse, but I prefer to refer to the Higher Self as the spirit because of the fact that it dwells in the spiritual realms.

The Higher Self plays an important role in the planning of each lifetime, and it acts as an overseer throughout its duration. The more attuned we are while on Earth to our Higher Selves (for which the best tool is meditation), the better will everything go for us. Sadly it can happen that people on Earth become so trapped in evil that they get cut off from their Higher Selves, and sometimes the damage can be so great that they fail to re-establish the connection even between incarnations. Fortunately, however, help is always available even for the most difficult cases.

Ultimately, when we have completed all our necessary incarnations, having learnt all our lessons and worked out all our karma, we will (as I explained in my book *SOULS UNITED – The Power of Divine Connection*[10]) firstly fuse with our twin soul and secondly become reabsorbed into our joint spirit. At that point, the soul, which is no more than the link between the spiritual and the physical, will cease to exist. The final stage (at least in the present cycle!), when individualism has been completely overcome and we have helped every last soul up the mountain, will be *Moksha* or *Nirvana* - the streaming of all the rivers into the Ocean which is God. Will this entail complete obliteration of our individuality? I do not think so. I myself like the idea – one which my reading has also led me to believe – of us each enriching the tapestry with our precious uniqueness, weaving into the whole, as Master Craftsmen and women, our own beautiful threads of varied experiences.

I am sure you could think of times in your life when you have felt guided by some sort of force more or less outside yourself. Well, during all of our lifetimes on Earth, each of us has, besides our Higher Self as a general overseer, firstly a guardian angel and secondly some spirit guides (normally two, three or even four in number). Clairvoyants tell me that we have each kept the same guardian angel from the very beginning, throughout every one of our lifetimes, and that it is he (or she?) who holds the 'map' of each life and has the job of ensuring that we do not take too many wrong turnings. Angels, often known as 'God's messengers', can be seen as extensions of the will of God, and they are no less active in the world today than they were in biblical times, whether or not people are willing to recognize their presence. Spirit guides, on the other hand, are no less human than anyone on Earth, and they are normally old friends from previous incarnations, who are not at present incarnate. Their tasks are more specialized than that of our guardian angel, and for this reason, though there will normally be one main guide who remains constant throughout each lifetime, the others will change according to the work we are doing.

When my involvement with spiritual things first began several years ago, I was always both amazed and mystified at how such things as Angel cards, Runes and so on worked. Each time that either I myself or, say, a Tarot reader, drew out a card for me, its appropriateness would leave me 'mind boggled'. Then one day it suddenly dawned! Since one's spirit (or alternatively one's guardian angel or guide) is not encased in flesh, it is no problem for him or her to read cards that are upside down, or to see inside a pack. This enables them to guide our choice even when we are not consciously aware of it.

The more evolved we become, the more control we have over each impending lifetime, and consequently the more active will be our participation in its planning. At the lowest end of the scale, all decisions for the incarnating soul are made by others who are more evolved, but even in these cases the general planning rules apply equally. A useful book on the subject of Life Plans has been published fairly recently, and I recommend it both to those who are skeptical about the concept and to those who would like to study it in greater depth. It is entitled *YOUR SOUL'S PLAN – Discovering the Real Meaning of the Life You Planned Before You Were Born*[11], and its American author, Robert Schwartz, did a great deal of research with people who had had very difficult lives, interviewing clairvoyants who were able to give information about their reasons for choosing the particular difficulties or traumata. I shall be making references to one or two of Schwartz's cases.

Though I do not doubt their existence, the civilizations of other planets are not the concern of this book (you can turn again to Neale Donald Walsch[2] for that); that of Earth is more than enough to deal with in a single volume. Edgar Cayce said that over the eons some souls had crossed over from one planet to another, but that the majority of those who were on Earth at the present time had done most of their evolution here. Anyone reading this book who senses that they have come from elsewhere (and I have in my life met one or two such people) will know that they chose to come to Earth for a reason, and so whatever I say will apply to them equally.

After the 'planetary' bit of the jigsaw has been done, one of the first things the Higher Self decides each time is which bits of negative karma are to be dealt with in the forthcoming life. There are times when we feel ready to pay off more debts than at others. But karma can of course be positive as well as negative. Just as those who seem to have everything stacked against them are likely to be paying off a great deal of negative karma, so are those people apparently born with a silver spoon in their mouth probably reaping the benefits of the good that they have done to others in the past.

Dr. Brian Weiss, the well-known American psychiatrist, became a regression therapist as a result of working with his client Catherine, who under hypnosis not only went sponta-neously into past lives that were relevant for her healing, but also channeled information directed at Weiss from Masters[12]. Here is a quotation from his book: "We have debts that must be paid. If we have not paid out these debts, then we must take them into another life...in order that they may be worked through. You progress by paying your debts. Some souls progress faster than others. If something interrupts your ability to pay that debt, you must return to the plane of recollection, and there you must wait until the soul you owe the debt has come to see you. And when you both can be returned to physical form at the same time, then you are allowed to return. But you determine when you are going back. You determine what must be done to pay that debt."

Once a decision has been taken about the pieces of karma to be dealt with, the next step is obviously to work out how this can best be accomplished. Someone who had spent a lifetime being cruel to animals could run an animal sanctuary or work volun-tarily for an organization like the Cats' Protection League. Someone (like myself!) who had plundered and killed as a Crusader could work, as I did for some years, for organizations helping the Third World. Someone who had murdered his parents simply because they were old and a nuisance could run a residential home for the elderly. And so on. On the positive side, someone who had learnt to give a lot of love would deserve to be born to loving parents and to make a very happy marriage. But on the other hand, as Robert Schwartz points out, we sometimes choose to learn what we need by working through the opposite of what we want. For instance: people who need to learn self-love sometimes achieve this by deliberately taking on the challenge of incarnating into an unloving family.

Another important decision for the new lifetime is geographical location. For instance, Europe or North America might be a more obvious choice for someone with a debt to the elderly than Africa or South America, which have a strong tradition for caring for them within the family. On the other hand, someone who had previously been racist and despised Africans, might choose to incarnate in Africa, or alternatively to be black in a country such as England, where racism is rampant. For the balancing of karma involves experiencing the suffering that we have inflicted on others.

The next decision – usually inextricably linked to the negative karma we plan to work out – must concern the lessons we are choosing to learn. A former client of mine whom I will call Doris, who had in the past repeatedly been the victim of abusive husbands, found out in a regression that she had chosen before coming in to her present life to learn to stand up to them. She did this by marrying in turn no less than three abusive men, and each time escaping from them. Through this painful process Doris has not only probably paid off several karmic debts, but has also firstly gained the strength to live on her own, and secondly become a healer.

The choice of sex can be a complex decision, since we are all basically androgynous. Apart from the fact that we all need first-hand experience of both sexes, just as we need experience of everything else in order to become fully rounded personalities, there appear to be no fixed rules. Some people seem to spend many more lifetimes as one sex, others to divide them more equally, but clearly the choice of sex will be an important factor once both karma and lessons have been decided upon. Someone who needs a lifetime devoted to work that requires considerable physical strength would be likely to be better off in a male body, whereas someone who needs to learn gentleness might choose a female one. On the other hand, we no doubt all need lifetimes in which we can learn to be gentle men (not at all the same thing as gentlemen!) or strong women.

Closely linked to our chosen items of karma will be the choice of family members and of all the people who will be the closest to us in a given incarnation. Karmic debts are accrued from a wide variety of things, from murder to petty theft. Another former client of mine is married to a man who, as her uncle, murdered her during the Irish Potato Famine. Fighting over food in such horrendous circumstances is understandable, but no soul can ever totally forgive itself for murder until retribution has been made, and that was no doubt James' reason for choosing Clare as his wife this time round.

So, close family members will often be people to whom we owe karmic debts, or who are paying debts to us, but we also return together with certain people over and over because of strong bonds of affection built up over many centuries. Some (or possibly all) of these can be described as 'soul mates', and, quoting Robert Schwartz's book again, it can even happen that someone will agree beforehand to take on the role of, say, abusive parent, purely out of love for a person who needs that particular lesson.

An interesting point here is that adopted children will obviously have to choose two sets of parents, but I am elaborating further on that point in another book, which is specifically on the subject of Adoption, Fostering and Step Families.

It can also happen – particularly in larger families such as the one into which I was born this time – that not all the siblings have close karmic links with one another. In my own case I believe that each of the six of us chose those particular parents for personal karmic reasons, and I have found quite a difficult karmic link with one of my siblings, but probably only my youngest sister was already an old friend of mine. She, on the other hand, has always been particularly close to one of our brothers, and it did not surprise her at all when she found out that they had been lovers in a previous life.

Another factor in the choice of family is hereditary patterns, for biology (in the form of genes) has its part to play besides the spiritual element. The heredity required will be linked both to the karmic paybacks decided upon and to one's life purpose.

Someone who needs to experience a particular illness, such as heart disease, may well choose parents who come from a line in which weak hearts are prevalent. Shared talents and weaknesses are both frequently apparent in families. Though there are always exceptions to be found, someone destined to be, for instance, a great composer, will almost invariably be born into a musical family. The 'nature or nurture' debate has not yet been fully resolved generally, but I am quite clear in my own mind that both have their roles to play. Parents who have always done their best to praise and encourage their children might well wonder what went wrong if, say, one of them turns out to be severely lacking in self-esteem. The answer to this is not that they have failed in any way, but simply that the soul concerned had an issue in that domain that (s)he wanted to work on and chose those particular parents because they would be sympathetic to it.

One of the reasons why we have so many incarnations is the need for balance. Someone who in one lifetime had been, for instance, a very rigid Christian and intolerant of people of other faiths, might choose to return another time as, say, a Buddhist, a Muslim, or even an atheist.

My friend Ann Evans, whose deceased husband and twin soul is a wonderful artist, and about whom I wrote in *SOULS UNITED*[10], believes that, in complete contrast to most of us, she comes to Earth only very rarely – to remind herself of how difficult it is being here. In her present life, besides being a sculptor and a poet, she is a healer, but she tells me that her normal work is in spirit, where she dwells in the mental realms. Those closest to Earth are known as the astral realms, while the mental or spiritual realms are the dwelling place of our Higher Selves. There is a very common belief that there are seven of each, that we progress through them in between incarnations, and that our starting point will depend upon the way in which we have led our most recent life. It is easy for the spiritually minded to skip the lower astral planes all together in between lifetimes. Ann says that her and her husband Ken's home is a place of light to which she can return very easily at any time. She describes it as somewhere where people are "really interested in development, progress and insight, but find it difficult to get enthusiastic about the more ordinary details of life. They are the sort of people who, when on Earth, forget to eat. Everything there is unlimited; anything is possible; there is no feeling of curtailment of ideas."

Ken's work, when he had first returned to the other side, consisted of helping people who had just died – especially those whose death was so sudden that they could not understand what had happened to them. He has more recently, as I mentioned in my book on Twinsoulship[10], moved on to much 'higher' planes, but Ann's work is helping people to plan their incarnations. She steps in at the point when the initial decisions have been made. When souls are planning a new incarnation, she discusses their needs with them and then introduces them to possible parents who she feels could meet at least some of the requirements, although it is rarely possible to achieve absolutely all of them. Then she leaves them to make their own choice.

Ann stresses that, as a general rule, the incoming soul makes the choice, since at the present time the majority of parents are not sufficiently aware. This was confirmed for me by my Greek student client Alex, who, when I regressed her to the planning stage of her present life, found herself very eager to be born, in a waiting queue of souls. In her eagerness she allowed herself to be, as she put it, "kicked" towards these particular parents. Her mother was "sort of aware on one level", but did not yet really want to face the fact of another pregnancy, which had occurred as the result of her husband coming home drunk one evening.

Unless plans are made a very long time in advance, which I imagine is unusual, the possible parents will of course already be incarnate. Meetings with the incoming soul can, however, be arranged when the parents leave their bodies at night, which we usually do in sleep. Once the choice has been made, the incoming soul normally overshadows the parents before entering the womb for the first time.

In her present incarnation on Earth, one of Ann Evans' particular interests is past-life healing, and the incoming soul's *samskaras* (karmic residues) are one of the things that she needs to bear in mind in her spiritual work when she is advising on the selection of the parents. Here I should like to quote Dr. Roger Woolger[13], my mentor in Deep Memory Process (formerly known as 'Integral Regression') therapy. In discussing the findings of Dr. Gerhard Rottman and of Thomas Verney and John Kelly[14] regarding the effect of the parents' emotions on the child in the womb, he says: "What past life research and therapy add to the extremely valuable findings of Rottman and others is this: The incoming soul or protopersonality is attracted to a mother (and father) who will help mirror his or her unfinished karmic business during pregnancy and birth. An incoming soul still dominated by catastrophic memories of violent death, deprivation or abandonment will easily be attracted to Rottman's Catastrophic Mother. When such a mother harbors the unconscious thought 'I really don't want this child', it will be mirrored directly by 'I don't want to be here. Nobody wants me.' in the fetal unconscious of the unborn child.'" Woolger stresses that: "For the child these thoughts belong to the remnant of a past life trauma; they are not caused by the mother, but only evoked by her unconscious ruminations. Fortunately the obverse is also true: where a pregnant mother wholeheartedly wants a child (Rottman's Ideal Mother), she will attract to her a child who is relatively free of negative or violent karma."

Although it is normally the incoming soul who is chiefly responsible for the choice of parents, there are exceptions. Very aware souls, who are incarnating with a clear purpose, need to have aware parents in order to be able to carry out their intended work on Earth. One such is undoubtedly my Norwegian friend Ivar, who comes into Chapter Eight, whose family have taught the same philosophy for about fifteen hundred years; and I strongly suspect that the case of Naomi, born several years ago to some friends of mine, is another such exception. Another notable exception is the Evans family itself. Ann and Ken had two daughters. Ken died in 1987 when Christine was only fourteen months old, and in recent years the rest of them have been doing a great deal of healing work together as a trio. They are all very clear that the four of them made the plan for this incarnation together before Jessie, the older daughter, was born. Ann says that, as a baby, Christine knew that Ken was going to die long before she and Jessie knew, and consequently she never allowed herself to get close to him.

Jessie is now a graduate of Art College, is working in film and has a partner and two young children, while Christine is making jewelry, but the two of them talked many years ago about their prior decision to come in together. Further evidence of this family's joint plan is that from a very young age Jessie kept asking for a sister. She had to wait six years, however, partly because Christine decided to be born first to a woman in Cornwall whom she did not like. She died that time at just a few months, and Ann feels that this cot death was undergone for that family, because parents sometimes need such tragedies for their growth or to repay some of their karma.

Ann maintains that the planning has to be done on a global level as well as a personal one. She feels that individualism is a phase that we have to go through – a necessary stage in our evolution if you like – because we in the West have got ourselves so deeply involved in karma. "We want all the time," she says, "to know what is going to happen to us personally, and so a certain amount of egotism will come through at the planning stage also, even though in the *Bardo* we are as a general rule more aware of the whole than we are while on Earth." She explains, however, that the more evolved we are, the more our lives are geared to the interests of the whole rather than to working out our individual karma, and this will be reflected in the Life Plan that we make.

Ann thinks that tribal planning is easier in a way because people in tribal societies understand their links with each other, but that there are also instances in the West where it is clear that groups of people have come in together for a global purpose. She gives as an example the twenty-one-year-old student who led the demonstration in Seattle against the World Trade Organization a few years ago, defending the rights of the Third World, because he obviously knew very well what he was doing and had a great deal of support.

Where Ann works when she is not incarnate – and also during her present life, when her soul returns at night to her 'true home' (as we all do as a rule, but most of us have no memory of it on waking up) – she says that there are "seminars where everyone says what they think and feel. There's no formal instruction – it's more sensing things – but there are nevertheless group leaders who share their ideas about what could best help the whole progression. It's looser than on Earth. It's very exciting! A growth industry – like organic cafés where people meet for the joy of discussing." Ann, Jessie and Christine all sleep a lot, which I take as an indication that they have a great deal of work 'up there'. Another indication that Ann is still doing her usual work during her present incarnation is that she sometimes meets people younger than herself whom she remembers having helped with their Plans.

At Ann's level of planning, *Devas* also have an important role. Ra Bonewitz, in *The Cosmic Crystal Spiral*[15], defines *Devas* as "the overriding fields of consciousness that evolved for the lower Kingdoms....." He says: "The word itself comes from Sanskrit, and means "a being of light". But none of them really describes what it **is**. The *Deva*...is basically a field of consciousness, which

27

has as its purpose to bring itself into manifestation in the lowest possible levels of energy; for us, the physical plane. Thus, all that has form has a consciousness behind it." Ann refers to *Devas* as the spirits of mountains, rivers and trees, and she says that "they are much wiser than we are. People are too knowledgeable and clever. We keep forgetting and muddling our priorities. *Devas* are more one-track minded. We've got amazing potential, but we can't manage ourselves."

So Ann Evans' work is at the highest level of the planning, where the global blueprint is also an important consideration. After carrying out the initial stages of discussion and making suggestions as to possible parents, she passes people on to other guides whose specialties are different. Rebecca, the subject of a book by the well-known French authors Anne and Daniel Meurois-Givaudan[16], was at the time of her decision taken by her guides to a place where she was shown scenes of her future life. This gave her an idea of what her tasks would be, and she was able to say "yes" to each one of them, but she explained that it was by no means compulsory for all reincarnating souls. It was the prerogative of the fairly evolved, and served the purpose of accelerating the process of awareness and choice. In our society it is surely fairly easy to distinguish between those who went through such a process before incarnating and those whose arrival was more (as Rebecca puts it) "like a shipwreck"!

It may be difficult for some people to understand why anyone would <u>choose</u> to be born with a disability, but more advanced souls often volunteer for such lifetimes for the sake of parents who need to learn more about caring. Karma can be a factor here as well, and Robert Schwartz has a case in his book[11] of a deaf person called Penelope, who in a previous life had heard her mother's boyfriend shoot her. The trauma of the sound of the gunshot that had killed her mother was so great that this time round Penelope, very understandably, <u>wanted</u> to be deaf, but the particularly interesting thing about this case is that she has put her disability to good use by becoming a teacher of the deaf.

Once all the main points concerning an incarnation have been taken into account, our astrology has to be worked out, as this determines our best method of creating the piece of the jigsaw that we have designed. Advice on this is always readily available to the incoming soul. The precise moment of birth needs to be selected in order to acquire the personality traits most suitable firstly for the working out of the soul's karma and secondly for achieving its life purpose.

According to the Meurois-Givaudans, in each new life we are born into the sun sign in which we died in our previous life; this ensures continuity in the cycle. But within that sign there is much scope for variation. Our Life Plan is revealed in our birth chart, and analysis of the chart can give an indication of our talents and weaknesses, the chief lessons we need to learn, and what our destiny could be if (and only if) we express the higher energies of the chart. Some people go right through life never expressing their true selves or fulfilling their complete destiny, but here again a person's level of evolution will be a strong determining factor. Not being an astrologer myself, I discussed the subject briefly with my astrologer friend Gertrude, and she provided me with a couple of examples.

Sagittarius is, *par excellence*, the sign relating to freedom. It indicates such things as long distance travel, philosophy, broadcasting, academia, sport, flying, cycling, horse riding, casting one's net wide. No-one in my own family is actually a Sagittarian, but we all have that sign strongly aspected in our chart. Well, my husband and I met in Geneva and we have traveled widely as a family throughout the thirty-seven years of our marriage. My husband and our elder son are both mathematicians, our daughter works in publishing and took riding lessons when she was at school; our younger son was a professional basketball player and now recruits American graduates for basketball jobs in Europe. My husband always cycled to work, and all the children always cycled to school (as did I).

In Gertrude's family, on the other hand, the strongest influence is Capricorn. Capricorns live by rules, and for them discipline and the establishment are always important. Gertrude's paternal grandfather was a lay preacher and a Capricorn, and he had a strongly puritanical influence on both his son and his two granddaughters. Gertrude's older son is a Capricorn, while her younger one is a Cancer – the diametric opposite – and all three of her children have had to surmount enormous odds. She says that they all "have to run to stand still, and all the money in the family has been worked really hard for." Attachment to the family is a strong characteristic of Capricorns, and in Gertrude's family they all help each other financially. Capricorns also tend to have an interest in property, and Gertrude's children are always buying and selling houses.

There are various systems of astrology, and one can always find relevance in all of them. I have a particular interest in the Japanese Nine Star Ki system, and another is Numerology, which was elaborated by Pythagoras. Numerology, as its name implies, is based on numbers – Pythagoras said that <u>everything</u> was number – and we incarnate in cycles from One to Nine. One's number can be obtained by adding up the numbers in one's date of birth – I was born on 9 February 1940 and am therefore a Seven (9+2+1+9+4+0 =25; 2+5 =7) – and I would consequently be an Eight if I needed to return. The chief features of Sevens are spirituality and unconditional love.

Jesus said that in his Father's house there were "many mansions", and our home in other realms is populated only by those with whom we have an affinity. One of our biggest challenges on Earth is getting along with people to whom we feel an aversion. This is an important part of our learning, but we can have a rest from it in between incarnations. Many people on Earth attach immense importance to family, but in fact Earthly families are as a general rule somewhat artificial creations. My client Alex said that she always felt like a stranger or guest in her family, and she was hoping to find true companionship if she married and had children of her own. 'True families', or groups of friends who really understand one another, are found mainly on the other side, and saying "Goodbye" to them when coming into a new incarnation can be painful. Exceptions to this are those societies who believe that reincarnation takes place within the family. American Indians, for instance, African tribes such as the Dagara, and my friend Ivar mentioned above.

The period of 'time' spent in between incarnations varies immensely, and a consequence of this is inevitable constraint upon the period available for the planning. Normally the most successful projects are those which have been given the most careful and detailed forethought, and our lifetimes on Earth are no exception to this. Dr. Joel Whitton, the co-author of *Life Between Life*[17], found during his many years of regressing clients to the *Bardo*, that sometimes no plan at all was made, occasionally with rather dire consequences. But I query this, for I doubt whether Dr. Whitton's subjects were able even in the *Bardo* to see far beyond their own individual perspectives. I have already said that our participation in the planning increases with the level of our evolution, and it may well also be true that some lifetimes are planned in more detail than others. No lifetime, however, can ever be left completely to chance, for the Masters are always there guarding the overall blueprint of the planet.

So, just as towns and buildings have to be planned before they are built, so is there a firm structure underlying all of our lives. People who believe their lives to be a total mess can be greatly helped by being made to see that there is logic behind every aspect of the mess. Each instrument in the orchestra has a vital role, even though some may apparently predominate over others. Each melody or rhythm has an important contribution in the symphony as it weaves its way in, out and around the other melodies or rhythms. How often do apparent catastrophes turn

31

out to be blessings in disguise? We vary immensely in our ability to hold on to our blueprint, but before embarking on the adventure of life, I wanted to make clear that every single incarnation has some sort of blueprint – that there is method in every type of madness!

Notes

1. The discourses of the Indian avatar Sathya Sai Baba are published in many volumes by Sri Sathya Sai Books and Publications, Prashanthi Nilayam, India.

2 *Conversations with God, Volumes 1-3,* Neale Donald Walsch, Hampton Roads, USA, and Hodder and Stoughton, London, 1995.

3 All available from the ARE (Association for Research and Enlightenment), Sixty-Eighth and Atlantic Avenue, P.O. Box 656, Virginia Beach, VA 23451-0656, USA.

4 *KARMIC RELEASE – Journeying Back to the Self,* Ann Merivale, Sai Towers Publications, India, 2006, and *SOULS UNITED – The Power of Divine Connection,* Ann Merivale, Llewellyn Worldwide, USA, 2009.

5 *Sathya Sai Speaks, Volume XI – 48,* Discourses of Bhagavan Sri Sathya Sai delivered during 1972, Sri Sathya Sai Publications Trust, India.

6 See, for instance, *Reincarnation – True Stories of Past Lives,* Roy Stemman, Piatkus, London, 1997.

7 *JESUS AND THE ESSENES – Fresh Insights into Christ's Ministry and the Dead Sea Scrolls,* Dolores Cannon, Gateway Books, Bath, 1992.

8 *The Prophet,* Kahlil Gibran, Mandarin, London, 1991.

9 *A Soul's Journey,* Peter Richelieu, Thorsons, London, 1996.

10 See *Twin Souls – A Guide to finding your True Spiritual Partner,* Patricia Joudry and Maurie D. Pressman, MD, Somerville House Publishing, 1993; and also my own book *SOULS UNITED – The Power of Divine Connection,* Llewellyn, 2009.

11 *YOUR SOUL'S PLAN: Discovering the Real Meaning of the Life You Planned Before You Were Born,* Robert Schwartz, North Atlantic Books, (Random House, USA), 2009.

12 *Many Lives, Many Masters,* Dr. Brian Weiss, Simon & Schuster, USA, 1988.

13 *Other Lives Other Selves,* Dr. Roger Woolger, Doubleday, USA.

14 See *The Secret Life of The Unborn Child,* Dr. Thomas Verny with John Kelly, Warner Books, London, 1999.

15 *The Cosmic Crystal Spiral,* Ra Bonewitz, Element Books, Dorset, 1986.

16 *Les Neuf Marches,* Anne and Daniel Meurois-Givaudan, Editions Amrita, France, 1991.

17 *Life Between Life,* Dr. Joel Whitton and Joe Fisher, Grafton, London, 1986.

EXERCISES

1 Have you ever thought much about whether your life was planned broadly before you incarnated, or is the concept new to you? In either case it could well be useful to look into the making of your Plan. The best way to do this is normally with the support of a qualified Deep Memory Process (or regression) therapist[1] but, failing that, it is always possible to do something on one's own. For instance, Dr. Roger Woolger's book *Healing your Past Lives*[2] includes a CD with five guided regression exercises on it. I suggest listening to No. 3 on this CD and, before you do so, asking to be shown your most recent life on Earth. Since the exercise is short, you will find your foray into that life will be brief, but you could pause the CD as soon as Roger has taken you to your post-death scenario. Then ask the guide whom you may have met there to move you forward into the planning stage of your present life. (If you do not meet a specific guide, simply ask your Higher Self to do this for you.) You can then

33

take as long as you like looking into it. If nothing happens the first time, don't despair; practice helps enormously with exercises such as this one.

2   Are you a parent of a young child or children? If so, his, her or their purpose in life may not yet be clear, but it will be of interest always to be on the lookout for any little signs that may be given you. They might, for instance, show particular talents early on, and these might or might not relate to your own special abilities. In either case, do all you can to foster and encourage them, never hesitating to praise their efforts and success, however small they might seem to you. And – MOST IMPORTANT – never dismiss anything a child says to you regarding any previous experiences that they claim to have had. Carol Bowman's book on *Children's Past Lives*[3] convinced me that there are increasing numbers of children incarnating at present who have conscious memories of some of their own past. If you are privileged to have such a child yourself, you might learn a lot from listening to him or her. You could also encourage your child to look further into the memory and maybe even find something about his or her own Plan.

3   Have you any older children still living at home? Do you remember any conversations that they had with you in the past that could have related to a previous life of theirs? If so, you might care to ask them whether they still remember it and this could also lead on to an interesting conversation. Very likely their memories will have faded – don't worry: that's quite normal – but it could well be useful for them to be reminded of it.

Notes

1   You can consult www.rogerwoolger.com for a list of his graduates to see whether there is one in your area.

2   *HEALING YOUR PAST LIVES – Exploring the Many Lives of the*

Soul, Roger Woolger, Ph.D., Sounds True, Inc., Boulder, USA, 2004.

3   *CHILDREN'S PAST LIVES – An intriguing account of children's past life memories*, Carol Bowman, Bantam, USA, 1997.

CHAPTER TWO

THE COMING DOWN

I am not yet born: O hear me.
Let not the bloodsucking bat or the rat or the stoat or the
club-footed ghoul come near me......
I am not yet born: provide me
With water to dandle me, grass to grow for me, trees to talk
to me, sky to sing to me, birds and <u>a white light</u>
<u>in the back of my mind to guide me</u>. (My underlining.)
Louis Macneice

Most of you are unlikely to remember anything about either your time in the womb or your birth, and not all of you will have had children of your own. However, an understanding of how it all takes place is important for setting the stage to the huge adventure that constitutes a lifetime. It is easy to get hold of books that elaborate on the purely physical side of pregnancy, so what I am looking at here is the non-physical aspects of the story, or anyway those that are less exclusively physical.

Once the Plan is complete, and the time has come to prepare for a new incarnation, the soul will, as a general rule, start its descent from the highest level, which is the level of pure spirit. The incarnating soul takes on subtle bodies as well as a physical one. The question of the subtle bodies is quite a complex one, and to anyone interested in a deeper understanding, I would recommend firstly Dr. Roger Woolger's article entitled *Past Life Therapy, Trauma Release and the Body*[1], and secondly David Tansley's book on the *Subtle Body*[2]. Tansley explains that we have in all seven layers, of which the four that come above the three subtle bodies are transpersonal. Moving upwards from the physical, each layer becomes less and less dense. Although we tend to think of the physical body as 'containing' the soul, in reality the other bodies are larger than the physical body, and so they 'overflow' it. This is why our auras, which are part of our subtle bodies and can be seen by clairvoyants, can easily be both measured and photographed. (You may well have heard of Kirlian photography.)

One very important point about this is that, although we create new subtle bodies for a new incarnation, the <u>seed for the new is carried over from the old</u>. This means that aches and pains and so on (known in Sanskrit as *klesas*), emotional traumata (*samskaras*) and also thoughts (*vasanas*) are imprinted on or in the physical body, via the subtle bodies, by the soul which has not yet shed its past memories.

Many people ask the question why, if the soul retains all the past memories, are they not in our conscious minds. The answer is simple: how many detailed memories do you have of your childhood? Or even of last year? In the case of past-life memories, there are so many of them that we would be completely overwhelmed and confused if we retained them all. If a fresh start is to be made with each new lifetime, the slate needs first to be wiped clean – amnesia is essential. Past-life memories sometimes surface in flashbacks or feelings of *déja-vu* (to which old souls tend to be more prone than younger ones), and Deep Memory Process/regression therapy can bring back traumatic memories that have not been dealt with in order to clear them, but that is not something that any of us would desire to take place every day.

The well-known American academic, Dr. Ian Stevenson, did a great deal of research into birthmarks and physical disabilities, showing their correlation to, for instance, wounds received in previous lives[3]. Mental or emotional 'disabilities' are obviously less easy to 'prove', but my experience as a therapist has taught me the extent to which awareness achieved in this way can be useful both for healing and in enabling us to escape from repeated patterns.

So, from the level of pure spirit, the first step is to take up a new mental body. This is much the largest of all the bodies and it has the highest vibrations, but it is also the finest, though it will with each new incarnation be slightly more thickly woven because it will have added into it the new learning from the most recent life. It is in the mental body that thoughts from our previous incarnations are stored, and these thoughts often impede or limit us. For example, in my own case, the thought "I can't dance" dates back many centuries to a lifetime as an Indian dancer who fell on stage and broke her back. I found this past-life trauma while on a workshop during my training with Dr. Roger Woolger, when searching for the cause of my fear of speaking in public prior to making the case history presentation required for graduation. Reliving and then letting go of that public humiliation greatly helped my confidence.

Following the soul's taking up of the mental body, travel through the mental realms to the astral realms is then likely to be quite speedy, and there a new emotional body (sometimes referred to as the 'astral' body), which looks exactly the same as the physical body, will be created. This will include the emotional progress made in the last life, and will consequently be more sensitive than the previous one. Emotions (for instance "I hate women", "men always let me down", or "I want to kill them") are stored in the emotional body. In that Indian dancer's life I never saw my lover again after my humiliating accident, and when I met him for the first time in my present life, the immediate sense of recognition was coupled with a certain feeling of sadness at not being young and beautiful. I did not understand this until a few months later, when I had done the regression, and only then was I able to shed my sadness over losing a lover.

The final step in the preparation for reincarnating is the creation of the etheric body, which is the exact counterpart of the physical body, i.e. although it is less dense, it has all the organs and so on of the physical body. Wounds, aches, pains and other purely physical problems are stored in the etheric body, and are then re-imprinted on to the physical body. This is why psychic surgeons can perform such miraculous healings by operating on the etheric body.

When I asked my client Suzy to focus on the pain in her hip that she had had ever since a fall on to sand many years previously, she said: "it's as though I've been kicked". Repetition of this phrase quickly took her into a past-life scene where, as a milkmaid called Anne, she had been kicked by a horse, and after she had worked through that life with me, her hip pain – obviously exaggerated in her present life since sand is not very hard – greatly improved.

Illness always manifests in the subtle bodies before it manifests in the physical body, and consequently those who can see auras (which is known as having 'auric sight') can detect sickness at a very early stage. Such people can also perceive our emotions and the principal aspects of our personality from the colors revealed in our auras.

Closely linked to the aura are the seven *chakras*[4], which are already formed on the emotional body before it enters the physical body, and whose function is to absorb the vitality that our body needs from the sun and the atmosphere. They are made up of the colors of the rainbow; the base (influenced by the moon) is red, the sacral (influenced by water) is orange, the solar plexus (influenced by fire) is yellow, the heart (which directs the functions of touch) is green, the throat (which controls the mouth) is blue, the third eye (the *chakra* of the spirit, the centre of spiritual consciousness) is indigo, and the crown (the seat of Christ consciousness) is violet.

The physical body is the last one to be formed, and whether it be weak or strong, male or female, black or white and so on, will – combined of course with genetic factors – be decided upon according to the lessons that the Higher Self has deemed necessary. The Higher Self, in choosing which karmic paybacks are to be made in the new lifetime, may also select a particular disability (such as blindness). So, while a birthmark, or even something more serious such as a deformed hand, may well be no more than the effect of a subconscious memory, anything that is incurable is more likely to be karmic. (Edgar Cayce gave a reading for a blind man, whom he found to have had a previous life in which his job had been putting out people's eyes and – most importantly – had enjoyed it.)

There are three exceptions to the general rule that the soul on reincarnating needs to clothe itself with new mental and emotional bodies. The first is children, i.e. those who in their last life died long before being able to complete what is normally regarded as a full cycle. Such souls do not tend to shed either their mental or their emotional bodies in between incarnations and so, when the time comes – usually fairly quickly – for their return, they only need to take on new etheric and physical bodies.

The second exception is the 'less evolved' – those who have had few incarnations and those who have abused some of their lifetimes to such an extent that they have become 'Earthbound' by fleshly desires and have consequently not gone beyond the astral realms in the inter-life state. Such souls have decisions made for them by more evolved beings and are simply 'pushed' back into a womb when a vehicle suited to their necessary next stage becomes available.

The third exception is those who are impatient to return to Earth, and sometimes do so against the advice of their guides. The reasons for such impatience can vary from a feeling that the Earth is all they really know to an over-eagerness to work off some more of their karma. Time is normally necessary for consolidating the experiences of each lifetime and preparing oneself fully for learning the lessons of the next one. Consequently, as

Dolores Cannon points out in her book on the Inter-life[5], those people who in life never seem to be able to "get it together" are likely to be the ones who have rushed into a new incarnation too hastily. Our guides can advise, cajole and point out the likely consequences of an action, but free will always prevails, and no-one who is quite determined to come back at any given moment can actually be prevented from doing so. As soon, that is, as a vehicle is available, for there are always more souls awaiting return than there are new physical bodies ready for them.

Here I want to deal not with the exceptions but with the norm. Whereas literature on the afterlife abounds, much less has been written on the subject of the preparation of our incarnations. An exception to this is the rather remarkable book, *Les Neuf Marches*[6] (*The Nine Steps*), by the French authors Anne and Daniel Meurois-Givaudan.

Anne and Daniel have developed the ability to travel astrally (i.e. out of their bodies) at will and to remember upon awaking all the details of the work that they did during the night. This practice was used widely by the ancient Egyptians (see Joan Grant's wonderful book *Winged Pharaoh*[7]), but most of us have sadly since lost the mastery of it. In this book they encounter a soul – Rebecca – who is preparing to reincarnate, and each of the nine steps is of course one month of the pregnancy, during which the authors watch Rebecca, a comparatively evolved soul, turn gradually into 'S'. 'S' is to be born to an American couple who are rather less evolved than she is, but part of the task that she has consciously taken on is to educate them in certain matters, and she is also aware that she has karmic links with both of them. Anne and Daniel lose touch with 'S' once she is about to complete her return to Earth, but the book ends with the information that she is now an intelligent little girl who is beginning to ask many questions of her parents.

When I became pregnant for the first time thirty-six years ago, it did not enter my head even for a moment that my husband and

I were welcoming not a 'new creation' but a mature soul, who had not only already come to Earth countless times before, but who, I discovered much later, had been our son on previous occasions. Despite my ignorance, I marveled throughout that pregnancy at those 'women's libbers' who argue for abortion on the grounds that the little creature they are bearing is their "own body". As Paul began to make his physical presence felt, I thought of him certainly as a friend rather than a stranger, but nevertheless as a being whose existence was totally independent of my own.

Since then I have met – both through my regression work and through my circle of personal friends – people who were much more 'aware' during their pregnancies than I myself was. Annie rejected her Catholic upbringing at a comparatively early age, when she found that it did not give her all the answers she was wanting. Since then she has spent a number of years exploring different paths, and has also received a certain amount of education in Buddhism. So when little Naomi was conceived, unplanned, Annie was very conscious of her womb being host to a soul that was very determined to be born. In fact Naomi's story begins a whole five years before the conception, which I find interesting since the clairvoyant Lilla Bek told me that the planning of an incarnation takes on average five years in Earth time. Annie was at the very beginning of her relationship with Naomi's father when, walking with him in a graveyard, she had a vision. It was only a little flash, but what she saw very clearly was two beings sitting on a rough-hewn plank of wood, looking down at them and obviously getting excited that "something that included them was about to happen". Naomi's father, who already had a son and many other responsibilities, was not at that point at all eager for another child, but when Annie mentioned the vision and her feelings about its meaning, he remembered that a clairvoyant had once told him that he would, after a big gap, have a daughter with red hair. (Annie is herself a striking red head!)

During the intervening five years – a period in which they were both very busy with work and other children as well as with their blossoming relationship – Annie gave little further thought to her vision. During the following year, however, she says that she had a strong sense of a whole group of people, including some far away Tibetan lamas, telling her to have a child. She put it off because her partner was less keen, but an unplanned miscarried pregnancy made her put her mind to the idea. Maybe the miscarriage was the first being on the bench, while Naomi was the second.

It is well known to students of the esoteric that every event, every new idea, every work of art or scientific discovery that takes place on Earth has already taken place on – for want of a better term for it – a 'higher level'. In the case of an incarnation, Rebecca informed Anne and Daniel, conception takes place on the etheric level about three months before it happens on the physical. The idea that Naomi's etheric conception had very likely taken place three months earlier than the physical one made a lot of sense to Annie, for whom that had been a rather special time. Whether or not a conception is planned on the Earth's plane, there will inevitably have been an agreement made on a higher plane by all the parties concerned. One of Dolores Cannon's regression subjects explained that you can stay 'up there' as long as you like, but that once the decision to reincarnate has been taken, you cannot go back on it, because the energies have been set up. ("Like water going down a slide: you can't collect it up again until it's got to the bottom"[5].)

The soul is merely the intermediary between the 'True Self' (as the Spirit or Higher Self) and the physical body, and as such it is consequently, unlike the spirit, capable of being subjected to things which one would normally think of as pertaining only to the physical body. Illness at the end of a life can necessitate a period of recuperation for the newly departed soul. I perform shamanic soul rescue work (known as 'psychopomp') and, on a recent journey, being concerned about a friend of mine who had just died after many months of serious illness as well as a lifetime of chronic depression, I was given a vision of him being tended in hospital by young, attractive nurses (something he would have reveled in!) and was told that his recuperation would take several months in Earth time.

Rebecca said that a reasonably evolved soul knows when it is time to reincarnate, and that teachers and guides telling one so simply reinforces the push that one is already feeling inside oneself. When the time for reincarnating is getting very near, she says, something in the body of the soul[8] (by which I assume she means the newly reformed emotional body) gets activated and increases in density, and this makes it harder to stay awake all the time. Sleep is normally quite unknown in other realms but, after her etheric conception, Rebecca found herself initially needing little *siestas*, which gradually increased to really long sleeps. At the same time as becoming aware of a need for sleep, she began to notice the days passing. In other realms time does of course not really exist and, since the light and temperature are always perfect, there is neither night nor day; so for Rebecca, becoming aware of time passing was one of the first signs that she truly was preparing to return to Earth.

At the moment of her physical conception Rebecca saw a ray of light coming towards her, which she described as "so big and solid that I wanted to envelop myself in it". When my friend Selma got pregnant several years ago, she too saw a light traveling round the room and was quite sure that it entered her body at the moment of conception. Later on in Rebecca's mother's pregnancy, Rebecca got a similar feeling of wanting to envelop herself in the light whenever her parents were thinking about her strongly, and she said that this always pulled her towards them.

So the soul does not normally enter the womb at the moment of conception. Or if it does (as seems likely in Selma's case), it does not remain there for long. Rather, it spends most of its time initially hovering around the parents – particularly the mother when they are not together – getting to know them, and accustoming itself to the idea of a forthcoming life to be shared with them. This, however, is NOT an argument for abortion. Every pregnancy is planned on the etheric level, and once the initial bonds have been established, abortion is inevitably painful and consequently creates karma. The two-volume Regression Therapy Handbook, edited by Winafred Blake Lucas[9], has a chapter on conversations with the unborn child, and some of the book's contributors recommend to mothers who are contemplating abortion that they discuss the matter with the incoming child before taking definitive action. There are cases quoted of the baby's soul agreeing to await a more convenient moment for its return, and even of such dialogue resulting in a spontaneous abortion. As regards abortions performed on medical advice on account of the fetus being 'defective', any malformation of a physical body will have a good reason behind it, such as the working out of a certain piece of karma, and so, if that is interfered with, the incoming soul will have to seek an alternative means of resolving the karma.

Rebecca entered the fetus briefly for the first time at twenty-one days, with the first heart beat. She found the noise rather disturbing, however, and so she shot out again straight away. Yet even that fleeting visit was enough for the formation of an indestructible bond, and she knew from that moment that she would have to enter again, repeatedly. This she did until her guides intervened and told her that she was going to Earth too quickly. Her reply to this was that, knowing the incarnation and the separation from her astral friends to be inevitable, she wanted to get it over with. Her guides then explained to her that the transition to Earth was easier the more consciously it was done, and that it was therefore wise at that stage to keep contact with Home as much as possible.

Annie had not previously given this particular matter a great deal of thought, but she told me that the concept of the soul popping in and out during the first few months corresponded with her intuitive feelings, for she had at certain times felt much more aware of Naomi's presence than at others. In fact she says that there were even times when she said to herself "That's funny. She's not there at the moment."!

My friend Joy felt this too. I would not wish Joy's dramatic gynecological history on anybody, but her story is a wonderful example of the power of a woman's intuition and so I am recounting it with an exhortation to you women who may be contemplating having children or are having them already always to trust your own instincts. Joy's three children were all born by Cesarean section, and she had in addition no less than five miscarriages. The first of these was her second pregnancy, and it was to her first husband. She was thrilled at the thought of a second child, and it was that husband's adverse reaction to the news that caused the break-up of their marriage and probably, Joy feels, the miscarriage also. Dominic was miscarried at twenty weeks, was perfectly formed, and to this day, many years on, Joy has not got over losing him. Miscarriages and cot deaths can occur when the soul in question only needs to spend a very short time in a physical body in order to complete its karma, but my research has also shown that in many instances of miscarriage, abortion or early death, the prematurely departed soul returns later to the same parents. However, Joy, who is very intuitive, is convinced that none of these is the case with Dominic. She still feels very aware of him as a soul with whom she has a strong bond, and she is quite sure that he is neither of her sons, and also that he was none of her four subsequent miscarriages. She has a strong feeling that he will in due course return as one of her grandchildren. On the other hand she says that Joel, her youngest child, was first Zoë (the second miscarriage) and then Heather (the third), "because I felt exactly the same way about all three of them, whereas the others were different." She adds (and as a mother of three I agree) "You know how you feel differently about each of your children even though you love them all equally."

The loss of Dominic was the most traumatic of Joy's five miscarriages, since that pregnancy was the most advanced. Twenty weeks were more than enough for her to make a very strong connection with the baby and to be aware of him as a human being with a history of his own. With him, as with the three children who were born to her, she says that she was often aware of when he was inside the fetus and when he was not.

When Annie was pregnant with Naomi she also made a very strong connection to a being who, she said, "felt like an adult, like someone very ancient". She says that she felt as though she could look down a central channel to the being in her womb and that they made a mental connection. Both Annie and her partner talked to Naomi a lot, as did Ruth, Annie's older daughter, who was sixteen when the baby was born. Ruth liked to put her head on Annie's tummy and feel the baby's movements, which began quite strongly at sixteen weeks. When Rebecca's mother was pregnant, Rebecca had a friend incarnating at the same time whose parents set aside some time every evening to talk to her. At the appointed moment each day a sort of aura was sent out from the house, which drew the baby's soul there, and the parents knew that she was present. Rebecca stresses the importance of parents talking to their unborn child. (My older son and his wife read stories to Adam while he was in the womb!) However, although it clearly helps the relationship on all sides if parents do this consciously, there is always night-time too, when the future child can meet and talk to the parents while they are out of their bodies.

In the third month Rebecca says that she felt scared to enter the womb. What scared her was the fear of solitude; the memory of the pain that one suffers on Earth – pain both self-inflicted and inflicted on others. She was fully aware, however, that her karma made the pain unavoidable, and by the fourth month she was already feeling denser and more at one with both the fetus and her mother, whom she saw at that point more as a sister. In fact she later became aware that she and her mother had been sisters in many previous lives.

In the fourth month of the pregnancy Rebecca's mother had a fall and had to go to hospital. The shock of this sent Rebecca straight out of the body. She explained that had she not left, the energy of her mother's anxiety would have been damaging to her etheric body, for, although the soul pre-exists the fetus, once the connection has been made, the fetus affects it very profoundly. It is only comparatively recently that psychologists and the medical profession in the West have become properly aware of the effect of the environment on the unborn child, and this new knowledge is something for which our present-day society can be very grateful. My client Mark was adopted at an early age, and when I regressed him to the womb his distress was acute. He knew that his mother had decided to give him up for adoption, and this aroused in him intense feelings of both rejection and anger, with which, at thirty-five, he was still wrestling.

Just as the human being living in the physical world has both a conscious and a subconscious existence, so is the embryo or fetus in a sense two beings: the conscious adult (later to become the subconscious in the new personality) who has chosen to re-enter the world and make a fresh start, learning new lessons and rectifying old mistakes, and the conscious baby. The psychologist Morris Netherton describes the latter as a tape that records every single remark, thought and feeling in its environment. A potential problem for this conscious baby is that in absorbing all these external stimuli it makes them its own; while the soul is able to remember exactly who it is whenever it is <u>out</u> of the womb, the baby <u>in</u> the womb identifies so strongly with the mother that it is unable to distinguish between her feelings and its own.

For an elaboration of this complex subject, I strongly recommend Dr. Roger Woolger's book *Other Lives Other Selves*[10]. In Chapter Ten, dealing with prenatal and perinatal experience, Woolger points out a lacuna in Verney and Kelly's fascinating book *The Secret Life of the Unborn Child*[11] – namely that they view the mind of the fetus as a *tabula rasa* rather than a bundle of complex and conflicting memories and experiences. Woolger says: "As infants we are all conceived with pre-existent psychic dispositions or *samskaras* that are already laid down in the unconscious. These karmic residues latent in the unconscious are reactivated during pregnancy and birth by certain thoughts, feelings and events in the mother's experience, aided by whatever cast of characters – father, doctor, nurse, etc. – are involved during this period of time..."

And he goes on to say that "The period of gestation from conception to birth <u>is therefore one of the most important in the overall scheme of the formation of personality</u> [my underlining]. Not only is the fetal consciousness an uncritical observer and recorder of all the mother does, thinks and feels, but it is also engaged in a sort of deep rumination over all the still-unfinished business of other lives. The contents of these ruminations will constitute his or her ongoing karma post natum. These two streams of consciousness, unmediated by any discriminatory ego, form the matrix of the personality later to emerge."

Although she had left the body after her mother's accident, Rebecca followed her mother to the hospital, empathizing with her distress, and she was amazed to discover, when the doctor did an examination, that the fetus could move independently of her. The same is true at the other end of life, when the soul sometimes leaves the body prior to the death being evident. Rebecca commented at this point that she was able to care for her mother's whole being and for her body, placing her hands on, for instance, the nape of the neck, forehead, or soles of the feet –

areas where the *prana* (energy) can stagnate.

In the fifth month of the pregnancy Rebecca was still attending preparatory lectures. The lecturer stressed that we have to learn to be born – just as we have to learn to die – "with serenity and confident joy". Rebecca's teacher points out, though, that this is the prerogative of the more evolved; those attending the lecture were only those who were ready for it. The less evolved arrive on Earth "like a shipwreck", whereas those who have reached Rebecca's level of evolution should have a well-prepared, fully desired, and conscious landing. There are, Rebecca says, many more souls arriving on Earth today with this preparedness and awareness, and this is something that it is useful for parents to be aware of.

The sixth month of the pregnancy was particularly important, as it was then that Rebecca's silver cord was formed. The silver cord attaches the soul to the body, and facilitates return to it when we wake up after leaving it in sleep. Its functions (as explained by Robert Crooke in *The Supreme Adventure*[12] are firstly "to transmit impressions from the physical senses via the soul body to the mind" and secondly "to carry orders from the mind to the physical body." It is attached at the solar plexus, and transmits to the physical body vitality collected by the soul body during sleep. Rebecca described it as made up of a multitude of little threads, and the thickness to be that of about three or four fingers together.

Even at this point, however, Rebecca was still by no means always inside her new body. Sometimes she simply did not feel like entering. For instance, when her parents were in a huge, crowded, department store, and she felt that they were abandoning their personalities to the energy of the crowd. On one occasion her father had to get up during the night to go to the office to sort out a computer problem, and she followed him. Although he was aware of a "sort of breeze" behind him, he was still, unlike his wife, unwilling to admit that Rebecca already existed, yet she felt a very strong desire to communicate with him.

Rebecca always entered the fetus by the fontanel, and she said that a sort of automatic sucking occurred rather than it being deliberate on her part. At first it was a bit painful and the body felt to her like an ill fitting glove, but in the sixth month the sound of the heartbeat, the blood throbbing and the breathing, which had at first seemed "aggressive", were more like "music" to her, like "waves on a beach", and she felt pulled towards it. She knew that these experiences were all quite normal from keeping contact with others who were incarnating at the same time. Another feature of the sixth month, however, is a rigidity given by the formation of the bones. She and her friends were afraid both of inhabiting a restricting body and of forgetting the resolutions about their new lives that they had made at the time of making the decision to return.

When Anne and Daniel met Rebecca in the seventh month of the pregnancy they found that she had shrunk considerably in stature and now looked more like a little girl of only six or seven. This is not difficult in an emotional body because one's other bodies are much less dense than is the physical body, and it is easy to change one's appearance at will; (I shall be looking at that again in the final chapter). By the seventh month she was realizing that her Rebecca days were over and, to help ease herself into the completely new life, she chose a new name. Being a reasonably evolved soul, she found that she was able to influence her mother in the choice: she whispered it and her mother picked it up, regarding it as her own idea.

Rebecca says that besides influencing her mother in the choice of name, she was able to tell her about the purpose of her new life. She said too that a big wave of these "worker souls" was incarnating at present, and that it would be useful if parents could see something of their destiny. By the eighth month Rebecca was no more. She had now become 'S' completely, and

Anne and Daniel found her to be inhabiting the body much more and really getting used to it. The two auras were interpenetrating, which not only gave 'S''s mother a sense of oneness with her child, but also made 'S' herself feel "physically pregnant" with her mother. This inter-penetration of the auras, which continues for some time after the birth, helps with the bonding between mother and child and is one of the main reasons why adoption or any other form of separation at an early stage can be permanently damaging to both parties. However, having adopted a baby myself at the age of two weeks, I personally believe karmic bonds to be at least as important as physical ones. Awareness on the part of adoptive parents has a big role to play, and Earthly family ties are both ephemeral and artificial. 'True families', or groups of friends – whatever one likes to call them – are best found on higher planes, and the strength of ties with either natural, adoptive, foster or step parents will vary with the strength of the links already made karmicly.

Rebecca was also at this point still sufficiently in touch with Home not to forget the fact that for each lifetime we have both a personal target (connected with remedying an error made in a previous life or lives) and a bigger target, relating to help for others and the planet. However, remembering her targets was already becoming more difficult. She said that the trouble was that, if one's target did not seem particularly grandiose, one's ego could cause one first to ignore it and then even to forget it. As the weight of the fetus increased and her need to inhabit it also increased, the Earth's vibratory rate had a numbing effect, making her intellectually lazy. She stressed, however, that this was not inescapable, and of course parents who appreciate that their new-born child is not a virgin soul can help him or her to remember their purpose.

The peoples of Africa tend to have a better understanding than most people in the West of the fact that each incoming soul has a particular purpose. In his beautiful autobiography, *Of Water and the Spirit*[13], Malidoma Patrice Somé, a member of the Dagara tribe in Burkina Faso, explains that the first few years of a boy's life are spent not with his father but with his grandfather. The reason for this is that grandfathers know that they are heading for where the young child has just come from, and communication is therefore of mutual benefit. For the boy is able to talk about the place where "the value in which the elder has an interest exists the most purely" and the elder is qualified to remind the child of what is his mission on Earth. In fact the grandfather begins his involvement with the new life very soon after conception. The Dagara, like American Indians among others, believe that reincarnation takes place within the tribe, and they always want to know who the new baby is before the birth. So a ritual known as a 'hearing', in which the pregnant mother, the brothers, the grandfather and the priest are participants, is organized by the father, who is given a report on it afterwards. During this ritual the mother goes into a trance and the incoming soul uses her voice to answer the priest's questions. The child's name, which summarizes its life purpose, is chosen as a result of these communications. Somé himself is a reincarnation of his grandfather's brother, and the name he was given, meaning 'the one who makes friends with the stranger', denoted his future mission in the West.

But it is not necessary to be African in order to find out something about a child's mission prior to the birth. My client Helen already had four children before she finally met the right partner, and was already well into a pregnancy with him when she first came to see me. A conversation with her new son happened more or less spontaneously, when we had failed to get to the root of a particular problem that she wanted to solve, and it proved fascinating. Jimmy, as I am calling him, revealed to Helen that he had been her maternal grandfather who had died of cancer when he was fairly young. Her grandmother's death the previous year had left him free to reincarnate, since he no longer felt the need to watch over her, and so he was now coming back to Earth not only for Helen and Spencer, her new husband, but also for Helen's mother (previously his daughter). It was evident that he was fearless, with a very quick mind and a great love of people, and the main purpose of his new life would be to help his father, whose first born he would be, and they would do athletic things together. Jimmy further said that he was already good friends with all his siblings, especially the eldest one, who had taken care of him before, and that he had something important to tell people. Interestingly too, Helen when she was pregnant was expecting the baby to have red hair like his father, but she emailed me a couple of months or so after the birth and told me that in actual fact Jimmy looked exactly like the baby she had seen during the session and that he had his grandfather's chin!

The practice of performing scans of the fetus has caused a big change in recent years, since this makes it now possible to know the sex of the baby at twenty weeks. Desire for this knowledge varies among individual couples (and even within couples, which can sometimes cause problems!), but, when they were expecting their first child, both my sons and their wives were keen to be given the knowledge that was available. I clung to my 'old-fashioned' feeling that a surprise was preferable until my daughter-in-law, Becky, commented that she felt that the knowledge would help with the bonding. That suddenly made a lot of sense to me and, as his grandmother-to-be, I started feeling particularly excited about the imminent arrival of "Boing" (temporarily so named on account of his very vigorous kicking!) – especially since we already had one wonderful granddaughter. Also, since blue is my favorite color, the knowledge of the sex gave me an extra excuse for purchasing blue baby clothes.

While the fetus' aura begins to interpenetrate with that of the mother, etheric ties are also being formed with the father. This is the case even when biological fathers absent themselves, and it is only a man who is very detached from his emotions that would be insensitive to these ties. (Our adopted son's biological father, who at the news of the pregnancy expressed only a desire to wash his hands of it, was nevertheless sufficiently curious to go and have a peep at the baby in the foster home prior to our collecting him. The foster mother told us that, on seeing Christopher, he had been unable to hide his emotion).

Another feature of 'S''s eighth month was an increase in communication with her mother, though she said that her mother saw it more as intuition on her own part than as direct communication. Annie, however, is in accord with 'S'. At a late stage in the pregnancy Annie was meditating with a friend who was undergoing Buddhist training, when she received what she interpreted as a very clear message from Naomi about how she would like the birth to be organized. She wanted a Buddhist prayer for enlightenment to be chanted by three people as she entered the world, and Annie and her partner were able to arrange this.

'S' said that babies feared birth just as much as mothers did, and in her own case her mother's fear of pain affected her a great deal. On the subject of birth, volumes and volumes have already been written and doubtless have yet to be written, so I will be brief. The circumstances of birth, and the emotions induced by it, can have an effect that lasts a whole lifetime, so good preparation is vital. And here I speak, as a Deep Memory Process therapist, from very personal experience; a regression to my own birth was by far the most powerful (and uncomfortable!) that I have ever undergone. The experience of my friend and teacher Roger Woolger must have been similar to mine, for he says in his book on Deep Memory Process Therapy[10] that his own thought at birth was "I don't want to be here"; and in the same paragraph he makes the interesting point that, just as at the moment of death, people's whole lives flash before them, so at the moment of birth there tends to be a "brief period of heightened consciousness".

My Greek client Alex was, as we saw, an unwanted child, and when I regressed her to her birth I momentarily forgot two of my own oft-repeated statements: that no two people, and therefore no two regressions, are ever alike, and that the therapist should never start out with any particular expectations. Knowing about Alex's difficult background, I could not help myself expecting her birth experience to resemble my own, but in fact I was quite mistaken. Throughout her time in the womb I found Alex to be brimming with hope and optimism about her forthcoming life, looking forward to "playing happily in the Grecian sun", and confident that she would be able to survive her family's lack of caring. She knew at the time of her conception that her mother did not want the pregnancy, that another child was going to be an enormous burden, and that her mother wanted to get the birth over with as quickly as possible. She took on board her mother's pain to such an extent as to actually choose to come a whole month early. A further regression to a previous life revealed a karmic connection when the two of them had been the same age. The mother was a slave girl in a well-to-do family and Alex the youngest daughter of that family, who always leapt to the girl's defense; and later, when she was old enough, Alex took her off with her and set her free to marry a man she loved. The pattern has unfortunately not been repeated in the current life, as Alex's relationship with her mother has always been extremely difficult, but this regression helped Alex to appreciate her mother's reasons for expecting too much of her.

The decision about the moment of birth is made in the planning stage, because the astrology has to be chosen in accordance with the lessons needing to be learnt. 'S', who had been Rebecca, knew when the moment had come for her birth because she recognized the sound of "her" planet, even though she did not know which one it was. This obviously applies too even in the case of premature births, because there is no reason to think that they are not also planned beforehand.

Annie had the problem that from the thirty-fourth week Naomi was in the breech position and, though confident that she would manage without a Cesarean, she felt sure that the baby would be born breech. Her partner, however, thought otherwise, and it was his confidence that eventually won the day. Annie performed various antics, such as turning somersaults in the swimming pool, and in due course Naomi responded by turning. I once met an Indian gentleman who, when his daughter was late on in pregnancy, visited Sai Baba's ashram in Puttaparthi. He and his wife were extremely concerned about both their daughter and their new grandchild, who was then in a breech position, but one day during *Darshan*[14] Sai Baba stopped in front of them and said "Don't worry. Everything's going to be all right." They noted the time, and later, when they contacted their daughter, she told them that at that precise moment she had felt the baby turn in her womb!

Not everyone has such good fortune, however, and Joy has a gynecological history that I feel few of us women would be strong enough to have survived. With Amber, her first child, a Cesarean section was deemed necessary, firstly because she was breech, and secondly because she was large, and Joy accepted these arguments without difficulty. Jack, who arrived after five miscarriages, was born by Cesarean section because he was three weeks late, but (despite what I have just said about the time of birth being planned astrologically!) in retrospect his mother feels that this was a mistake. She wishes that she had been stronger in resisting it, but any woman who has been a victim of hospital desire for control can sympathize.

Joel the one whom Joy feels to have been so very determined to be born to her, believing him to have made two previous attempts – was so big that the doctors at the hospital were quite sure that she had got her dates wrong. They performed the Cesarean a whole six weeks before Joy herself believed the baby to be due. After the operation Joy had two massive hemorrhages, during the first of which she had an out-of-body experience. She still remembers the feeling of being out of her body as the most wonderful sensation she has ever had, but she knows that she was not permitted to go very far because Joel needed her. She watched everything that was being done to her body and to the baby painlessly and with interest, and she longed to explore beyond the confines of the hospital ward, but felt something on her shoulder firmly holding her down. She then re-entered her body reluctantly, knowing that there was a job to be done.

Joel, who Joy is still sure was indeed six weeks premature despite his enormous size, screamed relentlessly after the birth, and when they laid him on her chest to try to calm him down, he started to have fits. He was then taken into intensive care and given every possible test, each one of which showed him to be "grossly abnormal". Joy, who was given several blood transfusions, had constant battles with the hospital staff overseeing the baby, and when in desperation she took herself down the corridor to try to see him, she collapsed with another massive hemorrhage.

After about six weeks in a side ward all to herself, "attached to all sorts of drips and so on", Joy decided to take matters into her own hands. Lying to the hospital staff about the amount of help she would have at home, she escaped in a wheelchair with the baby. She ignored the doctors who informed her that Joel was seriously brain damaged and would never be normal, and maternal intuition won! Convinced that her baby's only problem was a premature birth, Joy decided to "put him back into the womb". She bought a sling to strap him to her body, covered him with a massive T-shirt, and literally never put him down. The two older children accepted straight away that this baby needed to be with her all the time, and she frequently took them all swimming, with Joel clinging on to her neck just like a baby monkey. The hospital staff insisted that she take Joel back for frequent checkups, but each time she did so he again had a fit, whereas he was perfectly all right at home.

The silver cord, which forms during pregnancy, gets attached to the physical body at the moment of birth. 'S' was aware of "two powerful beings of light" doing this for her. This cord – at least in the case of evolved souls – can apparently stretch more or less infinitely, as the more evolved often travel a long way away from their bodies at night to do important work, and it is severed only on death. (See the Book of Ecclesiastes: "Yes, remember your Creator now while you are young, before the silver cord of life snaps...."[15].) Though the book does not say so, I suspect that these beings of light were 'S''s 'spiritual midwives', for at birth, as at death, we always have helpers from another plane as well as Earthly midwives to deal with the physical side. My clairvoyant friends tell me that the Archangel Uriel is the overseer of the spiritual midwives; that it is he who presides over both birth and death.

Birth can never be totally easy for two reasons: firstly there is the difficulty, for both mother and baby, of pushing one's way through an extremely narrow canal, and secondly, returning to the physical plane from such a very different one is bound to be a shock. Obviously, with regard to the second, the parents' attitude is absolutely crucial. I have witnessed on Roger Woolger workshops many painful 'births' to parents who were rejecting their offspring.

These are normally part of a difficult Life Plan which has been chosen for a reason, and we do not normally bite off more than we can chew. However, Rebecca had a friend who chose to reincarnate at more or less the same time as she did, but who did so against the advice of his guides. His ego was at the time rather inflated, and he was anxious to pay off a lot of karma in one go, so he plunged without sufficient forethought into a situation which was going to be exceptionally painful and difficult. At the moment of birth he suddenly funked it, and the result was that he 'committed suicide' by getting the cord around his neck. Rebecca's comment was that such cases are not uncommon. One has to feel great sympathy for the parents in instances like these, but does it not make it easier to accept if we realize that such a tragedy must be a part of their karma?

Babies in the womb are, as we have seen, not virgin souls but intelligent adults, and as such they know what is and is not good for them. This includes food, and obviously their only way of obtaining this is via the mother. Herein, as Joan Grant points out in her chapter on the Supra-physical in *Many Lifetimes*[16], lies the explanation for the cravings for certain foods and the nausea from others experienced by so many pregnant women

I have quoted Rebecca's various adventures simply because *Les Neuf Marches* is the only book I have come across that follows a pregnancy in this way. This pregnancy was, however, only one out of millions that are taking place all the time, and there is no reason to suppose that the pattern is always identical. All the clairvoyants of my acquaintance seem to be agreed that the incoming soul will begin by overshadowing the mother and then pop in and out throughout most of the pregnancy, but one thing that appears very clear is that – as with most other things in life – there are no hard and fast rules. (My client Alex appeared to have entered at an early stage, but was still able to keep in close touch with Home and remember her decision about the incarnation.) Although I believe that the soul is normally fairly well-anchored in the body by the time of the birth, there are said to be cases (for instance that of Edgar Cayce's wife, Gertrude) where it does not enter for the first time until after the birth.

Birth is never easy and is often traumatic, but I prefer to end this chapter on a cheerful note! Little Naomi, who dictated to Annie her requirements for her birth, did not arrive with the greatest of ease, as she was facing the wrong way and had one hand above her head, which made it more painful than Annie's two previous deliveries had been. Yet Naomi seemed nevertheless to be very relaxed and calm, and she cried very little when she emerged. She was born at home, and Annie, besides feeling that she knew exactly what her little "adult" child was wanting, was determined to retain control right through the birth process, and in this she was successful. The midwives co-operated when Annie explained to them that she planned to listen to her body rather than obey orders about when to push and so on. One consequence of this was that Annie found herself standing up for a whole hour and a half of the labor. The result of this rather unusual birth was a beautiful little personality, who seemed to her mother to have adjusted more quickly to the world than did either of her older children. At three months she was looking around, taking everything in, and appeared to her doting parents not to be doing the "baby thing" very much at all. Annie says "While Ruth slept through it all and took the early days a lot more gradually, and Chico was a Buddha for about six weeks, Naomi seemed to me to have entered with a lot of consciousness that being in the world was what she was doing. People who saw her in her pram often used to comment 'She's been here before!'". Nowadays she is doing really well at school and developing into quite an exceptional and interesting child.

No doubt many of you have such a child or children yourselves.

Notes

1   Dr. Roger Woolger's article on *Past Life Therapy, Trauma Release and the Body* is published in *Body Psychotherapy*, edited by Tree Staunton, Brunner Routledge, London, 2002.

2   *Subtle Body, Essence and Shadow* by David Tansley, Thames and Hudson, London, 1977.

3   See *Where Reincarnation and Biology Intersect*, Dr. Ian Stevenson, Praeger, London, 1997.

4   *Chakra* is the Sanskrit word for "wheel". To people with auric sight the energy centers are observed to spin like

wheels.

5   *Conversations with a Spirit*, Dolores Cannon, Gateway Books, Bath, 1993.

6   *Les Neuf Marches*, Anne and Daniel Meurois-Givaudan, Editions Amrita, France, 1991.

7   *Winged Pharaoh*, Joan Grant, Duckworth Press, London, 2007.

8   She calls this the "esprit de fer" (iron spirit).

9   *REGRESSION THERAPY – A Handbook for Professionals, Volume II*, edited by Winafred Blake Lucas, Ph.D., Deep Forest Press, USA.

10   *Other Lives Other Selves*, Dr. Roger Woolger, Doubleday, USA, 1999.

11   *The Secret Life of the Unborn Child*, Verney and Kelly, Warner Books, London, 1999 .

12   *The Supreme Adventure – Analyses of Psychic Communications*, Robert Crookall, James Clarke and Co. Ltd. For the Churches' Fellowship for Psychical Study, Cambridge, 1975.

13   *OF WATER AND THE SPIRIT – Ritual, Magic, and Initiation in the Life of an African Shaman*, Malidoma Patrice Somé, Compass, Penguin Books, USA.

14   *Darshan* is a Sanskrit word meaning "Seeing and beholding the Lord or some other holy being". Sai Baba appears to His devotees at the ashram daily.

15   Ecclesiastes chapter 12, verse 6, in *The Daily Walk Bible* translation, Tyndale House Publishers, Illinois, 1989.

16   *Many Lifetimes*, Joan Grant and Denys Kelsey, Ariel Press, Atlanta, 1997.

EXERCISES

1   Did your mother tell you very much about your own time in the womb and your birth? If not, and if she is still alive and willing to talk about it, you might find it interesting to discuss it with her. You might even find that it helps to make sense of certain later experiences in your life. Alternatively,

you could make an attempt at regressing yourself to the womb. A shamanic drumming tape, or some music specially designed for meditation, can help to put you into an altered state, and curling up on the floor in the fetal position while you are listening to it could well trigger important memories. However, should anything traumatic surface – either from conversation with your mother or from regressing yourself – I would advise you then to deal with it with the aid of a well-qualified therapist.

2   Are you by any chance pregnant or thinking of it? Then here's your exciting chance to dialogue with the incoming child! All you really need to do is to sit quietly, go inside yourself, ask questions and wait and see what answers you get. Don't despair if nothing seems to happen straight away. All it takes is a bit of patience and perseverance and then – above all – to trust the words that come into your head. If you are a man contemplating fatherhood, do not feel excluded from this exercise. Your role in the child's life is every bit as important as the child's mother's.

3   Are you already a parent? If so, think back to the time when you were expecting a child and reflect on what was going on between you. If you feel that the relationship did not get off on a perfect footing for any reason (such as a difficult pregnancy or birth), it is not too late to make amends. Children appreciate openness and honesty, and if you can really talk to them now, truly opening your heart, it will pay off in later life for all of you.

CHAPTER THREE

THE FIRST SEVEN YEARS

Love unfolds first on the lap of the mother. The eyes of Love fasten themselves on the caressing face of the mother. It then spreads towards the father, brothers and sisters, kith and kin, friend and playmate, region and language, world and its Maker.
Sathya Sai Speaks, Volume X

I suppose one can say that the first seven years are the first truly visible step of our eleven. And what an important step they are! Just think about some of the main things a child will normally learn during this period: drinking, eating, crawling, toilet training, walking, talking, reading, writing, drawing, adding, subtracting, cycling, swimming…<u>What</u> an achievement! When I started to think about all this, I suddenly recalled my older son Paul's first sentence: "Mooken giddis". "You call that a sentence?" do I hear you ask? Well, yes, it <u>is</u> a sentence if you understand its meaning. This was perfectly clear to my husband and me at the time, because we were not only familiar with our son's very individual vocabulary, but had also witnessed the event he was describing. The sentence meant "I showed the milkman the picture of the chicken." Reflecting on this, I found myself thinking that our encouraging response to Paul's early attempts at putting words together must surely have helped in his rapid development towards producing sentences that were intelligible also to people outside our own family. Then, however, I discussed this point with our daughter, whose degree was in Linguistics. Alice replied as follows:-

"Your response to Paul's sentence would presumably have helped to some extent, but I don't think you can say that the way you responded to him was the crucial factor in his language development. There's a large amount of evidence to support the theory that there is an innate ability for language, and that it is independent of other cognitive abilities such as memory and intelligence. Although the quality of the interaction that a child gets may help to some extent in the early stages of language development, its main effect would be on social skills, confidence and so on, which are not really to do with language acquisition. All children acquire language in roughly the same way provided they hear it around them."

Alice then told me that in some cultures, such as certain American Indian tribes, "parents don't talk to their child at all until it has reached a reasonable level of language ability, because they don't see any point in talking to the child until it can understand. When children in these cultures start to speak, they are mainly ignored until they are able to produce intelligible sentences. In spite of this, the children still develop language in the same way as children in different cultures."! Chomsky was the first to outline the now-accepted theory that children are born with an innate ability to acquire language. He showed that (again in Alice's words) "from a minimal amount of input, very young children try to work out the rules that govern morphology, syntax and phonology, and they then apply these rules to new phrases, rather than just copying what they hear. (This can be seen from the mistakes they make when they overapply rules, such as 'I seed the sheeps', 'you goed home', etc.)" Here we have confirmation of the reincarnationist view of the young child being anything but a *tabula rasa*!

Conversely, it is interesting to note that in some cultures children are 'taught' to sit up, walk and so on, the parents believing that this would not happen naturally! Alice agrees that language is a good example of the vast amount of difficult and intricate stuff that is generally learnt during the first seven years, but she also maintains that it is learnt in a very different way from certain other things such as tying shoelaces. She explains "It isn't conscious, and it isn't taught by other people; it's something that develops naturally because of the way people and the brain are designed."

The Jesuits are well known for their saying "Give us a child for the first seven years and we have him for life." Certainly the child's environment during these early years is of great importance, for souls inhabiting small bodies have needs which only parents, or good parent substitutes, can fill. That order, however, was founded a long time after 553 AD, when the Christian doctrine of reincarnation was officially suppressed. Consequently, they regard the young child as a clean slate, rather than an experienced soul full of memories both of previous lives and of Home, and – to a greater extent than most of us who have lived a great deal longer – still able to keep contact with what he or she knew before coming in. So, while I will not argue with the Jesuits over the importance of external influences during the first seven years, I would love to be able to explain to them that what children have brought in with them from their past is equally influential in the formation of their characters. A child such as Naomi, or my grandson (whose name when he was born was changed from Boing to Adam), whose parents instantly recognized in them a "tremendous sense of wisdom", have had a head start over a baby whose parents see her as something to mold in the way they want her.

In his book on *Soul Mates*[1], Richard Webster quotes a gynecologist who found that, by looking into a newborn baby's eyes, he could distinguish old souls from young ones. "Some babies' eyes were filled with apprehension and fear, while others looked around 'much more casually as if appraising their new situation'." It is good to be aware of the fact that souls vary so much in age and experience, and also to appreciate the merits of having both young and old in a family. Our children may come to us mainly to be guided and helped, or they may come more as teachers for us. Older souls may well have more wisdom, but younger ones may have enthusiasm and energy that are both refreshing and necessary to the world.

Babies, as we all know, sleep a great deal, and the reason for this is not only the fact that growth occurs in sleep, but also their need to keep close contact with Home as protection against the shock of being newly back on Earth. Communication with guides, guardian angels and friends on the other side is much easier when we are out of our bodies in sleep, and frequent contact also makes it less difficult for the new arrival to remember his or her life purpose. It is all too easy to become ensnared by 'the illusions of *Maya*' (*Maya* meaning the Illusion that this physical world is the real one), and parental awareness can make a big difference.

Tiny physical bodies are obviously much more vulnerable than adult ones, so babies need extra protection – on the spiritual level as well as on the physical. This is provided not only by guardian angels and guides, but also by etheric ties to the parents, visible as cords to clairvoyants. The well-known clair-voyant Lilla Bek explains that these cords are particularly strong during the first two years. And the child's aura, which initially is intertwined with the aura of the mother, continues to be so for some time after the birth. Opinions – and no doubt individual cases – differ as to the amount of time it takes for the child completely to detach itself and fully to assert his or her identity as quite separate from that of the mother. Joy, who has auric sight, maintains that the auras of her two older children (Amber and Jack) continued to interpenetrate her own until they were about five, and in the case of Joel, who had such a difficult start to his life, it only really separated completely when he reached the age of eight.

Babies and very young children also have charms which few can resist, and this is surely Nature's way of providing extra protection, because who – apart from those sadly distorted characters who commit such horrendous things as child abduction or rape – could possibly bear to see harm being done to a young child? Also, in his book *A NEW EARTH – Awakening to Your Life's Purpose*[2], Eckhart Tolle makes the point that, in contrast to, say, a beautiful flower, crystal or bird, which will attract even the least sensitive among us ("Because of its ethereal nature, its form obscures the indwelling spirit to a lesser degree than is the case with other life forms."), all new-borns (babies, puppies, kittens, lambs and so on) are "fragile, delicate, not yet firmly established in materiality". He then goes on to say that "An innocence, a sweetness and beauty that are not of this world still shine through them. They delight even relatively insensitive humans."

I once had a brief but moving encounter with a little baby who had very obviously only just come from a better place. This was in answer to a prayer made at Prasanthi Nilayam, Sai Baba's ashram in Puttaparthi, India, only a few months after having broken my hip. Sitting on the floor for long periods of time does not come easily to me at the best of times, but that particular afternoon I had reached my limit of endurance long before Baba had appeared. Wondering how I was going to survive the remaining time, and praying for assistance, I was suddenly overcome by two irrepressible calls of nature: thirst and the consequence of quenching it. So I set off on my dual mission, thankful for a brief respite from my uncomfortable sitting position. Once my two needs had been satisfied, and I was queuing at the metal detector to re-enter the Hall, I found myself standing behind an Indian woman holding a tiny baby. This baby's eyes were open, and the image of them will remain forever engraved in my memory, for this was my first real glimpse of ecstasy. That baby, though in the world, was very clearly not yet of it. It was obvious to me that it was still seeing the world that it had just left, and the look of rapture on that little face is indescribable. Once back with my group, I was so engrossed in thinking about the baby that, while awaiting Sai Baba's appearance, I completely forgot about the ache in my leg and the discomfort of sitting on the floor.

I have already mentioned Dolores Cannon's book on *Jesus and the Essenes,* but now there is an equally fascinating one entitled *THE ESSENES – Children of the Light*[3] written by a regression therapist called Joanna Prentis. She has regressed people to previous lives with the Essenes including her co-author, Stuart Wilson, who in this previous life was an Essene named Daniel. Daniel speaks extensively about the knowledge and practices of the Essenes and, of the period with which this chapter is concerned, he says: "Children become much stronger and more anchored in themselves at one point, but for the first seven years the soul is still descending and integrating with the new self. By the age of seven the soul should be securely anchored within the new self, but any great shock within the first seven years will impede integration and set the whole process back." The author then comments that this ties in with the ideas of Rudolf Steiner and also echoes Maria Montessori's ideas about nurturing young children. So this is something important to bear in mind if you are the parent of a child in this age group.

In countries such as India, where the majority of the population take reincarnation for granted, parents are much more likely to be aware of their children's still-conscious connection with the realms beyond. This is the reason why Dr. Stevenson, the well-known researcher into "cases suggestive of reincarnation"[4] has worked on such cases mainly in the East. However, with spiritual awareness now spreading so rapidly in the West, more and more parents in Europe and America are becoming open to the concept of their children having lived before. Annie's partner had a son several years before Naomi was born. At the age of about three, he expressed to his father his sadness about not being able to "go back", even mentioning the name of his father figure on the other side. But then he added resignedly "of course if I did go back to him, I wouldn't be able to take you with me."!

Conscious past-life memories are present in young children much more frequently than most of us in the West normally recognize, but they tend to fade quite quickly, particularly when parents fail to acknowledge them. Carol Bowman, in her fascinating book on children's past lives[5], mentions cases of exceptional children who remember about Heaven and the reasons for coming to Earth. Particularly remarkable was a little girl called Courtney who, at the age of four, told her mother "you go to heaven, then you have a little time to rest, kind of like a vacation, but then you have to get to work. You have to start thinking about what you have to learn in your *next* life. You have to start picking out your next family, one that will help you learn whatever it is you need to learn next. Heaven isn't just a place you go to hang around forever. It's not just a place to relax and kick back. You have work to do there."! Carol Bowman further makes the point that babies and children can have past-life dreams – even nightmares – and in the latter case she says that parents can help their children to overcome the trauma by talking to them about it during the nightmare, without waking them up.

Carol Bowman's research was prompted by her own children's traumatic past-life memories, which were alleviated by regression therapy, and she consequently encourages parents to listen to what their children tell them about their past and to take it seriously. My client Elaine did just that when on holiday with her teenage daughter Yasmin and her four-year-old nephew Nathaniel. Nathaniel, who was explaining something to Yasmin, said to her at one point "Do you remember when I was your brother before, a long time ago? We were twins, don't you remember? And another time I was your daddy." He also once said to his grandmother whilst she was laying the fire: "Nana, you have to be careful with fires, you know", and then he proceeded to tell her a story of how in a previous life he had died in a fire with his father. As for Yasmin, she has been having *déjà-vu* experiences since she was two, and on this same holiday, she said to Elaine: "Mum, I don't know why, but when I go into Olhao (an old Moorish fishing town), this sadness comes all over me and I feel like crying. I have this picture of a man who feels like my husband, and I lost him. It feels so real yet I know it's not true."

Sleep fosters spiritual awareness, whether or not this includes actual past-life memories, but it is not for everyone the only means of keeping contact with Home. As a young boy, Edgar Cayce[6] had spirit friends with whom he played regularly in the garden, and my friend Ann Evans had encounters with Jesus when she was a child. Joy's middle child, Jack, has always been very psychic, and for some time after her father had died, before Jack was seven, he communicated with him. Jack called his grandfather by his Christian name of Fred, and he sometimes told Joy things about her earlier life that she knew she had never told him herself. One day he announced that Fred had said "goodbye" because he was returning to Earth three days later, and exactly three days later the wife of one of Joy's brothers gave birth to a son!

On a slightly more mundane level, many parents have stories to recount of their young children's 'imaginary friends'. My son Paul's invisible friend Ben used to accompany him to play school, while Alice's companions had the rather more unusual names of Box and House. It is so easy for us parents to wax lyrical about our infants' "wonderful imaginations", but is it not at least equally likely that they are displaying powers of mediumship, which, in the majority of cases, are lost in later life? So if your child talks about contact with anyone that you cannot see yourself, please don't laugh or dismiss it as "imagination".

Another thing that I cannot stress too strongly is the importance of trusting maternal intuition. However well qualified and learned doctors, midwives, pediatricians and so on may be, only the mother has borne the child in her womb for a whole nine months. Only the parents (and of course often siblings or – in the case of tribes such as the Dagara[7] – grandparents) have communicated with him or her on a deep subconscious level and are welcoming him or her into their family as a previous acquaintance.

Joy, whose child-bearing story I started in the previous chapter, knew that her 'grossly abnormal' baby needed nothing more than to go back into the womb from which he had been prematurely extracted. Because of Joel's fits each time she took him back to the hospital for further tests, she stopped taking him when he was three and a half months old, despite continual telephone calls from the hospital authorities. They then threatened to put Amber and Jack into a foster home for assessment, and to take Joel forcibly back into hospital. Joy, whose husband was unable to cope and had fled to his parents, then put the three children into the car and drove to her own parents, who had retired to Spain. While driving she could not of course keep Joel strapped to her as she usually did, but she put him into a baby seat beside her, and when she was unable to hold his hand, Amber did so.

After three weeks in Spain, Joy's father told her to go back and face the authorities. So she went back to the hospital to show them how well her five-month-old son was doing. Amazed, they insisted also on inspecting her at home and, finally convinced, and apprised of the difficult circumstances in which she was bringing up three children on her own, they sent her a home help every day for the next several months.

Joy's husband later returned from his parents and took the family off to make a new life in Spain. Joel, who had walked at ten months, started swimming before he was two and learned to ride a bike at three. Before he started school he was fluent in three languages (English, Spanish and Valenciano), and he later taught himself to read in English, which he did not learn at school. Later he knew his tables better than his brother who was three years his senior, and he often complained of boredom at school on account of being ahead of his peers in all subjects. This is the child who had been diagnosed in his first weeks as irreparably brain-damaged!

Birth is rarely easy. For the mother a certain amount of physical pain is inevitable. For the child, returning to Earth from a place where pain is unknown must surely be akin to having a nightmare after falling asleep while lying comfortably on an idyllic beach. For the normal mother, however, the joy of the safe arrival of her new-born child is usually enough to obliterate the memory of the pain. For the child, the best antidote to the pain of returning, complete with the knowledge of the karma to be dealt with in the forthcoming life, is love. Learning to give love is one of the most important tasks of any lifetime, and also the best way of dealing with our karma, and those who are greeted with love on arrival into the world have a head start in this lesson on those who are not.

Joel was born to a mother who was made dangerously ill by the birth and a father who was scarcely around at all and later disappeared from the scene all together. Yet Joy's immense love for him, combined both with her strength of character and the qualities of the evolved soul that Joel clearly is, helped him to overcome both these handicaps. Naomi, and my grandson (born much more recently) had the further advantage of being born in the presence of two parents who were bursting with love for them, and Naomi's birth was also attended by a good friend who was joining in with their chanting of the Buddhist prayer for enlightenment.

In contrast to both of these, my client Miriam was born to a father who never met her, and to a mother who, after marrying someone else, dumped her (Miriam's own words!) in an orphanage at the age of four and only took her back ten years later to help her look after her five younger step-siblings. This was, however, an important part of Miriam's Life Plan. She realizes now that had her childhood been happy, she would neither have become a nurse nor set out on the journey of self-discovery which enabled her to break free from certain karmic patterns, and also to give more help to her patients. Furthermore, her own negative experiences made her resolve very determinedly to do things quite differently for her own children.

Another example of an adverse childhood not necessarily being disastrous is that of my friend Jemima, who was born a few years before the Second World War to an alcoholic mother and a father who had to go off as a soldier. Forced by circumstances to move in with her grandparents, who were extremely wealthy, she and her sister were brought up mainly by a series of rather awful nannies and a governess. Her grandparents were always aloof, communicating with the children only when they felt they needed correction. Jemima regarded her 'privileged' background as a handicap, and says that as a girl she longed to live in an ordinary house like the other children she knew, rather than in their immense one with butlers. A sensitive child, rather than reveling in her own privilege, she would lie awake at night worrying about the fate of the poor. When, many years later, she had her own children, though never short of money, Jemima knew that the most important thing to give them was love. Ensuring the happiness of their childhood was her greatest pleasure and, now that they are both adults, their continuing happiness is still the most important thing in the world to her. Though Jemima herself is at present an atheist and therefore disagrees with me on this subject, she is clearly someone who, like Miriam, chose prior to this incarnation to learn the hard way about the importance of giving love. Her own children, like Miriam's, benefited from her negative experiences.

So the baby and young child's greatest need apart from food and security is love. We have nevertheless to appreciate that, however adequate or inadequate the parents are in meeting their child's needs, they will be working with what is there already: the centuries and centuries of lifetimes that have molded a personality, and the memories of these lifetimes which are deeply embedded in the subconscious. Why should Jemima, brought up by unloving, snobbish grandparents, and nannies who were regularly sacked for their incompetence, have shown compassionate characteristics at such an early age? Why did I, reared in a Conservative and racist family, join a group at university aimed at helping the Third World, choose as my first job to recruit teachers for Africa, start voting Labour, and later adopt a black child? My father in his conscious life knew nothing of my blueprint, and successfully brainwashed me into believing in the depths of my being that I was no good in any way at all. Yet without these initial difficulties, I would certainly neither have become a therapist nor thought of writing books, so it is clear that overcoming them was an important part of my blueprint.

But keeping in touch with one's blueprint is often extremely difficult. How I felt for Elizabeth, the heroine of Helena McEwen's autobiographical novel *The Big House*[8], when her nanny gave her horrendous punishments for things that were not her fault at all, and she was quite unable to defend herself! You will doubtless be able to think of many equally painful experiences – either your own or others' – which made keeping the blueprint in mind far from easy. In fact the healing profession is in my experience very largely made up of people whose painful childhoods gave them this difficulty, but whose experience has equipped them to help others to discover their blueprints. Louise Hay is an obvious, very famous, example of this.

The basic needs of the baby and young child are food, security and love and, although the father figure is important, these three things are normally best provided by the mother (who will hopefully feed the baby at her breast). The psychologist D.W.Winnicott maintained that the first year of life was crucial for the integration of the personality. I once worked for a few months in a school founded exclusively for children who had missed out on a relationship with their mother, or mother substitute, during their first twelve months. The result of this early deprivation is very distressing to see. I am filled with admiration for the teachers and care workers who not only coped so well with the disturbed behavior of their charges, but also succeeded in giving them, despite repeated rejection, what they had missed out on as babies. By their love, understanding, compassion, and also skilled training, these colleagues were able – in certain cases – to bring about the integration of the personalities of these children so badly damaged by neglect. In some instances the damage was apparently too great to be completely redeemable, and the very destructive behavior of some of these children made me personally feel unable to cope well with caring for them. I would love now to know the fate of Frank, Tracy, Simon and Kelly, to mention just a few, but I fear that it may well have been prison for much of this lifetime. So how fortunate that this was not their last chance! On return to the astral realms they will hopefully absorb their painful lessons and maybe choose a less traumatic blueprint next time round.

Energetic Therapy, which my young friend Yann was studying when we first met, goes further than Winnicott, for it maintains that during the first seven years for boys and six years for girls (it is generally accepted that girls mature earlier) the child builds the basic links with the people close to him that will help him to do the same later on with others. Yann explains that it has been discovered that 'resilient' people are those who had the good fortune to create strong and safe links with someone during the first six/seven years of their life, and that for people who do not receive love at that time it is much more difficult to attain a stable and balanced life later on. Children need first to feel safe and then they will be able to discover the world. But it is never too late for people who did not experience a good birth or who had big problems during their childhood. Yann says: "With regressive or energetic therapy we can really change people's past and help them to relive their previous experiences happily."

Even though the mother is normally the primary carer during these early years, I would not like in any way to diminish the importance of the father's role. Nowadays of course there are (particularly in the West) very large numbers of single parents, and one has to admire the excellent job that so many of them do, often in the face of immense difficulties. But it is important during these early years for both boys and girls to have role models in adults of both sexes and so, however fraught may be your relationship with your 'ex', please remember that your mutual child and he or she need to keep contact with each other wherever possible. And, when this is not possible, it is vital to find alternative role models of the opposite sex.

Babies' behavior can vary as much as that of older people. Conditions in British maternity hospitals have no doubt improved in the thirty-six years since my eldest child was born, but one of the things that I had to suffer was only being allowed to feed Paul every four hours. Perhaps some babies do have an internal clock that makes them hungry exactly every four hours, but mine certainly did not! Once safely home, however, I fed Paul whenever he cried, and he rapidly turned into a very contented baby, who had apparently read the books and dutifully started to sleep through the night at six weeks – the very age at which they said he should. But it is all too easy for the parents of a baby that 'follows the rules' to congratulate themselves on providing an 'ideal environment'! Fortunately for my education, Alice, who was born twenty months later, had not bothered to read the baby books, and she only started to sleep through the night at the age of four.

Finding out about the karmic links with the members of one's family can often explain a great deal. Just as parents' attitudes to each of their children will be governed, whether or not they are aware of it, by the nature of their previous relationships with them, so too will that of the siblings. When I was taken into hospital for Alice's birth, I dreaded leaving Paul for the first time, and his distress at our separation made me fear that he might resent the new baby; but my fears were quite unfounded. He was perfectly happy with 'Daddy' looking after him and, when we came home, he obviously recognized his sister instantly as an old friend and companion soul mate and, above all, his one-time twin sister. Besides looking alike, they behaved like twins from the moment that Alice was old enough for them to play together. Now aged thirty-six and thirty-four, they are still as emotionally close as ever although they live in different cities.

When Christopher, our adopted son, arrived, however, the reaction of each of the older children was quite different. Paul, who was just about to turn five, was besotted from the first moment, but Alice showed a few little signs of jealousy. At the time we attributed this to the fact of her having been the 'baby' for a whole three years, and consequently did our utmost to reassure her both of our unchanged love and of her continuing importance. But many years later my friend, the well-known clairvoyant Edwin Courtenay, (who also first told me about Paul and Alice having been twins), explained that Paul and Christopher had previously been blood brothers and extremely close, while Alice and Christopher had difficult mutual karma to work out between them. During the years when the behavioral symptoms common to adopted children disrupted the whole family, I was more surprised by Paul's tolerance than by Alice's intolerance of Christopher's misdemeanors.

One will not invariably have close karmic links with every member of one's family. Several people might have reasons for choosing the same parents without having a particular reason for choosing one another as siblings. Most of you are probably acquainted with siblings who appear to be virtual strangers to one another. In a large family I imagine that it would be rare for them all to be bonded closely already. My husband is very close to one of his older brothers, but generally only meets the other one at weddings and funerals.

Karmic links are, however, not the only factor relevant to the dynamics within families. In the Japanese Nine Star Ki System of astrology[9], one's personality number is governed by the year of one's birth, while the date determines one's 'driving force', which is normally apparent in childhood. Thus, someone who is a Six (Metal)/Three (Tree) will be destined to be a rather controlling adult with strong qualities of leadership, but as a child, when the Tree element is more greatly in evidence, will be very creative, with masses of energy, but tending to dart from one project to another without completing the first one. A trauma such as adoption in the early stages of life can throw a child straight into his or her adult number, as was the case with Christopher, a Three Tree. He had hyperactive tendencies from babyhood, and I never remember him completing anything he started until he was forced to by impending examinations. Christopher's second number is Six, and another characteristic of Sixes is stability, but 'stable' is the last adjective one could have used for him when he was small. However, at eighteen he had the good fortune of winning a basketball scholarship to do his degree at a College in the United States, and now at thirty-one, having ended a successful career as a professional basketball player, he is working as an agent for other players. He is becoming more and more stable, while his energetic 'Three Tree' qualities have remained a great asset in his sporting career.

I always find it fascinating to analyze families in the Nine Star Ki System. While Tree supports Fire, Fire supports Soil, Soil supports Metal, Metal supports Water and Water supports Tree, Metal cuts down Tree, Water puts out Fire, and so on. In my own family, my husband, daughter and myself are all Metals (though my husband is a Seven, which is gentler than a Six), while Paul is a Soil, and Christopher, as I said, is a Tree. So Paul has to support three of us, whereas Christopher challenges all of us, all of the time. All of this was evident from very early on. Paul was very protective of his sister from the moment she arrived – Soils are the world's carers, and there are three classes of them: Twos, Fives and Eights – and he even showed a protective attitude towards me from an exceptionally early age. Alice, a Six Metal like myself but a double Metal, her second number being Seven, started to assert her leadership qualities after becoming fully embarked on her career, and she and I sometimes clash when we are together. In big contrast to both the boys, Alice's Seven qualities were much in evidence in the care she used to take as a child both of her own appearance and of all the things around her, and in those days she was gentler too towards me!

In an ideal world, these first seven years would of course be mainly a rapturous, exciting time for both children and parents. I shall never forget our joy when Paul uttered his first word, the delight I took in the beautiful, intricate little models that Alice used to make from Plasticine, the poems that Christopher wrote in his early years at primary school. My husband, whose early childhood memories are almost entirely joyful ones, can still recount a whole catalogue of adventures, such as fishing in the nearby stream with nets for tiddlers, exploring by candle light in the underground passages of Kew Green (the excitement increased by being slightly tinged with fear), and running around a big hollow that he found in Kew Gardens.

But of course such happy experiences are by no means universal. While some who are born into difficult circumstances do not really survive them, for reasons which are most likely to be karmic, nowadays, in my work and personal life, I encounter many survivors. One such is my young friend Andrew, whose survival I regard firstly as miraculous and secondly as the mark of an evolved soul. Andrew has not yet discovered quite why he chose to be born this time to a prostitute mother and a sailor father who disappeared back to his own country before he was born, but it is not of great concern to him at present. What is of concern to him is to give his own three young sons the love and the fathering that he himself was deprived of.

Andrew finds this easiest with the middle one, John, who is six. The bond between the two of them is so strong that they often communicate telepathically, and Andrew says that when John climbs on to his knee, he feels their two auras "clicking into each other", making him feel totally at one with his son. John, Andrew says, is wise beyond his years and extraordinarily spiritual, always asking his father questions about the meaning of life, and he remembers the answers he is given. Since Andrew himself became acquainted with Sai Baba, John has been having regular dreams about Him.

This is interesting because, of the three children, John is the one who apparently had the worst start to life. Tessa and Andrew were not together when John was born, and Tessa rejected John, believing him to be the offspring of a man she did not like. Andrew returned to Tessa later, and formed a very strong bond with John by the time he was four. He then had a DNA test done and found, to his delight, that John was indeed his son. John is the only one of the three who was not breast fed, and he was fatherless until he was two, when Andrew returned to the family. Yet he is much more popular at school than his older brother David, who has always been very close to Tessa. John may be the exception to prove Winnicott's rule! David, despite the excellent relationship that he has always had with his mother, holds a lot of anger, which he sometimes expresses by punching other children at school. But Sai Baba promises to His devotees the care of their whole family, and David once had a dream in which Sai Baba was punching him on the leg just has he was wont to do to others. This made David realize what it felt like!

When talking to Andrew about his background, one would imagine that it would be virtually impossible for him to have any happy memories. For instance he was born covered in eczema from head to toe, and the only man with whom his mother ever had a long-term relationship abused her physically in the children's presence. Yet he says that he was never short of friends and that, while always unhappy at home on the estate, where windows were constantly getting broken and so on, his school days were positively idyllic. He simply loved learning, and shone in every subject from the very first day. This is why I regard Andrew as an old soul, and also maintain that evolved souls can survive even the most difficult circumstances of early childhood.

More important still than walking and talking is surely the development of morality. Here, I think, we can return to the Jesuit contention. The Jesuits would no doubt maintain that the first seven years were crucial for the formation of a good Christian, and that anyone with this advantage is unlikely to deviate into immorality in later life. While I am sure that there is a great deal of truth in this theory, it surely cannot explain either the Andrews of this world or the children of 'good families' who sadly go off the rails later in life. This latter must always be tragic for parents, but it is my hope that the spreading of belief in, and under-standing of, karma will help such parents to stop blaming themselves entirely.

On the subject of morality, a question that has occupied my attention for many years is that of racism. When our adopted son, who is half Sierra Leonean, was in his first elementary school, I got tired of going in to the school to complain about the racist taunts of his fellows. Christopher was clearly suffering so much on account of it that we eventually moved him at the age of six to a school much further away which had a firm rule against name calling. Some people maintain that children "do not notice color", but this is patently untrue. They do <u>notice</u>, but they do <u>not</u> judge. Racism, like any other prejudice, has to be <u>learned</u>, and this teaching (as Christopher's first Head constantly informed me!) comes from the parents. This Head fell short in failing to appreciate her staff's moral duty to curb the verbal abuse to the same extent as they endeavored to curb stealing and lying. It took Christopher a long time in his new school to gain sufficient trust in the teachers to follow my instructions to report any abuse he suffered, but gradually his confidence was built up. This move, to a little Catholic school where he was no longer the only black pupil, was one of the best things that we ever did for him. There he was encouraged to be proud of his racial origin, to paint self-portraits using nice brown colors, and also to talk openly about having been adopted. Here I will not argue with the Jesuits, for the education Christopher had at that school was, I believe, one of the major factors in his development into the moral adult that he is now. Is it any wonder that crime rates are high among the black sector of our population, when the suffering inflicted on young black children naturally makes them rebellious?

When children are adopted, it is important that they should be told about it as early as possible, to avoid trauma in later life. In *The Primal Wound*[10], Nancy Verrier maintains that the adopted child's subconscious feeling of having been rejected at birth is responsible for a wide variety of behavioral problems. Where the book falls short for a reincarnationist is in failing to look deeper: what were the child's reasons for choosing such a difficult start to this life? What are his or her karmic links with both sets of parents? In the case of our own son, the well-known English clairvoyant Edwin Courtenay reckoned that Christopher had not been particularly close to his birth mother before; she was mainly, as far as he was concerned, the vehicle for his getting to the four of us, with all of whom he has strong karmic links. (In fact, in my first book[11] I recounted a life in which Christopher was my firstborn son. His then father, who is a close friend of mine now, taught him to play *Pelota*, which explains the great interest he has always taken in Christopher's basketball!)

This brings me to the final point that I wish to make on the subject of the first seven years. I have already mentioned the 'karmic residues' that are brought into a new incarnation. In a lifetime these can, if one is fortunate, be resolved, but they can also – particularly in the first seven years – unfortunately be overlaid by new problems. On second thoughts, 'new' is probably not the correct word to use. Dr. Roger Woolger maintains that – like a gramophone needle that gets stuck in a groove – a newly incarnated soul will attract to itself, rather than new difficulties, a repetition of the same old patterns.

A child who is loved and respected by her parents during her first seven years will have a good self-image, whereas if a child is constantly criticized, this will show up in her body. My own troublesome back is a good example. One result of my father's negative attitude towards me, which made me unable to look the world squarely in the face, was very bad posture. This was no doubt accentuated by the system in school of awarding marks each term for 'deportment' – red girdles for the juniors who got 'A's for their straight backs, green belts for the seniors. Knowing that I would never obtain anything higher than a 'C' increased my inferiority complex, which in turn had a deleterious effect on my deportment! I did not become aware of any physical problem until I first became pregnant, but then pregnancy must have triggered a host of subconscious memories: rejection at birth, a difficult childbirth undergone in Egypt, which damaged my back, an eighteenth century lifetime in which I developed a back problem from taking too much on...The emotional manifests in the physical, particularly when a body has experienced real physical injury previously. In other words: emotional abuse inflicted on a child by her father is likely to cause bad posture at an early age; bad posture will deform the spine; and a deformed spine – which could have been actually broken in previous lives – may cause pain in later life. Usually there is a trigger for the pain. That is the reason why Roger Woolger trains his students to focus so much on the body, and it is also the reason why I have found his methods in Deep Memory Process therapy to be so effective. The physical body holds memories imprinted on it by the subtle bodies. The subtle bodies do not themselves feel physical pain, but the memories of experiences of previous lives are transferred by them to the physical body when incarnation first takes place. So focusing on a physical pain can lead one into pictures of, or feelings about, an old story (often a traumatic death) that one no longer gains from holding on to. It is then up to the therapist to encourage the client to let go of what he or she no longer needs. 'Getting into the body', however, is not always easy for those whose first seven years were painful ones, but we shall look at that some more as we move on to the next stages in life.

Notes

1   *Soul Mates*, Richard Webster, Llewellyn, 2005.
2   *A NEW EARTH – Awakening to Your Life's Purpose*, Eckhart Tolle, Penguin, USA, 2005.
3   *THE ESSENES – Children of the Light*, Stuart Wilson and Joanna Prentis, Aark Mountain Publishers, USA, 2005.
4   *Twenty Cases Suggestive of Reincarnation*, Dr. Ian Stevenson, University Press of Virginia.
5   *Children's Past Lives*, Carol Bowman, Element Books, Shaftesbury, Dorset, 1998.
6   See, for instance, *THERE IS A RIVER - The Story of Edgar Cayce*, Thomas Sugrue, ARE Press, 1997.
7   See *Of Water and the Spirit*, Malidoma Patrice Somé, Compass (Penguin), New York, 1994.
8   *The Big House*, Helena McEwen, Bloomsbury, 1999.
9   See, for instance, *Nine Star Ki*, Michio Kushi with Edward Esko, One Peaceful World Press, Massachusetts 1991.
10 *The Primal Wound*, Nancy Verrier, Gateway, USA.
11 *KARMIC RELEASE – Journeying Back to the Self*, Ann Merivale, Sai Towers Publishing, Bangalore, 2006.

EXERCISES

1   Were your first seven years mainly happy ones or not? If they were, I hope you are eternally thankful rather than simply taking your past for granted. If not, have you ever given much thought to what you learned from your negative experiences? I hope by now that I have convinced you of the fact that there were good reasons for them! And if you feel that you are still suffering from the consequences of a far from ideal childhood, it is not too late to deal with your problems. As a therapist one of the things that I recommend most frequently is 'inner child work', and for that the book that I recommend most strongly is John Bradshaw's *HOMECOMING*[1]. My own book, *Karmic Release*, also contains a number of exercises that many people have found useful for inner child work.

2   Are you the parent of a child or children in this age group? Do some of the points that I have raised in this chapter ring bells with you? If not, you might care to think about anything you might have missed. If, on the other hand, you think of anything important that you feel I have missed, please do not hesitate to write and tell me!

3   If your child or children have now gone past the age of seven, think back to their first seven years and what important things you learned from them.

4   If you are in a stable relationship with your child or children's other parent, you might care to discuss the points raised here with him or her. There is nothing more valuable to a child than mutual understanding!

5   If you are a single parent, are you endeavoring always to put your child or children first in your dealings with the other parent? Remember that the blood tie is important and that your child's view of the other parent may be quite different from your own. If you have lost contact with your 'ex', are you doing all you can to find other good adult role models of

the opposite sex from your own? This is no less important for the child whose care-taking parent is in a gay relationship.

Notes

1 *HOMECOMING – Championing the Inner Child,* John Bradshaw, Piatkus Books, London, 1991.
2 *KARMIC RELEASE – Journeying Back to the Self,* Ann Merivale, Sai Towers Publications, Bangalore, 2006.

CHAPTER FOUR

SEVEN TO EIGHTEEN - THE AGE
OF TEMPTATION

The more you do, the more you will rediscover your talents at fathering and your own unique style. There is nothing as satisfying as raising great kids.
Steve Biddulph (Raising Boys[1])

Age seven can be seen as the beginning of the outward journey, following, for most people anyway, seven years spent mainly in the safety of home and family relationships. This outward journey entails separation, the literal meaning of which is 'division into parts'. For our origin is unity, in the world of spirit, where all is light, and, as God points out to Neale Donald Walsch in *Conversations with God*[2], if all is light we need darkness to be able to recognize our own light. This is the reason why we descended into the darkness of matter in the first place. Hence the role of temptation, the lure of the material world, which begins to impinge more and more as the child emerges from the shelter of the home environment.

By the age of seven, children will normally be well settled into a routine of school, and will have an established circle of friends and acquaintances outside the intimacy of the home environment. This contributes to the discovery of the self as a separate entity – an individual – and for some this discovery comes earlier than for others, probably depending mainly on upbringing. So the years from seven to eighteen are those in which we begin to establish our identity, and this establishment involves experimentation: trying on different costumes in order to find out which one fits the real you. Drama at school can make a valuable contribution to this. A group of children for whom special activities were laid on while their parents were attending a Justice and Peace conference, were each asked in turn "Are you special?". The replies were all negative until one nine-year-old boy had the courage to say "Yes...because I'm a unique part of God's creation"! Identity is, however, closely related to ego, and establishment of the ego necessarily involves a certain amount of 'selfishness'. So parents, rather than being alarmed or upset by our offspring's apparent selfishness, can accept it as an inevitable part of their development at the same time as doing our best to educate them to care about others.

Peer influences obviously increase gradually during this period, peaking in the teenage years, when rebellion against parents is not only normal but also healthy. I am calling it 'the age of temptation' since so many different kinds of temptation – from sweets to drugs and sex, for instance – are thrust at the developing youngster without his going out of his way to look for them. Many children who can in no way be described as delinquent occasionally steal from each other or get tempted into little acts of shoplifting and, as they get older, desire to exper-iment with such things as drugs is also very natural. A Benedictine monk speaking on BBC Radio 4's 'Thought for the Day' in October 2010 mentioned how shocked a friend of his had been when, on taking her child to apologize to the manager for stealing something from his shop and pay for the item, the reaction had been "Well, everybody does it." It may be normal behavior for children in this age group, but this does not make it less important to educate them to be honest citizens.

At this stage of life, focus is predominantly on the lower energy centers, and the first two *chakras* (the 'root', 'base' or – for the Hindus – *muladhara*, and the second *chakra*, called the *swadhishthana* in Sanskrit, which is located in the area of the generative organs and is considered by the Hindus to be the source of our creative potential) are more crudely physical, regulating, in the words of Dr. Samuel Sandweiss[3], "biological and physical development and the early aspects of personality". For Piaget this is the first sensorimotor stage of cognitive development, and Sandweiss says that "the development of these two *chakras* can be related to Freud's oral, anal and phallic stages and Erikson's stages of basic trust versus mistrust, autonomy versus shame and doubt, and initiative versus guilt. Development issues center around the child's acquiring a basic sense of security, developed through consistent loving care by the mother, and a sense of autonomy and strength, which is developed through the child's struggle with the parents as he or she becomes more mobile and willful. This sense of autonomy is influenced by the attitude and behavior of the parents in this challenging stage". Everything at this stage tends to be up front, and sex is more on the outer level. As we mature and progress to the higher *chakras*, sexual feelings move more to the inner level and can thus become more spiritual. It is important for parents to instill in their children a right attitude towards sex before they (inevitably!) absorb a wrong one from their peers and/or the media.

While we are focused on the lower centers, dependency and identity predominate. And linked to identity at this stage is of course the ego. Paradoxically, the more ego there is, the less real power; by getting rid of the ego we attain the Self. Hopefully by eighteen we will have taken the first steps towards finding this Self, and good parenting is the best contribution to this. 'Ego trips' are caused by a need for attention from others because you are not in touch with your Self, and their effect is the exact opposite of what is desired, i.e. they drive people away, while the stillness that comes from connection with Self draws others. Dr. Wayne Dyer, the well known American spiritual teacher and author of numerable books, defines EGO as "edging God out". (I strongly recommend his recently made first film, *The Shift*.)

Survival, commitment and the rediscovery of the material world are all linked to the first *chakra*, as is reaction to difficulties, and this last has to lead eventually to acceptance. To quote Ngawang Rigdzin, a French lama who completed all the Woolger training at the same time as I did: "ALL our *samskaras* (the *karmic* residues which force us back to Earth over and over) come from 'Noes' – non-acceptance of what is". Linked to the second *chakra* are both dependency and family relationships, but the enjoyment of social interaction and the discovery of self through relationships with other significant people are also important aspects of what is known in Buddhism as the Hara.

Moving upwards, the third *chakra* is located in the solar plexus, which is in the abdominal area just below the navel, and is generally recognized as the seat of power. The solar plexus is also the seat of both fear and excitement, so we can say that this is the *chakra* of adventure. This could often involve, for instance, a first trip away from the family, even if it is only a school outing or a scout camp. The third is also the *chakra* of individuality, and the discovery of identity can bring with it happiness, fun and sociability as well as personal power. The third *chakra* (and also the fourth and fifth, which we come to at a later stage) are, again quoting Sandweiss, "associated with the development of the distinctively human personality...The development of higher emotions and mental capacity." The years seven to eighteen are, surely, particularly important ones for coming into our own power, and Sandweiss says that this *chakra* is "associated with the psychological quality of expansiveness, power and self-expression" and that it "has to do with the drive to express the real power within, such as that found in great generals and kings", being "different from that [power] found at the anal stage, where the struggle for dominance and control is in reaction to a feeling of weakness and vulnerability and is primarily a defense against being manipulated, controlled and humiliated".

During these years, when focus is on the lower *chakras*, the physical tends to take precedence over spiritual interests. After all, we come in with a physical body and need to get to grips once more with all that that implies before we can focus fully again on what lies beyond; i.e. you have to experience the physical before you can break free from it. Identity seeks sensation, and while new sensations can be very exciting, the impressionable youngster can also very easily be hurt. Hurt of course calls for response, and as protective walls are built up as defense, gradually the cells become less open. The great American prophet Edgar Cayce said that we build our cells all through life with our mental attitudes, and while more layers are built around them, all our experiences, values, expectations and so on become locked in as conditioning. This makes radical change in attitude in later life very difficult, but in some lifetimes it is a particular challenge that we choose for our learning and growth, as my next character clearly did.

For Sharon the following words of Plato ring very true. In his Republic (X, 620e), he says "When all the souls had chosen their lives, they went before Lachesis. And she sent with each, as the guardian of his life and the fulfiller of his choice, the daimon that he had chosen, and this divinity led the soul first to Clotho, under her hand and her turning spindle to ratify the destiny of his lot and choice, and after contact with her, the daimon again led the soul to the spinning of Atropos to make the web of its destiny irreversible, and then without a backward look it passed beneath the throne of Necessity."

Sharon says that even at the age of seven she was aware of having chosen to be in her difficult family for a purpose. Her father was an alcoholic, and her mother, who has been bi-polar ever since Sharon was ten years old, gave all the attention to her older brother, about whom she was obsessive. Sharon's mother was appalled when she found herself pregnant for the second time, for fear that her son, two years Sharon's senior, would be jealous. While he was over-mothered and protected from any emotional feeling of hurt, Sharon was told (implicitly anyway) "you don't need anything; you're strong." Consequently she never cried, and people used to say that she was a doll. Though she endeavored to put on a normal front to the world, in reality Sharon lived in an independent bubble with no contact with either family or friends, and it was only her intuitive knowledge that she had a 'script' that made her life bearable. Even at that remarkably early age Sharon saw her difficult circumstances as a challenge to be got through, and she was somehow fully aware that the second half of her life would be all right. She made up her mind not to get "sucked into their drama", and she used to say to herself "Once I can detach myself from those three, I can become acknowledged as a full person."

Long before this better second half of her life could begin, however, Sharon had a great deal to endure. As a young child she was never allowed to be close to her brother, and his behavior often annoyed her. She was quiet at home but extremely disruptive at school, and got expelled twice. At meetings with the teachers, her mother used to say "the person you're describing is not my daughter"; and, while running wild at school, Sharon never really quite understood why she was always in trouble. The first major difficulty of her teenage years came when her brother was killed on a motorbike when he was only seventeen. Her mother blamed herself for the accident, saying that it was her fault that her son had been late for work; but she dealt with it by never mentioning his name again. Sharon says that her brother died in the morning and by four o'clock the same day he had ceased to exist, so that no real grieving was permitted to any member of the family. She herself, however, felt very angry at being left alone "to cope with these two nutcases", and that is surely more than reason enough for running wild somewhere!

When Sharon's brother died, her parents sent her to a boarding school, but, despite being happy there and not short of friends, she got expelled from the lower Sixth Form. She then went to the local college to try to finish her Advanced Levels, but got pregnant when she was only halfway through the course. The relationship which led to the pregnancy began with a rape by a young man whom I will call Ron, and after the rape Sharon went on to go out with him even though she had a huge fear of him. Her mother forced her to have an abortion, which was an incredibly traumatic experience for Sharon. Although she knew that she was too immature to have a child, she saw the abortion as murder, and Sharon now, in her more mature years, is convinced that she relived a past-life experience, for she screamed abuse at the surgeon to such an extent that she found herself asking "is that really me saying this?" Ron did not know about the pregnancy until Sharon wrote and told him, and later she met him in a pub with a girlfriend who looked to be at the same stage of pregnancy as Sharon would have been if she had kept her baby.

Sharon maintains that she coped because of the fact that she knew she had chosen it all beforehand, and she even blamed herself for the rape. (This is common also in cases of incestuous sexual abuse, often making it doubly difficult for the victim to seek help.) Sharon says: "When you choose an incarnation, you choose your parents accordingly. My choice was to be strong for them, and my father recognized that when he was dying of cancer. He told me then that he was proud of me." After her abortion, Sharon made up her mind never to be a victim again, and she is glad of her experiences, which she knows have made her a stronger person. She feels that there can be little that is more frightening for a child than to see her parents not in control, and she says that, though her father was verbally violent, her mother's depression was even more difficult to cope with than her father's alcoholism. Yet, "like water finding its natural course", Sharon comments that: "when you're in the drama it's different to how it might appear to an outsider, and we human beings have an extraordinary ability to find our own salvation".

Sharon found her salvation in nature and animals, with which she has always had a close connection. As a child she owned both a dog and a horse, and walking other people's dogs as well was another lifeline for her.

For many years Sharon had a recurrent dream, from which, when she was young, she used to wake up screaming. It was of a revolving spherical shape like the surface of Mars, which would divide into two, then four, then eight, and so on, growing enormously and coming closer and closer until she finally became absorbed by it. Now she sees this dream as an image of conception, and she believes that she entered the womb at an early stage in order to get the full impact of her mother's negativity. She says that "the horror of the dream is of losing knowledge" and that as a child she knew that she had had to lose her previous memories and that she would see clearly again once she had died. So, like Joan Grant, who I believe coined the phrase 'far memory', and whose beautiful past-life books[4] may be known to many of you, Sharon endorses James Hillman's 'acorn theory'.

The well-known American therapist, writer and lecturer, Dr. James Hillman, whom my mentor, the Jungian psychoanalyst Dr. Roger Woolger, describes as his mentor, writes very interestingly about what was known to the Greeks as the *daimon*, coining his own word for it. In *The Soul's Code*[5], Hillman says that today's Western paradigm for understanding human life, namely the "interplay of genetics and environment", omits the essential. He defines his 'acorn' theory thus: that each person bears a uniqueness that asks to be lived and that is already present before it can be lived. He further attempts to trace this *daimon*/'acorn' right through history, saying that for the Egyptians it could have been the *ka* (spirit) or *ba* (soul), with whom you could converse, while the Romans named it your *genius* and the Christians your 'guardian angel'. The Neoplatonists referred to an imaginal body – the *ochema* – that "carried you like a vehicle. It was your personal bearer or support", and later Michelangelo's intuitive eye saw an image in the heart of the person he was sculpting; and the Romantics, like Keats, said that the 'call' (which I suppose is used here as another word for *daimon*) came from the heart.

Hillman says that Plotinus (AD 205-70), whom he describes as "the greatest of the later Platonists", explained that we elected the body, the parents, the place and the circumstances that suited the soul and that, as Plato's myth says, "belong to its necessity". However – hardly surprisingly for someone born in 1926 and achieving prominence before such notions had begun to be taken seriously in the West – Hillman stops short of giving any clear definition of the *daimon*. So his successor Woolger, who was born nineteen years later, which is a long time in terms of the developments in this field, is bringing American psychotherapy forward immeasurably thanks to his understanding of the workings of karma. (Woolger is English, but has for many years worked on the other side of the Atlantic as well as in Europe.) Or should I perhaps say rather that he is taking it right back again? Back to the understanding that modern man (and woman) has so sadly lost, but that the Greeks describe admirably.

Sharon, now that she is a mature woman, sees clearly that she chose her difficult family in order to make her a stronger person. Though she is different from most of us, who do not understand what Plotinus says because we have forgotten, I am sure that she is by no means unique. (For example, Naomi in Chapter Two is being encouraged by her parents to remember that she chose them, and New Age literature abounds in stories of amazing children who are aware of having come in with a very clear purpose.)

Hillman says that "these many words and names [of the *daimon*]", which he comments contemporary psychology and psychiatry are unique in omitting from their textbooks, "do not tell us <u>what</u> it is, but they do confirm <u>that</u> it is. They also point to its mysteriousness. We cannot know what exactly we are referring to because its nature remains shadowy, revealing itself mainly in hints, intuitions, whispers of the sudden urges and oddities that disturb your life and that we continue to call symptoms". Well, this book of mine is an attempt to define and describe the *daimon*! I disagree with Hillman when he equates the *daimon* with our guardian angel, preferring myself to see it as our Higher Self or spirit (the *ka* for the Egyptians) and the guardian angel as the *daimon*'s colleague who helps the soul, while clothed in the physical body, to adhere to its Life Plan. And I suggest that the Life Plan is what Plato in his Myth of Er calls (again quoting Hillman) the *paradeigma*.

Hillman, however, describes the word *paradeigma* as "similar" to *daimon*, saying that it is a "basic form encompassing your entire destiny". But if we, along with, in Hillman's words, "Eskimos and others who follow shamanistic practices" see the *daimon* as "your spirit, your free-soul, your animal-soul, your breath-soul" or – my addition – your *atma*, then surely *paradeigma* is <u>not</u> similar. On the contrary, it is clearly the root of the English word *paradigm*, and *paradigm* is perhaps a good synonym for Life Plan. I believe Hillman is confusing the two when he says "Though this accompanying image shadowing your life is the bearer of fate and fortune, it is not a moral instructor or to be confused with conscience".

The very act of coming into material form from the purely spiritual one is, as I said, separation, and separation entails fear. Fear is, in varying degrees, a common characteristic of all human beings, and while one layer of it comes from this separation from the world of spirit – our true Home – another is caused by our *samskaras* from previous lives. Some souls (like Sharon) take this to extremes. For Sharon it was a case of choosing greater darkness to enable her greater light to shine, but often those living in the greater darkness are souls who have strayed so far from the light, over a series of incarnations, that they have completely forgotten its existence.

We have looked at how the different bodies are formed progressively and, just as the physical body carries on developing for a long time after birth, so the subtle bodies do not reach completion straight away. Richelieu's guide in *A Soul's Journey*[6] – a book that, though quite old now, I recommend very strongly – explains that, when the fetus is enclosed in the protective womb of the mother, the etheric, emotional and mental bodies are in turn each enclosed within the womb of the universe in the protecting envelopes of 'ether', 'desire stuff' and 'mind stuff'. He says that this protection continues after birth until the different bodies are sufficiently mature to withstand the conditions of the world – a thing that cannot be hastened any more than can the development of the physical body – and that before full use can be made of each vehicle, its positive qualities have to ripen. During the first seven years, while you are just getting to know yourself again as a physical being, the etheric body is coming to completion and its negative qualities are in operation. It is these that give young children clairvoyance, making it normal for them to have playmates who are invisible to others.

Following the birth of the etheric body, at about age seven, we move on through the next seven years to the consolidation of the emotional body. During this stage, which coincides with the establishment of individuality, developing emotionally is very important, as is sensation. All the senses are very alert, and so everything around the child can be a tremendous cause of excitement. In contrast to Sharon, who chose such a difficult and painful childhood for her growth this lifetime, my friend Carmen chose a reasonably happy one, yet there are nevertheless certain similarities between them.

Carmen, as her name suggests, was born in Spain (in the North), and she feels that she has been on a spiritual path ever since her childhood. An only child, she longed for siblings, yet was nevertheless always happy in her own company, and she was very close to her parents, particularly her father. The mark of an evolved soul is often said to be a desire to skip childhood, and Carmen always felt different from other children, who were just happy playing. "Playing was OK <u>some</u> of the time," she says, "but I daydreamed a lot and read a great deal as an escape, because I couldn't fit into the world very well, and I couldn't connect at school." Carmen was very unhappy in the state school and eventually persuaded her parents to move her to the convent school. She was always very drawn to the Church despite the fact that her father, who went through a period of being a Communist, was very anti-clerical and never accompanied his wife to church. Her mother never pushed her either with regard to church going, but she always got very good marks in Religious Studies at school.

Just as Sharon found her lifeline in nature, so Carmen's very happiest times were when her father took her on walks in the Pyrenees. She describes the beauty of the mountains, the sight and smells of all the flowers, the joy of drinking from the crystal clear streams and so on, as an overwhelming experience that she was unable to share with any of her peer group. Looking back now at her early years from the vantage point of a mature adult who has learnt a great deal about reincarnation, Carmen realizes that as a child she must have been very much in touch with previous lives as a monk and a pilgrim. For instance, her taste in food was quite abnormal for her age – in fact she regarded eating as a waste of time – and all she ever wanted was soup, brown bread, yoghurt and liver. Her parents used to get the local baker to bake specially for her, and she used to look in monasteries for yoghurt, which in those days was not widely available as it is now, and for goat's cheese in little market squares. Though educated by nuns, she found their lack of freedom repellent, and she feels that she has been a contented monk in the past, and that their spirituality goes deeper than that of nuns. People were puzzled by her eating habits, and some said that it stemmed from being an only child, but Carmen herself is sure that its roots are deeper. She points out that the medieval pilgrims used to eat the livers of animals that they found. I feel too that Carmen must have had a lifetime around Jesus for, even when she was being prepared for her first communion, she says that she could not connect Jesus to the Church, and she has retained a great devotion to him.

Age seven, when children tend to lose their natural psychic ability (clairvoyants excepted of course) is the time of the First Saturn Square. Saturn's task is to make us more Earthbound, and so hand in hand with the loss of the natural psychic ability comes an increased awareness of the physical body. This ties in with the point about all the senses being very alert. Like a young tree whose new leaves are very bright and fresh but also vulnerable, the cells of the young child are very open, so that everything will penetrate easily and make an impression, as on a soft sponge. That is why adult influence – particularly that of the parents – is so important at this stage. Young children are very imitative and it takes an exceptionally strong, advanced soul such as Sharon not to suffer permanent damage from an adverse home background. On the one hand the young child is exploring enjoyment of the senses, while on the other hand he is coping with shocks and traumas, some of which come from the deep past. In the interlife we suspend the working out of our *karma*, and clearing that is our chief reason for coming to Earth.

Another aspect of Saturn is to give an understanding of the concept of death. Traumatic though loss can be, the life of the Buddha shows the futility of any attempt to protect anyone from suffering, and the sooner we can learn that grief is as inevitable a part of life as joy the better. Having pets is often a valuable way for children to learn about death and the intense grief that it can cause. Also, learning to let go is as important a lesson as learning to love.

One of the most important things for the parent of a grieving child to do is to empathize with the reality of his or her experience rather than encouraging suppression of the feelings. Cutting off from our feelings is detrimental to the health and can even lead eventually to something such as cancer, and it can be done all too easily when the feelings are not seen as 'permissible'. As a child I did not suffer anything quite as traumatic as my daughter did at seventeen, when her first dog died at the age of only two and a half, but I still have a very vivid memory of the intense grief I felt over the death of the fictional character with whom I was 'in love'. Like most girls of my age at that time, I read the *Anne of Green Gables* books avidly, and the object of my affections was Anne's son Walter. When one of my school friends discovered in the library a lesser known sequel to the most popular of the books, Walter's death rendered the two of us inconsolable. For days on end I cried at school and I cried at home, which naturally worried my poor mother. When she eventually got out of me what had happened, she exclaimed "Oh, is <u>that</u> all?!" Though her relief is understandable, this reaction was not what I was needing at the time, and it took several Woolger workshops many years later to teach me fully to acknowledge and honor my feelings.

Bereavement through the death of a pet is a common occurrence at any stage of life, and people who are not, say, dog lovers normally find it hard to understand quite how painful it can be. I myself did not start life as a great dog lover and am consequently grateful to my daughter for having persuaded us to buy her a dog when she was fifteen. Though the deaths of three dogs have caused me some of the greatest grief that I have ever experienced, I would not have been without the lessons in love that our spaniels brought me.

Some children, however, (though fortunately fewer nowadays than in previous centuries) suffer the bereavement of a sibling or a parent, which will inevitably mark them deeply for life. In such cases professional counseling is very important, and they should always be encouraged to go on talking regularly about the person they have lost, have photographs of them around and so on. And as well as offering sympathy and understanding, it is useful to appreciate that this particular loss was something that they chose beforehand to experience as part of their learning, and also that 'loss' is never permanent since we come together with those closest to us over and over again.

Saturn, too, is connected with discipline and responsibility. As the child gradually becomes conditioned into society, going to school and having to fit into schedules and conform with rules and regulations, she becomes aware of boundaries and also begins to take responsibility for certain aspects of her life.

The next astrological landmark is the First Jupiter Return, at the age of twelve. Jupiter is concerned with philosophy and the meaning of things, and can help the just pre-teenager to become aware of abstract thinking rather than the purely concrete, and to expand her mind to incorporate a view of the world and of her own place in society. Then at fourteen, when the emotional body has been 'born' and the mental body starts on its road to completion, mental development becomes very fast.

In the Japanese Nine Star Ki system of astrology, our second number, which is our driving force, is manifest in childhood, while our personality number, derived from the year of birth, becomes fully operative in adulthood. So, following the landmark of the First Jupiter Return, the teenage years see the transition from the second number to the first in the Nine Star Ki system. Whether this transition is smooth or choppy will depend upon the relationship between these two numbers. If the two numbers are either in the same element or in supporting elements, the transition will be smooth, while if there is challenge between them, it will be choppy. Sharon is a Two/One (Soil/Water) and since Water challenges Soil, her transition can be expected to have been choppy, and we have already seen that it was. In contrast, my friend John is a Two/Nine (Soil/Fire), and the fact that Fire Supports Soil made his transition to adulthood quite smooth.

The same goes for my homeopath friend, Lawrence, a Nine/Two. Nine and Two, along with Four and Seven, are the feminine numbers, and John and Lawrence give evidence of the fact that it is possible for men who appear very masculine to have a strongly feminine side too. They are both evolved souls who matured early, and both got married young to women older than themselves. (Lawrence is another example of someone with the desire to skip childhood. He says: "I was old before my time".) Unlike many in the profession, both John and Lawrence became aware of their blueprints as therapists and healers at an early age, but there the similarities between them end.

John makes use of the Japanese Nine Star Ki System in his own therapy. The middle child of three, he was the only member of his family to be very spiritually inclined, and he has been a Buddhist for many years. His parents are Anglicans, and from the age of about fourteen John was drawn to monasticism. He says that he might well have become a monk had he not been advised against it by a clairvoyant friend who could see that he had already done enough of that in the past. Gurdjieff outlines three paths: that of the monk, that of action and that of the intellect. John studied Gurdjieff only briefly, finding his philosophical language difficult to cope with, but he decided in due course that his own path was Gurdjieff's fourth way, namely a combination of the other three.

As a child John went to boarding school, where he was happy, though always very dreamy (a prerogative of Twos). He formed an immense contrast with both his older sister and his younger brother, who rebelled during their teenage years. John's sister ran away from school at the age of twelve and never went back. She had a series of rather unsavory boyfriends and trained as a hairdresser before, at eighteen, undergoing secretarial training, which led her in due course into several high-powered jobs. She eventually married and is now engrossed in looking after two young children. Similarly, John's younger brother was really rebellious until the age of eighteen and also refused to go to school. Paradoxically, his healing was brought about by a serious accident. At seventeen he bought a motorbike and promptly smashed both his legs, ending up in hospital for seven months. A blood clot in his heart caused his life to hang by a thread, and this brush with death produced an overnight change. Upon his recovery John's brother buckled down to Advanced Level examinations and then went on to university.

The Tibetans say that the teenage years are the most dangerous because during this period we have the potential to create the most mess, and may then have to spend a large part or all of the rest of our life sorting it out. John, who has already fathered (or rather step-fathered) four teenagers, comments that they are like wild horses, that they can be disjointed and difficult to control. Tempted in many different ways – especially in the Western world at the moment, where their peers often seduce them into drugs, cigarettes and alcohol – they tend to be awkward with their emotions and consequently either over the top or excessively reserved. Despite its obvious dangers, John points out that over-indulgence can be good, as it spurs you into growth and exploration.

The attempts at establishing self-identity tend to peak during the teenage years, but, as with everything else in life, there are no hard and fast rules about timing. Christopher, our adopted son, was, as the head teacher at his second primary school used to remark, "more or less <u>born</u> a teenager", while others might start breaking out at nineteen, just after the end of the period that this chapter is dealing with.

Christopher, like John's second stepson Timothy, who was born just three days later, is a Three/Six, but he got through his extremely choppy transition to adulthood somewhat earlier than Timothy did. They are both extremely intelligent, but Timothy messed up his 'A' Levels and took longer to find his path.

Christopher's passion for basketball, combined with the discipline and dedication typical of a Six Metal (his driving force), gave him the ability to succeed in both the academic and sporting fields under immense pressure from all sides at his American college.

Anyone whose adult number is masculine – One, Three, Six or Eight – will have a bigger, more assertive ego to establish, and girls who are Sixes will be frustrated if their environment is not conducive to their having a career. My daughter has the advantage over me of being in a generation in which girls are expected to have careers, and has taken very much less time than I did to find her path. Fives, being in the middle, take their gender from their other number. But when Five is the adult number, finding one's path can be made difficult by uncertainty as to who one is. Kate, the eldest child in John's family, had a choppy transition to her number Five, which included making a change of university.

In contrast to the older two, Jeffrey, the third child in John's family, had a very smooth transition, going straight from school to Cambridge. His numbers – One/Six – are the most masculine of all, but Metal supports Water, and so Jeffrey has manifested very few problems, even getting himself a job lined up well in advance of completing his degree. Anthony, who comes after Jeffrey, is another double feminine (Nine/Seven) and, though his transition can be expected to be choppy, he has learnt from the mistakes of his older siblings and is also very clear in his choice of a degree in Computing.

Another "dreamy Two" with whom I have strong past-life bonds is Jonathan, who, though no-one meeting him nowadays would ever imagine it, claims to be following the Tibetan dictum and sorting out the "mess" caused by his choppy transition (Two/One). He is the father of three teenage girls, of whom Emma is only fifteen months older than her twin sisters Sarah and Harriet. Not surprisingly, he comments that the sheer physical task of caring for three young children – one could almost call them triplets – was relentless for at least the first six years. Jonathan and his wife invariably felt themselves to be one hand short. However, the plus side of all that hard work and getting through their most intense period of parenting unusually quickly, is that it left them both with more freedom to pursue their separate careers.

The twins, who are not identical, are Four/Sixes and so, once fully grown into their adult numbers, will to some extent challenge not only their parents, who are both Soils, but also Emma, who is a Six/Four. On the other hand, having the same numbers entails a certain amount of understanding between the three girls, and now that they have mutual teenage interests, they are becoming increasingly good companions. Jonathan says that, "since the twins were a more powerful unit than any or all of the rest of us, and having consequently in their very early years rather deprived Emma of attention, it is lovely to see them now looking up to their older sister". Choppy transitions to adulthood can be predicted for all three of these girls, but Jonathan's own experience will no doubt have prepared him for coping with that. He moved from a masculine to a feminine number, and his twins will too, while Emma will do the reverse.

It is not the purpose of this book to add to the numerous studies already done of twins, but I was very interested when, talking about the establishment of identity being an important feature of the Seven-Eighteen period, Jonathan told me how, at the age of about nine, Sarah and Harriet began to display a fierce determination to be independent and separate from one another, needing to mix with separate friends and pursue different activities. This is still the case even now that all three girls are sharing similar teenage interests, and Jonathan has always encouraged that. At the same time, he does not expect them to share his, deeply spiritual, interests, nor even to be interested in his activities, thoughts or values. He comments that "teenagers today have so many carefully targeted things of their own that the adult world seems irrelevant to them", and that "even the pop stars nowadays seem to be teenagers". He is, however, confident that one day they will "wake up and remember some of what their parents used to go on about".

Despite feeling some concern in retrospect that having the twins when Emma was only fifteen months old made them unable to give her sufficient attention, Jonathan is very happy now that she is fifteen to see her really blossoming. A major change started for Emma at the age of ten, when she got a place at "the perfect school", and Jonathan says that her blooming into young womanhood really started at fourteen. As Emma grows into her adult number, which is Six Metal, she will have the support of her Soil parents, while the twins, in maturing from Six Metals to Four Trees, will be more of a challenge. (Though Fours, who are like mature oaks, are less challenging than the very vibrant Threes.) In spite of the inevitable squabbles of three children so close in age, Jonathan is very positive about the "powerful frictions" of the teenage years, which he sees as an opportunity for parents themselves to progress, and so he says that it is important for parents at this stage not to close up. "As teenagers seek freedom and expression of their own souls, so too the parents, if they allow themselves to do so, can break out and seek their own freedom and expression again, because these so often get suspended during the period of early child care with its many trials and burdens".

Jonathan is realistic, too, about the mood swings which are a normal feature of teenage years. He says that they "have learnt a little as a family about allowing each other to be in a foul mood, which seems to mean that they don't last too long". And, unlike those parents who yell "Help, I've got a teenager!", Jonathan found it wonderful and exciting to watch his daughters "going off on their own journeys and developing their own lives". He endures the "grunge" (fashion, make-up and horrible clothes and language), which his older daughter is now into, recognizing it as a passing phase ("like roses, she will bloom again!"), and he is enjoying watching the fourteen-year-old twins "beginning to fill out into their maidenhood". As for his daughters' attitude to him, Jonathan relates very much to the quotation from Mark Twain: "When I was a boy of fourteen my father was so ignorant I could hardly stand to have the old boy around. But when I got to be twenty-one, I was astonished at how much he had learnt in seven years." For they will say more or less in the same breath "My Dad's great" and "My Dad's a complete idiot".

Another acquaintance of mine, Pauline, has twins of a similar age to Jonathan's, but they are identical boys, and she says that they do share her spiritual interests. Although they do not yet read the same sort of books as she does, they listen with interest when Pauline talks to them about her beliefs, and one of them recently asked his long-deceased grandfather for his help in a test he had to do and believes that this was given to him. Like Sarah and Harriet, however, Paul and Philip started at about the age of nine to express a desire for independence. In fact it was at this very time that they were first given the option of being in separate classes at school, and, though Philip feels more strongly about it than does Paul (the older of the two), they both leapt at the opportunity and have been in different classes ever since.

Pauline has always taken care to dress her boys differently, and at primary school it was always a source of annoyance to both of them, as well as to their mother, when the teachers made no effort to tell them apart. That has changed now, thanks mainly to their being in different classes, but being identical does make it difficult for outsiders to tell them apart when they are not together. They are both extremely bright, though Philip tends to have the edge academically and is always very determined not to be beaten by his brother. Pauline says that he will most certainly want to go to a different university from Paul. Paul, on the other hand, has the edge socially, being more outgoing and apparently more confident than Philip.

Paul and Philip would really have liked to do different Advanced Level subjects from one another, but it so happens that the sciences and music are what they are both best at; and doing the same subjects also means that they now tend to have mutual friends, whereas they had previously made efforts to have separate ones. Although they bicker in a way that is quite normal for siblings, they get on well, and the fact that they both play in an orchestra (one the flute and the other the clarinet) inevitably makes them do quite a lot together. They also travel to Newcastle together for lessons from professional musicians, which are paid for by the County Council on account of their gifts. This shared talent is a very interesting point, since Pauline says that it is certainly not genetic, much though she herself loves music. Perhaps one of the reasons that they chose to incarnate together was a mutual desire to express this particular talent this time round.

In Jonathan's family, fourteen appears to be the age for blossoming, but, in contrast, my twenty-three-year-old niece Nicola says that "fourteen is the worst age because no-one understands you. Adults claim to know what's going on, but that's rubbish. Only Kittypuss understands! (Or perhaps, on second thoughts, the really close relationship with one's family cat is more when you're twelve.)" Nicola, who has always been a very pretty girl, says that when she was fourteen she looked into the mirror and burst out crying "because I was so revolting". Certainly my own feelings at that age were identical – in fact they carried on for very much longer – but I shared with Nicola the disadvantage of having a highly critical father. We were both put down at a time when it is crucial for the developing teenager's confidence to be built up. My sister's divorce was in many ways Nicola's salvation, and in any case my sister was good at counteracting her husband's negativity towards the children. Emma, Harriet and Sarah are blessed with a father who would always do all he could to make them feel good about themselves, but were Nicola's feelings about her appearance caused <u>entirely</u> by her father, I wonder? Do many young teenagers share them? It is of course the beginning of the "acne phase", when hormones are wreaking havoc in young bodies, and pre-menstrual tension can also have powerful effects.

According to Nicola, seventeen is the "perfect age for a girl", because you can "just about get away with being eighteen but are still a child, so you can have the best of both worlds". She was at boarding school in Oxford, and says that at seventeen she got good at climbing out of the dormitory window and passing as a student. She used to meet up with boys who were three or four years older and then climb back in before dawn without getting caught! John Cleese did a television program in which he described fifteen to twenty-four as "the window of attractiveness, and Nicola herself reckons that seventeen is the best age physically – for both looks and fitness – and that girls then "have all the attributes that they know they're made for". Boys, on the other hand, she considers unattractive at seventeen, and says that they become attractive at about twenty or twenty-one.

Nicola's parents divorced in time for her to reap the benefits of being seventeen, and she now has a wonderful stepfather. My former client Louise, on the other hand, was seventeen when her parents separated, and that had a devastating effect upon her. Louise, who is now in her thirties, is another exceptionally attractive young woman, but the fact that her father never told her how lovely she was makes it to this day very difficult for her to overcome her low self-esteem. Although she remembers that she never thought her parents were well-suited to one another, Louise's childhood was happy, and the discovery at seventeen that her father had been constantly unfaithful to her mother was an appalling shock to her. She reacted by moving out more or less straight away into a relationship which lasted six years but was never very satisfactory, and she has since had several other relationships that have not lasted. Her father's failure to provide a model of commitment has been a major disadvantage to her.

But there are worse ways of reacting to trauma than Louise's. How many teenagers, at the height of 'the age of temptation' get pregnant or badly into drugs? Drug Abuse Help Centers, Alcoholics Anonymous etc. seem quite unable to keep up with the ever-increasing problems of the present century. What the real answer is I am quite unable to suggest. I can only assume that all of the really horrible things that are going on at the moment are part of humanity's learning and the *Kali Yuga* of Hindu philosophy. We have, it seems, to sink to the very depths before we can return to the Light. Corruption has destroyed a large part of the Earth before (Atlantis!) and will no doubt do so again, but the encouraging part of it is that some of us at least do learn from the errors. Edgar Cayce said that many of those who contributed to the downfall of Atlantis were back here today working to avert a similar disaster. Dr. Roger Woolger, in his Deep Memory Process therapy training courses, is always keen for students to explore their 'shadow side' as well as reliving and releasing traumas. My personal experience of this makes me sure that we have all been, at some point in our past, oppressors and abusers as well as oppressed and abuse[7].

Abuse is another important aspect of this phase of life. Verbal/emotional abuse, physical abuse, sexual abuse – all are devastating to the developing child. In my youth I suffered only from the first of these, and I particularly recommend the books of Alice Miller on the subject. My knowledge of sexual abuse has come only through my work as a therapist, and it is now well recognized that incestuous sexual abuse – so hard for so many of us to even begin to contemplate – is infinitely more common than we have previously been willing to acknowledge. It is an extraordinarily complex question involving so many different elements besides the feelings of guilt which are common in the victims. For instance, in my book *Souls United*[8] I wrote about

"Olivia", whose twin soul "Patrick" had in a previous life as her father made her pregnant. In that case the twin-soul bond caused the attraction between them to be so strong that it overrode the natural taboo against an incestuous sexual relationship, and "Olivia's" difficulties in that life were compounded by confused love/hate feelings for her then father, who is her ex-husband in her present life. Nowadays, fortunately, it is becoming generally recognized that sexual abusers are normally people who were previously similar victims themselves and – though such behavior can never be condoned or fully excused – I hope that it will soon be recognized too that prison is not the answer. The scandals of Catholic priests in both America and Europe have at least encouraged people in the Churches to take power into their own hands!

When I discussed with my client Madge the fact that her sexually abusive father never wanted to visit his own parents suggested that he had himself been similarly abused, she asked me "So how come I would not feel capable of abusing any child that I had?" My reply was that I had come to the conclusion that, once a cycle had been deemed in the spirit world to have gone on for long enough, a particularly strong soul would volunteer to step in and break it. This I certainly believe to be the case with Madge, whose experiences of abuse from her father since babyhood, from her older brother from a young child, and then rape by a total stranger on her university campus would undoubtedly have completely destroyed many weaker souls. Plagued by flashbacks which had been disturbing her sleep as well as making study very difficult for her, Madge took first the brave step of coming into therapy and secondly, perhaps even more difficult, of reporting her father to the police. Though she probably has a long haul ahead, I hope and expect that she will ultimately achieve her ambitions of becoming a wife and mother as well as of finding herself a worthwhile career. In this life she is no doubt paying off some karma connected with sexual abuse, but while doing that, thanks to the fact that she is probably more evolved and stronger than either her father or her brother, she should be able to break the cycle. Some people who have had such negative experiences later turn them into something positive with which to help others who have been abused.

Most aspects of sexuality are fortunately not abusive. Whatever Freud may have had to say on the subject, sexuality and all that it implies begins fully with puberty. We are all 'halves' feeling a need for completion, and so that is what attraction to the opposite sex (or sometimes the same sex of course) is all about. However, when adolescents begin to experience sexual feelings, they do not normally have any idea that they are really seeking the other half of their soul, and so these feelings can sometimes cause confusion and problems, such as teenage pregnancy. Education in this area is therefore of paramount importance and can never start too early.

In their search for their own identity, teenagers have a natural need to destroy old patterns. This is part of the evolution of society as a whole as well as that of young individuals, and rebellion is therefore not a thing to be feared. This period is a time for acute self-analysis, integrating the different aspects of the self, and exploring one's subconscious. When taken to extremes, this exploration can lead to problems such as anorexia, but on the whole it is very healthy.

The years seven to eighteen are an exciting, fascinating time of life. Anyone who has brought up teenage children themselves will know this, and if you have not done so, then you were certainly once a teenager yourself. It is the period when physical and mental development are both very rapid, and during which influences from outside the home gradually increase in importance. Those who have had the secure base of a loving home during their first seven years will usually integrate more easily as they spend increasing amounts of time outside it, but advanced souls sometimes select difficult homes as a particular challenge. The extent to which the Life Plan begins to become clear at this stage varies as much as do individuals, but the best thing that parents can possibly do during these years is to enjoy them.

Notes

1   *Raising Boys,* Steve Biddulph, Thorsons, London, 2003.

2   *Conversations with God – An Uncommon Dialogue, Books.1, 2 and 3,* Neale Donald Walsch, Hampton Roads, USA, and Hodder and Stoughton, London, 1997.

3   *Spirit and the Mind,* Samuel Sandweiss, M.D., Sri Sathya Sai Books and Publications Trust, India, 1985.

4   *Winged Pharaoh,* probably the best known of Joan Grant's 'novels', is published, like all her other books, by Ariel Press, Columbus, Ohio, 1985.

5   *The Soul's Code – In Search of Character and Calling,* James Hillman, Bantam Books, London, 1997.

6   *A Soul's Journey,* Peter Richelieu, Thorsons, London, 1996.

7   See my first book, *KARMIC RELEASE – Journeying Back to the Self,* Ann Merivale, Sai Towers, Bangalore, 2006.

8   *SOULS UNITED – The Power of Divine Connection,* Ann Merivale, Llewellyn, 2009.

EXERCISES

1   Thinking back to your childhood and teenage years, were they predominantly happy or unhappy, easy or difficult? Do you think that your parents handled them well or that they could/should have done better? If the latter, do you feel you can learn from their mistakes in the raising of your own children?

2   Did your own path in life begin to come clear during this period, or did it take a lot longer? Both are quite normal – life would be boring if we were all the same! Looking back over some of your difficult experiences, can you see how they

helped you to gain strength? Perhaps even that they caused your life – either directly or indirectly – to take a turn for the better? (My adopted son would not have discovered his career in basketball had it not been for his having been sent to a different school after being excluded from the first one we chose for him!)

3   If you are the parent of a child or children in this age group, do you expect them to take after you and/or your partner, or are you doing all you can to encourage them to find their true Selves? Heredity is certainly a big factor, but their own past lives (in many of which you may not have figured at all!) may well be just as strong an influence upon them. Are you willing to encourage and guide them in finding their path without putting pressure, and also to appreciate that they may be either more or less intelligent than you are and that a good heart is much more important than a good brain?

CHAPTER FIVE

EIGHTEEN-TWENTY-SEVEN - KARMIC RELATIONSHIPS

The age period from 16 to 30 years is a crucial stage, when man achieves best and struggles hardest to achieve. Once frittered, these years of life can never be regained! Take no devious path, but move in the footsteps of God and the godly during this period of your life.
Sathya Sai Speaks, Volume X

Probably the most obvious thing about eighteen is that – in our society at least – it is regarded as the moment when young people "come of age", i.e. become adults, and so it is at this point that the dissolution of ties with parents really begins. Alongside this of course goes learning to stand on one's own. The years from eighteen to twenty-seven are generally the best ones for doing this, equipping us to make a truly satisfactory and lasting relationship, rather than one of co-dependence. Some people learn to stand on their own much more easily than others, and I am sure that those who start life in a secure and loving environment have a big advantage over those who do not. For is not giving love the best way to instill self-confidence in a child?

The issues of making the break with home and of learning to be on one's own pose questions in my mind, one of which is that of cultural differences. In England and in North America it is common for those who 'come of age' to leave home for university or college, or for a job in another city, and this is an obvious first step in these two developments. However, this is certainly not the case in a country such as India, and even in certain European countries – for instance France – it is more common for young adults to go to university in their own city than to leave home. So are these developments during this period at least partly dependent upon the attitude of parents?

My Indian friend Jyothi has lived in England for many years because her husband works here as a doctor. She lived at home with her parents until her marriage at the age of twenty-seven, which is the norm in India, as it is in many other countries. Jyothi agrees with me that learning independence is important for this age group, but feels that it is not necessary to leave home in order to do this. Her own nineteen-year-old daughter, Shruti, is at present studying at the local university, but this is mainly because it happened to offer the best course for her. Jyothi and her husband are encouraging Shruti to mature as an independent person, just as their parents in India did for them at a similar age, and they accept the fact that living in England will probably mean that she will in due course make her own decision about a husband.

A loving environment is a big advantage, but we parents should always remember that one of the most important aspects of loving is being able to let go. It is during this period that the etheric cords between children and their parents should begin to weaken or disappear. Endeavoring to keep control over one's 'children' after they are eighteen is not love. It is possessiveness, and possessiveness is self-love, whereas love for one's offspring should be entirely selfless. My husband once had a colleague whose widowed mother went with him firstly to Cambridge, where he was a student, and then to the city where he got a job, and he eventually married in his forties as soon as his mother had died! That is of course an extreme case, but parents do not need to be actually living with their children in order to exercise excessive control. In Volume Two of Winafred Blake Lucas' valuable handbook for professionals in regression therapy, there is much discussion of the question of 'spirit releasement', and in the relevant section there is a chapter by the well-known Dutch regression therapists Rob Botenbal and Tineke Nordegraaf on 'attachment by living parents'[1]. Letting go is perhaps the most difficult thing of all about parenthood, as well as the most important, and it is probably the chief cause of friction between young adults and their parents.

Some souls, however, choose to incarnate without a loving environment as a challenge for their growth. In the last chapter we left my friend Sharon – a prime example of a survivor of a non-loving home – having had an abortion against her will at the age of seventeen, and having made up her mind never again to be a victim; but the very difficult times, that she had been aware for so long of having chosen, were nevertheless to continue for longer than the period of this chapter. At the age of twenty-one, having successfully broken away from her parents and gone to agricultural college, Sharon met her first husband, Norman, who was only eighteen. This was an obvious case of a 'karmic soul mate'[2] because she felt a strong revulsion to him at their first meeting, and when she did her first past-life regression many years later, she found herself being killed by Norman on a battle-field. She says that she recognized his eyes!

It must be difficult for anyone without experience of regression therapy to appreciate how people in a different life can be recognized, since we take on a new physical body for each lifetime, but the well-known regression therapist Dr. Brian Weiss says in *Only Love is Real*[3] that he always tells his clients to look into the person's eyes for soul recognition. (After all, are not the eyes said to be the 'window of the soul'?) Being a visual person is not necessary either – feelings are more important – and even those who think of themselves as "very poor regression subjects" can with practice learn to trust whatever comes. My own experience endorses that of Brian Weiss' clients when they say "I just <u>know</u> it's so and so". So often, (as Weiss has found too), encountering present friends or relatives in previous lives explains things that are happening in the present.

In Sharon's case, her first husband clearly had a karmic debt dating from the time when he had killed her (then a man) on a battlefield, and it will no doubt have been this rather than any real feelings of love that drew them together in this lifetime. In fact Sharon says that they both grew a lot during the fifteen years of their relationship, so she regards her marriage as a valuable, if often painful, experience, and the split, which was her decision, was not made until after Norman's karmic debt to Sharon had been paid, which enabled her to cut ties with him.

Karmic relationships, formed so frequently during this period, are often extremely painful. My one-time client Suzy, mentioned in Chapter Two, fell in love at the age of twenty with a Malawian called Kingsley, who was the captain of a ship that docked in Hull, and she had a daughter by him. Kingsley's father, however, who was a chief, could not permit his son to marry a white woman, and much to Suzy's distress, he was forced to return to Malawi when the baby was only three weeks old, and she has never seen him since. The affair was painful for two reasons. Firstly because Kingsley – presumably because hurting her was so very hard for him – simply told her that he had to return to his ship, and she only learnt from a friend of his that he would not be coming back to England. And secondly because, after re-establishing contact with him thanks to the friend, he asked Suzy to go out to Malawi and marry him, and even sent her the plans of his house. She had got as far as having injections in order to go out there with the baby, when he suddenly wrote again saying that he had changed his mind and was marrying a woman from his own tribe. She feels sure that Kingsley's father-chief stepped in there!

Twenty-eight years later, though still feeling somewhat sad about it, Suzy said that she believed that one's life has a plan and that marrying Kingsley and living in Malawi was not part of hers. It took her about a year of smashing things in the house to work off her anger and then, when her daughter was about two years old, she married a man from Eritrea who also worked on a ship. This turned out to be another relationship that was doomed to failure as, due to the conflict in Ethiopia at the time, the small minority of Eritreans on the ship were in severe danger from their Ethiopian colleagues. While the relationship with Kingsley had been a true love match, this case was more one of Suzy putting herself into the role of rescuer, and she ended the relationship after her husband became involved in guerrilla activities which took him constantly to Italy. Since then she has had other relationships with African men that have not lasted, and she had a son by one of them.

Wondering why she appeared to have a preference for black men, I took Suzy back to a lifetime in which her cruel father had had a black servant hung simply for having been seen kissing her. I expected the servant to turn out to be Kingsley in a former life, but this was not the case. In fact it was no-one she had known in her present life, but it was clearly that guilt that had made her get trapped in a series of relationships which brought her nothing but suffering. Seeing this will hopefully enable her to break the pattern in future lives.

Returning now to Sharon, two sons were born of her marriage, and the first, Robert, has caused her endless problems, while the second, Owen, has been a constant joy and support to her. However, she was twenty-nine when Owen was born, so he is not relevant to this chapter. Robert, who is a Two/Four (Soil/Tree), can be expected to have had a choppy transition to adulthood, and he got into drugs at school at the age of about thirteen and was still, when I talked to her eight years later, struggling to break with both heroin and cocaine. In fact Sharon described Robert as "a nightmare from the moment of birth" and said that when she first held him, her overwhelming feelings of maternal love were coupled with feelings of "holding a monster"; (she even thought of Hitler's mother holding her much-loved child!). Sharon sees Robert now as someone with a difficult past whom she took on because she had a karmic debt to him, and throughout his life she has devoted much time and energy to helping him. She has been sustained throughout her very difficult life by the awareness of her blueprint – the knowledge that her life had a Plan which she had chosen herself before coming in – and by the conviction that the second half of her life would be a great deal better.

The resemblances between Sharon and Carmen ceased when they became adults. In the northern part of Spain, where the latter grew up, there were few openings for young women. The only real career available to girls was teaching, which she knew she did not want to do, so instead she learnt secretarial skills and crafts such as leatherwork, embroidery and lace making. She was obviously subconsciously aware of her blueprint, because she wanted at a young age to learn languages and communicate with other cultures, as well as to earn money and travel abroad. She achieved all of this in due course, but she began by working as a weaver in a local factory, where she greatly enjoyed making patterns, and even after she had mastered the machines, trained another girl in the craft. However, this caused jealousy among her older colleagues, and she also got rheumatism from the humidity, so, when she was eighteen, her parents persuaded her to think seriously about a move.

A job in Andorra as a hotel receptionist increased Carmen's independence and kept her happy for a few years, as she so enjoyed meeting people from all over the world. In Andorra she joined a group which met weekly, where she made strong friend-ships that she has sustained to this day, and she firmly believes that the reason for the strength of these friendships is that they are all people with whom she has also been close in previous lives. This group was mainly a social one whose principal aim was discussing different philosophies, which suited Carmen's enquiring mind, and she was able to discuss her doubts about her religion with a very open-minded priest who was also a member of the group. So her years eighteen to twenty-seven were very full and mainly contented.

Louise's, on the other hand, were less contented, though probably equally full, because she went first to university to do a B.A. degree, and then worked for a while before going to another university to do an M.A. Louise, who also had a choppy transition to adulthood, went, as we saw, straight into a relationship at seventeen when her parents separated, and this relationship was, as she put it, a "tempestuous one". Greg was very jealous of people who were close to her, which made Louise lose friends, and that in turn bred more insecurities in her. Greg's problems were no doubt partly caused by his having been sexually abused by a teacher at the age of thirteen. This made him leave school at fifteen, Louise was the first person he told about the incident, and he has never had any real help over it.

Greg is four years older than Louise, but was still living at home, and so she moved in with his family, who were nice to her despite seeing her as something of a threat. The tensions were relieved a little when she started at university and lived in a hall of residence, only returning at weekends, but when Greg left her for somebody else, she was completely shattered for a couple of years. Later she recognized the extent to which the relationship was not a healthy one, but felt that at least it taught her a great deal about "how not to act". She is also now rather ashamed of having felt vindictively pleased when Greg's new partner left him. When that happened he telephoned her every day for a while, but she knew it would not be right for her to go back to him.

Because of her fear of being alone, Louise did not lose any time after Greg had left her before entering into other relationships, and by the age of twenty-seven she had not yet learnt to be on her own. Neither, I hasten to add, had I! But Louise also appeared to have a problem with making a commitment, which may have stemmed mainly from the breakdown of her parents' marriage, or may have its roots in a previous life, or (more likely!)

both. Like so many young people today, she was excessively influenced by peer pressure, television and so on, which tend to encourage promiscuity. The West is at present recovering from several hundred years of sexual repression instigated by the Church, and that is all to the good in many ways. Inevitably, however, the pendulum has swung completely the other way, because that is what pendulums do. The Church divorced sex from love by regarding it as an 'evil necessity', while present-day society divorces it from love by treating it as essential to any comedy program. Hopefully, once enough people have come to appreciate on the one hand the sacredness of the sexual act when it proceeds from love, and on the other hand the difficulties caused by AIDS, unwanted pregnancies, and easy abortions, a better balance will ensue. (In *Many Lifetimes*[4], written jointly with her third husband, the psychiatrist Denys Kelsey, Joan Grant quotes an Anglican vicar of her acquaintance, who used to point out that the real meaning of the word 'adultery' is 'sex without love'.)

Another real difficulty for young people nowadays, which was not nearly so much the case for the preceding generation, is in finding jobs. On the one hand there is more choice of career than there was for us older ones, but on the other hand there is more competition, which means that even very well-qualified graduates often find themselves unemployed for long periods of time. My younger son's college in the United States was a particularly prestigious one academically, whose graduates used to expect to more or less walk into good jobs immediately, but 2002 saw a sudden big change there and some of his friends were still searching for jobs several months after graduating.

Some school leavers and graduates are clear about what they would like to do but unable to find openings, while others find it extremely difficult to make up their minds. Again this is all part of their karma. For the very lucky ones the Life Plan is straightforward, whereas others have a real struggle to achieve it. A young friend of mine, who knew from an early age that she wanted to be a vet, got all the required very high grades and the necessary work experience, yet was turned down by all the veterinary schools in Britain two years in succession. Fortunately she is German by birth and was eventually offered a place in a German university, where she is now doing very well, but such a possibility is of course not open to everyone.

On the other hand, it can happen that people discover their Life Plan more or less by accident. When my older son was still at school, I had his astrology chart done and was told that he would be a teacher initially. I did not tell him this, and was surprised when he announced an intention to go into computing. However, while he was looking for a job in that field, his girlfriend of the time, who worked in the recruitment of supply teachers, suggested that he let her recruit him temporarily. He then found that he enjoyed teaching and was good at it, and so forgot about the computing, at least for the time being. (This all changed later, when he found more satisfaction in a job as a soft ware developer, but this was not during the period with which this chapter is concerned.)

Even though we consciously forget what our Life Plan is when we are born, it remains always in our subconscious minds and sometimes little intimations will come through in some way or another to prepare us for what is in store. Robert Schwartz, in his interesting book that I have already mentioned[5], cites the case of a woman called Jennifer, who became passionately interested in autism and some time later had two autistic sons herself. Similarly, although nothing at all in my family background encouraged it, I was interested in race relations for a long time before we adopted our half Sierra Leonean son.

My Greek client Alex (who got "kicked towards those particular parents") had no idea what sort of career she wanted, and at the time of our therapy her greater concern was the matter of a relationship. She had an appalling childhood and adolescence, with very little love indeed, and it is therefore not at all surprising that she was through her twenties excessively anxious to make a relationship. For someone who is desperate for love, the obvious solution is to seek it from somebody else – from outside – and it often takes us a very long time to learn that the vital first step is to find it <u>inside</u>. Once we begin to love ourselves and cease to look to others for love, it will come from others of its own accord.

In Denise Desjardin's powerful book *De Naissance en Naissance*[6], an Indian 'Swami' regressed her to a tragic life in which her astrologer/guru agreed to marry her so that she could escape the cruelty of her foster mother. He then abandoned her as soon as he was tempted to break his vow of celibacy, and the Swami explains that if in a lifetime we fail to obtain the love we crave, we keep returning to Earth to look for it. Alex is clearly an example of someone who is doing that.

Alex describes her family, of which she is the youngest of three girls, as "dysfunctional". Her father had been having an affair with another woman for a long time before the divorce which occurred when Alex was eight, and she has clear memories of her parents discussing between themselves, but in front of the children, what should happen to her and her sisters should they separate. It was decided well in advance that the eldest would go with the father, the middle one would stay with the mother, while Alex would be sent off to her widowed paternal grandmother. This grandmother has never respected Alex's privacy, has always nagged her, and when things got too bad "at home" during her childhood, she would flee to her mother's house ten minutes' walk away, though the situation there was scarcely any better. The grandmother fluctuates between having good relations with her son, Alex's father, and good relations with her daughter-in-law, and the rest of the family are always expected to gang up against the one who is out of favor.

Apart from her favorite uncle, who died when she was twenty-three, the only people who ever gave Alex any affection were her maternal grandparents, but they lived quite a long way away and she never saw them more than a couple of times a year. Bad though her relations with her mother and her grandmother were, that with her father was worse still. He is very violent, and once when she was twenty-four and he came into her room drunk and she asked him to mind his muddy boots on her carpet, he beat her and kicked her repeatedly in the stomach.

Alex, who greatly wanted to be independent because the people who gave her money then tried to control her, worked for a few years after leaving school and managed to save enough money to get herself to university in England and thus escape from her family. One of her main reasons for wanting sessions with me was fear of her relationship breaking down, and when, as I had anticipated, the boyfriend did indeed break it off, he said it was because the "love attack" that she had launched on him was more than he could take. It is normal for someone who has been seriously deprived of love to try to obtain it by smothering another with demonstrations of affection, but this is not the answer to the problem. Over the weeks I encouraged Alex to read books on healing the inner child and to do the exercises in them. I also did my best to convince her that a more successful way to achieve her desire for a satisfactory relationship and a family of her own to whom to give love was to leave the boyfriend, Antonis, who was a few years younger than her, to live his own life and to concentrate on learning to love herself.

Alex was convinced that Antonis was her twin soul, and during our sessions she did indeed regress to a couple of previous lives in which they had been together, but I had to work quite hard to convince her that this was not necessarily a reason for them to be together again for the whole of this lifetime. The attraction between twin souls is usually strong as soon as they meet, but other factors come into play as well. For strong soul-mate bonds to work well, both parties need to be spiritually mature and not to need each other in the way that Alex needed Antonis.

Alex would only need to repeat a single phrase (for instance "I'm all alone") once, or to focus for a few seconds on a sensation in her body, in order to be plunged deep into a very vivid past life, and I would find it quite difficult to stem the flow of commentary sufficiently to get at the most important elements. I regressed her nevertheless to various previous lives in which she had also been "all alone", and this helped her determination to change the pattern this time. She also found a couple of previous lives in which she <u>had</u> experienced real love (either with Antonis or with someone else), and this helped her to believe that it would be possible again. Unfortunately we lost touch when she graduated and returned to Greece, but I hope that she will come to see that a lifetime shared with a companion soul mate can often be more satisfactory than a relationship with a twin soul for whom one is not ready, or who has chosen to work out some karma with someone else this time round. (As explained in my book[2], companion soul-mate relationships are often more comfortable than twin-soul ones. The intensity of the twin-soul bond can cause friction as well as bliss, whereas companion soul mates are close friends who may have often been previously, say, brother and sister as well as partners.)

Someone who was <u>forced</u> to learn to stand on her own at a very early age is my good friend Angela – a strong person and, I feel sure, a very old soul, whose blueprint for helping others has been clear all her life. As a child Angela received no nurturing or security, and she says that she has had to give these to herself, and that all her life she has been trying to establish roots. Her life has been characterized by people leaving. When she was seven, her mother kicked her father out because she had someone else, and the new man moved in for eighteen months. He turned out, however, to be unstable, Angela was frightened of him, and her mother threw him out when she started a new relationship that was to last much longer.

Angela's sister June was born of that third union, and they have always been very close. In a regression that she did with me, Angela found a previous lifetime in which she and June had been full sisters, and she also saw that she had a karmic debt to June from that time. She has been paying this ever since her mother's death from cancer when Angela was twenty-one and June was only twelve, because Angela's stepfather died not long afterwards and she was left to bring June up single-handedly.

But Angela had to learn to be strong and independent long before her mother's death. From the age of six or seven she had to get herself to school because her mother worked nights and did not get up in the mornings, and she always said that Angela did not need any nurturing. Nor did she have any nurturing to give. And although Angela's father visited twice a week until she was twelve and she went to his house occasionally, she has few memories of him from her early childhood. Here there are strong parallels with Sharon, as Angela's father says now that he always wanted a daughter and that he is sorry that he was not strong enough for her. She knew from a very young age, and also from a recent regression, that she had to be strong for him, and it is clear to her now that he is proud of that. Her visits to her father, however, are more out of duty than anything else, largely because his new partner has never accepted her. She says that her father, now around seventy, is stuck in the past and still loves her mother and, while empathizing with his feelings, she finds that his refusal to move on makes their relationship difficult.

Angela was working in a residential home for the elderly when her mother died, and so caring for young June as well was of course an immense burden, though one she took on very willingly, giving June a great deal of love. It was in the hope of finding some relief from this burden that, despite knowing deep down that it was not the best thing to do, she agreed to marry a man she did not love; her attempts to make the relationship work failed, and they parted after only six months. It could well be that she had a karmic debt to the man concerned, which it took only a short time to pay off; in any case she had no difficulty in cutting ties with him and has never had any deep regrets over the relationship ending. After it was over, Angela continued to put June's interests before her own, but managed at the same time to study for a degree in social work and then to become a very successful social worker.

Despite not having been brought up with any religion at all, Angela has always had natural spiritual inclinations, and when she was working in the residential home she made great friends with an old lady who was a devotee of Sai Baba. Clara found it very easy to interest her in Him, and so Angela was delighted when she read in a Baba magazine that a group was starting up in her area. She came along to the first meeting, which is where she and I first met, and has found her faith in Baba to be a tremendous support to her through many difficult times in recent years.

On the question of marriage, which so often takes place during these years, an interesting point is the difference in cultural customs and attitudes. It is only comparatively recently – more or less in my lifetime in fact – that arranged marriages have ceased to be common in France and Spain, and present divorce statistics in countries such as England and the United States give no support to the notion that 'falling in love' is the best criterion on which to base a marriage. We Westerners often feel sorry for people in countries such as India whose marriages are arranged by their parents, but my friend Jyothi assures me that it is not at all as most Westerners imagine it. First of all, she tells me that she herself turned down about forty possible suitors before agreeing to her marriage with Raj; and secondly, vital points such as astrological compatibility are taken into account. Knowing this couple, I am quite convinced that there is more love and happiness there than in very many so-called 'love matches' among Europeans and Americans.

One argument for the present-day freedom in relationships is that it allows people to work out karmic issues with one another before making a long-term commitment, and it would appear that many people nowadays choose to tie up various ends with several different previous partners (or perhaps 'would have been' partners) in one particular lifetime. The obvious time for doing this is during these early adult years, when people are beginning to establish themselves in careers and so on before starting a family. Certainly it is better if these ends can be tied up before children appear on the scene, as it is normally difficult to prevent them suffering when break-ups occur. Attraction that is caused by a karmic debt will often die a natural death once the debt is paid. Sai Baba likens it to logs floating down a river which drift together and then apart again.

Again, there are cultural variations here. This 'new freedom' has certainly not reached India – still less Saudi Arabia or Afghanistan! Jyothi says that living in this country did give her daughter some difficulties when her school friends reached the age for having boyfriends and girlfriends, and she inevitably felt "different", knowing that her parents did not want her to follow suit at such an early age. However, she accepted her parents' views without complaint, which endorses the whole contention of this book: the fact that we choose prior to conception the location and the cultural milieu for our birth.

In *Conversations with God*[7], God stresses to Neale Donald Walsch, that there is no such thing as 'right' and 'wrong'; simply that we learn over our many lifetimes what best serves us. So, though having myself been brought up as a "good Catholic" with an extremely strict code of "no sex before marriage", the very last thing that I would want to do is to pronounce judgment on which cultural custom is preferable. I can see arguments on both sides. The daughter of a friend of mine married at twenty-three while still (unusually in our present-day culture!) a virgin after a two-year engagement. The marriage lasted fifteen months, and she says that, had she lived with her partner beforehand, she would certainly not have married him. On the other hand, is the pain of break-ups even greater when people have been living together? Certainly there can be enormous complications if, say, a couple start to buy a house together and then separate.

I suppose that there are no real answers to these questions, and we always have to remember that every experience in life is part of our learning. I have mentioned the importance for parents of letting go, and is not the temptation to intervene in relationship difficulties with our offspring often great? At least, however, we always have the option of being there to offer support and a listening ear. (The trouble is that, good though we parents may be at letting go, when our children suffer we feel their pain as intensely as though it were our own! But that, too, is something we deliberately take on with each new lifetime.) My young Swiss friend Yann is someone who is during his twenties probably completing quite a lot of karma in regard to relationships, as, despite many attempts, he has not yet succeeded in maintaining one for any length of time. "Either I fall in love with them and they're not interested in me, or the other way round," he says ruefully, but by twenty-six he was securely on a spiritual path and confident that all his experiences had been for a good reason and that he would meet someone suitable when the time was right.

Yann, who is a Six/Three (Metal/Tree) in the Nine Star Ki system, says that he was quite rebellious and individualistic as a child (when his very active 'Three Treeness' would have been predominating). He remembers how, when he was seven, everyone in the class was expected to bring the teacher a present – his mother had even bought one for him to take – but he refused to do so because he did not like the teacher concerned. (When, however, the teacher asked them all to come up in turn with their present, he felt very bad!) Yann and his older sister were not given any religious education, but his mother talked to him when he was young about reincarnation, which must have been good preparation for the path he was to take later.

After leaving school, Yann started studying Forensic Science in Lausanne, his home town, but one mark of the choppy transition to adulthood which could have been anticipated in his case, was when he failed the examinations at the end of the first two years. He realizes now, however, that this was part of his Life Plan, because he subsequently decided on a career in alternative medicine. He chose to re-sit the exam straight away rather than take advantage of the option of repeating the year but, not being motivated, he then failed it a second time. So at twenty-one he went off to India, which was clearly part of his blueprint, for there he discovered Buddhism and felt an immediate connection with it. He went to a Vipassana Centre in Gujarat for ten days and then began meditating regularly, and he also started to read copiously - books ranging from ones on Buddhism and Sufism to Gandhi's autobiography. He has seen the Dalai Lama and met many Western lamas, and it was on a meditation retreat in Switzerland (run by Lama Ngawang Rigdzin and his wife Silvia, some of my fellow Woolger graduates) that Yann and I met.

Yann's difficulties actually date from birth, which was by Cesarean section because he had the cord around his neck, and he was then separated from his mother and put under surveillance for the first two days of his life. He has studied Stanislav Grof[8], who says that the way in which our birth takes place is responsible for the mental and behavioral patterns which we will probably keep all our lives unless we do specific work on them, and his own experience has convinced him of Grof's theory. Cesarean birth, according to Grof, gives people easier access to the transpersonal part of their psyche, such as past lives and the collective and ancestral unconscious, and makes them more open to the spiritual and mystical aspect of life. On the other hand, as

Yann has learnt through his studies of bio-energetic therapy, passing through the birth canal is important for one's grounding. So Yann now does things like walking barefoot to help him to be more grounded and to overcome being more 'in his head' than people who were not born by Cesarean section. He says that before coming across bio-energetics lots of things were jumbled up in his head, but that now things are becoming clearer, and his confidence is increasing immensely. His recent studies have led him to believe firstly that nothing happens by chance, and secondly that nothing is irredeemable.

More recently still, Yann has been given further help in resolving the problems caused by his birth through a regression that he did with my colleague Silvia. Since his English is excellent for someone whose mother tongue is French, I prefer at this point to quote Yann's own words (with just a few little corrections for the sake of comprehension):-

"I was lying down and Silvia pushed strongly on my chest. It was very painful, and I didn't even think to move to make this pain go away. As she was insisting that I make some efforts to avoid these sufferings, I started to move. And suddenly it became as if I was in the mother's womb, and I needed to move and to do everything I could to get out. It was very interesting, because I was born by Cesarean section; they opened my mother to take me out. And I feel that with this rebirth, it's as if I have completed something I never did before. Not to accept in a very passive way my sufferings, but to really try to do something about them. It is a situation that I lived very often in my life; I don't move, I can't move, say or do what I want, and then I feel guilty. So to relive this situation of my birth and to complete it helped me a lot in changing some habits and patterns I had which made me suffer..." (Tracing and acknowledging repeated patterns is one of the most important aims of Deep Memory Process therapy, because it is only their recognition that enables us to let go of them.)

Jann then continues, "And just before and after this I had very good 'signs' or 'omens': I was sitting in the train to go to Bienne (where Silvia and Ngawang live in Switzerland), and I had with me a book of a great Tibetan master that I bought in India one year ago. I was looking at the picture of the Lama, and I found it was a little grey. I saw that there was a plastic cover on the book. I took it out, and the picture was really colorful and beautiful after that. It was as if I had removed a veil.

After the therapy I went to a forest to walk. I needed to take many things into my mouth, like a little child. I took pieces of wood, stones, my fingers and so on. Then I saw a tree; I went to it, and I looked at a leaf on it. It was strange: the leaf I had chosen was quite an old one, and in the middle of it there was a new leaf, a bud which was growing, very green and incredibly beautiful. Normally new leaves don't grow in the middle of old ones! It made me think about my life: quite a lot of experiences, of things I've lived through, and now a new departure is just beginning to take off...The chances of my just happening 'by chance' on a leaf with an anomaly like that are absolutely minute. It was really a very beautiful, very powerful, moment."

In another regression with Silvia, Yann found himself a prisoner in France in the Middle Ages. He was there for a very long time, without a single visitor, and eventually died in the prison. He recognized the feelings of passivity and hopelessness, with nothing to do and no-one to talk to, as recurring occasionally in his present life, and so the regression has made him determined to overcome any of that lassitude and sense of extreme moral fatigue which might now prevent him from achieving what he would like to achieve.

On Yann's return from India to Switzerland, at the age of twenty-three, he decided to embark on nursing training, and he got accepted for that before returning to India just for three months. However, this second trip went really badly. At the time he was going through a great deal of anguish and irrational fears, which he now thinks were due to a past life surfacing, and, although he thought that he would calm down in India, in fact things got worse there. He sees this, however, as having been important for the discovery of his blueprint. Here again I would like to quote Yann's own words, as they are relevant to my whole subject:-

"Now I think this very hard experience changed the way I live. It pushed me very strongly; I had no choice, I had to change. If one of your friends is drunk and has fallen asleep in the snow, you will first ask him to get up, but if he doesn't respond, you will give him a tap. Then, if he still doesn't move, you will start to shake him until he wakes up. So God, who is a true friend, does the same with us...So since that difficult time in India I have really understood the fact that everything can change in my life in a few seconds, that I cannot escape my karma, and that I build my future every second. These hardships helped me to be sure that we can rely on nothing, that what we do is recorded somewhere and that we must be very careful about every single action, even the most insignificant one. (This, comments Yann, is quite scary when I read it again!) So that is when I really began to pray and to become convinced of its efficacy."

And now the would-be 'alternative therapist' continues the email. "Also, afterwards, I became convinced that there are no desperate situations, that with love human beings can recover from the worst possible traumas, and that even if we find ourselves completely lost in the worst situation, we can always call on our own healing power, the light and love that we have in ourselves, which are God or the nature of our mind. And as we all come from this light, we can pray for others too. I think every therapist, doctor or nurse should use the power of prayer besides his healing technique. A good healing method can only work if there is a sincere wish to make the patient recover at every level [and, I would like to add here, 'if the patient also desires it on the deepest level'], that means not to forget either the body or the mind. To heal body and mind we must learn to develop love for everybody, for everything, for every situation, even the most difficult one. In order to be really true and free, we have to untie all the knots in the heart, and prayer, abandonment to what is, help us enormously when we are trapped in the snare of emotions."

Upon returning home, Yann got better within a couple of months. He did think seriously at one point of becoming a monk, but now feels sure that his place is in the world. In fact his astrology chart confirms this: it makes it clear that if he were a monk he would turn inwards too much. Like my friend John, he has probably had quite enough lives as a monk already! Probably unusually for someone of his age (though echoing the Sai Baba quotation with which I headed this chapter), Yann sees eighteen to thirty as "the age for giving back to the world what one has learnt". At the time of our meeting he was working in a psychiatric hospital as part of his nursing studies, and he found that the young listened to him. He sees meditation as an invaluable tool for fostering compassion and enabling him to help the young. Being so sure about wanting to make his career in alternative medicine, he nearly gave up his nursing studies at one point, but then decided that the qualification would be useful.

Though young to take up meditation seriously, Yann is of course by no means unique. My Indian friend Jyothi is a 'professional meditator', and *Sahaj Marg* (The Natural Way), the system which she promotes, is spreading rapidly throughout the world. The Master of *Sahaj Marg*, who is known as Chariji, recommends starting meditation seriously at eighteen, and Jyothi's daughter did indeed take up the practice at that age, without any pushing from her parents. In this system, 'preceptors', who have been 'permitted' by the Master, channel his energy, and when they give 'sittings', this energy is transmitted through them to the fellow meditator(s). Weekly half-hour sittings are strongly advised, besides meditating each morning by oneself, and I personally found that the strong energy which I felt enveloping me when I was in Jyothi's presence helped my 'monkey mind' to be a bit more still. (I use the past tense because Jyothi lives in Hull and, since my move to Shropshire, there has been no 'preceptor' accessible to me.) The system is simple in the extreme, involving little more than morning meditation and evening 'cleaning'. The latter consists of imagining that the day's impressions (one's newly formed *samskaras)* are going out like smoke from one's back and that in its place the sacred current of the Divine is entering into one's heart through the Master's heart. (Jyothi adds that the word 'imagine' should not be misunderstood, because it is a very active process in which we are supposed to use our will power.) Jyothi is very appropriately named, as it means 'light', and during the meditation period the only injunction is to be aware of the divine light inside one.

Meditation has always been absolutely fundamental to every religious tradition, and although Christianity has tended to neglect it in recent centuries, the great Christian mystics – St. Teresa of Avila, St. John of the Cross, Julian of Norwich, to mention but three – were obviously as well established in its practice as any Buddhist. My friend Lawrence is a meditation teacher as well as a therapist, having started meditating himself at the age of only eighteen while studying for a year at Bennett's International Academy for Continuous Education. This was a spiritual school, which taught all kinds of practical skills (from gardening and building to psychology, art and craft, drama etc.) as well as meditation and other spiritual practices, and it also exposed its pupils to several aspects of alternative medicine. Lawrence's year there was one of the main triggers for the discovery of his blueprint, as it led him straight on to studying osteopathy and then homeopathy, running his first groups at the same time.

Lawrence says that "meditation is a word that covers a very wide range of practices, and so anything I can say is a general-ization which may not fit specific people or situations, and there are usually exceptions to these generalizations. As with most spiritual practices, I think that it is preferable to be drawn to it at the right time and to approach it gently and without force, but with a steady persistence". 'Persistence' is perhaps the word most commonly used by anyone who takes meditation seriously. But, although I am sure that Masters such as Chariji are right to encourage beginning at eighteen, I feel that – in our Western society at least – those who are ready to make the necessary commitment at this age are still the exception rather than the rule. When young people are first leaving home, starting college and so on, their lives tend to get very full with classes, preparation for examinations, social life and making new relationships outside the previously familiar circles, and sports or other hobbies. It takes real commitment and discipline to, say, get out of bed that half hour earlier every single day, which is essential for the necessary persistence. Lawrence had the advantage of an unusually (for that generation) enlightened father, who was a disciple of the great Indian Master Babaji, and so encouraged Lawrence in his spiritual practices. Though he thinks looking back now that at nineteen he was "in many ways absurdly naïve", he sees that he was well looked after at that time and learnt much, and feels himself to have been fortunate in being given the opportunity to have a spiritual grounding from which to establish himself in the world. And he finds now that, on the whole, the people who attend his classes are considerably older than he was when he started meditating.

Sathya Sai schools, which are steadily increasing in numbers throughout the world, teach 'silent sitting' even to quite young children. No doubt eighteen-year-olds who have been through such a system will tend to take to meditation as easily as did Lawrence and Shruti, and no doubt too, with the increasing number of more spiritually evolved beings who are incarnating into the New Age (if one cares to employ the term that is so often used disparagingly), this will gradually become more the norm.

Much has been written already about the benefits of meditation for health.

When I discussed with Yann the fact that he was rather an unusual twenty-six year old, he made it quite clear that the benefits he felt from his Buddhist practices and so on far outweighed any difficulties he might have about being "different". He has never been short of friends, though some of his relationships are on a fairly superficial level. The people to whom he feels closest are a friend about his own age who started meditating a couple of years ago, and a Frenchman four years his senior whom he first met in India and still sees regularly.

Eighteen to twenty-seven are of course years in which social life and peer influences are of particular importance. Often the necessary break with parents is accompanied by a desire to be 'with it' in the eyes of one's contemporaries, and this is another area where parents need to let go. The emotional body, which is 'born' at about age fourteen, is still developing at this stage, and diverse experiences with people outside the family are important for increasing subtlety and awareness. We are after all 'all one', and eighteen is normally the age at which we really begin to move out of the protective environment of the family circle and 'back' to the collective.

Though I do believe it to be taking over our lives to an excessive degree, the internet can be seen as a symbol of this collectivity. Internet cafés and so on are making it possible even for those who cannot afford their own computer to make relationships with people all over the world. It has obvious advantages and disadvantages, which most of you are probably much better qualified to talk about than I am. When, however, I mention the internet taking over our lives excessively, I should like to stress that I am talking here almost exclusively about Western society. You may find these statistics interesting. Apparently about eighty per cent of the world's population has never made a telephone call, and, although the internet connects a hundred million computers, the people who are connected make up only two per cent of the world's population! London has more internet accounts than the whole of Africa, and New York has more telephones than all of rural Asia. I recently met a young engineer from London who told me that his firm save a lot of money now by getting drawings done in India and sent over by email, yet India's population of almost one billion have two million computers between them, and the average rural wage in India is £20 a month while its cheapest computer costs £650!

When I asked Yann how peer pressures with regard to such things as drugs affected him, he replied that he saw taking drugs and alcohol as a phase that all the young nowadays more or less inevitably go through. He believes it to be the result of a lack of internal peace, and he does discuss the matter with some of his contemporaries and many admire his attitude. He says that he has taken cannabis himself even though he disliked the way in which it sped up his thinking, and admits that, though at seventeen and eighteen it was mainly peer pressure that made him do it, more recently it was simply because he liked it. When we met he had given it up completely, and, though he enjoys drinking a little bit too, he thinks and hopes that his personality is not an addictive one; (I am sure that he is right).

When I was myself a parent of three young people in this age group, I saw it as a rather wonderful time when they became more friends than 'children'. Not all young people of course find themselves able to talk to their parents about the things which are most important to them, but if parents have always shown themselves willing to listen, they are more likely to keep their children's confidence. Yann is able to talk about his spiritual interests with both his mother and his older sister (who is also interested in Buddhism, and has traveled a great deal, working in various countries for the Red Cross), but his father talks very little and he says that they never quite know what to say to one another. Yann feels nevertheless that there is a lot of love between him and his father, who respects Yann's religious views although he does not share them, and one of Yann's aims is to work at improving their relationship. He is also aware of a family pattern, which he is very keen to break when he himself gets married. His maternal grandmother is very dominating and has his grandfather completely under her thumb, and so Yann says that his mother was determined to choose a man who was the complete opposite. Though thirty-one years of marriage have calmed him down somewhat, Yann's father shouts a lot, always wants to complain to the neighbors and so on, while his mother is very accepting and always trying to make peace between them all. Yann himself would like a relationship of much greater equality, and I am quite confident that his prayers will be answered in due course. And he says himself that meeting his bio-energetics therapist and other people, such as Silvia and Ngawang, who have been really useful to him, was undoubtedly the result of prayer.

The people in this chapter are no doubt not completely typical of the age group eighteen to twenty-seven, but, unless we make a deliberate effort to step out of it, we are all limited by the environment that we have chosen. My own blueprint for this lifetime seems to have been a mainly spiritual one, and it is therefore natural for me to meet, and to want to write about, people whose interests are also spiritual. Nor do I regard my own three children as having been 'typical' of this age group, (apart perhaps from their tastes in music!). My older two are probably more introverted than the majority of their peers, while the younger, adopted, one (with of course different genes) has always been exceptionally self-confident. None of them has to date started to share my spiritual interests, but all three were at this stage busy finding their own way both career-wise and belief-wise, which is exactly how it should be during this period of life.

A person's blueprint and innate characteristics show themselves at this point partly through morality. Any parent whose offspring in this age group are leading moral lives and exhibiting a caring attitude towards others can feel very happy, even if their life style and interests are very different from their own. On the other hand, parents should not blame themselves too much if their children appear to have 'gone off the rails' at this point. Sharon's Robert obviously brought his difficulties in with him, and she, aware of that, is continuing to be there for him and will hopefully see him through them to a better future. He still has time on his hands in this lifetime alone, and she has the determination and strength of character to make a real difference for him. As Yann reminded us, "there are no desperate situations...With love human beings can recover from the worst traumas...". But those who <u>are</u> in touch with their Life Plan during these early adult years will be more ready to 'make their mark', which is the subject of the next chapter.

Notes

1   REGRESSION THERAPY – A Handbook for Professionals, Volume II: Special Instances of Altered State Work, ed. Winafred Blake Lucas, Ph.D., Deep Forest Press, California, 1993.

2   See SOULS UNITED – The Power of Divine Connection, Ann Merivale, Llewellyn Worldwide, USA, 2009.

3   Only Love is Real, Dr. Brian Weiss, Warner Books, Inc., New York, and Piatkus Books, London, 1996.

4   Many Lifetimes, Joan Grant and Denys Kelsey, Ariel Press, USA, 1997.

5   COURAGEOUS SOULS – Do we Plan our Life Challenges before Birth?, Robert Schwartz, North Atlantic Books, (Random House, USA), 2009.

6   De Naissance en Naissance (From Birth to Birth), Denise Desjardins, Editions de la Table Ronde, Paris, 1977.

7   Conversations with God, Books 1, 2 and 3 , Neale Donald Walsch, Hodder and Stoughton, London, 1997.

8   BEYOND THE BRAIN – Birth, Death and Transcendence in

Psychotherapy, Stanislav Grof, State University of New York Press, 2000.

EXERCISES

1. If you are in this age group and reading this book, there is no doubt that you must be on the spiritual path already. Be thankful for that, whatever difficulties it entails, because you will always find it to be an exciting one, with ever new discoveries to be made. Looking back at the family in which you grew up:-

(a) Were you close to them all, or were there difficulties between you? If the latter, can you appreciate the fact that you chose these people as family members either as part of your learning or in order to pay a karmic debt? Does appreciating this help you to forgive, say, your parent(s) for the wrongs that they may have done you? If you are still suffering from problems dating from childhood, have you thought of having therapy and/or doing some 'inner child' work? For the latter I particularly recommend John Bradshaw's books and also the exercises in my own book *KARMIC RELEASE* (published by Sai Towers, Bangalore).

(b) In some lifetimes we choose difficult family relationships for our learning, in others we incarnate together with people with whom we are already close friends and feel comfortable. Sometimes one comes across families who are exceptionally close and also work together. In such cases the likelihood is that they chose to be together with the aim of doing something important that they are all good at. (What better example could one find than the Bach family? Johann Sebastian had thirteen surviving children, most of whom were also professional musicians!) If you feel close to other members of your family, be thankful and always try to make the most of it.

2. Are you in a romantic relationship at present, or seeking one?

Have you had difficult relationships that have left you feeling scarred? Deep Memory Process can be one of the most useful types of therapy for dealing with relationship difficulties because, more often than not, it can help you to find out about the origin of the problem (which is almost certain to stem from a previous life when you were with the same person). This can then help you to decide whether to persevere in the relationship, or whether you have simply got trapped in a repeated pattern and that it is now time to break it. To find the DMP therapist nearest to you, you can go to Dr. Roger Woolger's website (www.rogerwoolger.com <http://www.rog erwoolger.com>).

3.   Are you the parent of anyone in this age group? If so,

(a) how do you get on these days? Would you like the relationship to be closer? If so, think back to when things began to deteriorate between you and look at whether there might be something for which it would be good to apologize, or simply to discuss. Openness, honesty and trust are vital ingredients for a good parent-child relationship at any age, and the bond is unbreakable however much you get separated by either distance or interests.

(b) Have you any offspring in this age group who are going through difficulties?

Do you tend to blame yourself for them? Well don't! It is important to appreciate that no parent can ever be perfect, and that they each have their own karma to work out that is independent of your own. The trouble with parenthood is that when they suffer we suffer with them, but the wonderful thing about it is that they will always appreciate our support whenever we are able to give it. So do try always to be non-judgmental as well as supportive, but remember too that this may not mean, for instance, bailing them out of financial difficulties that are of their own making! We are here to help them to learn their lessons as well as to give them our love.

CHAPTER SIX

TWENTY-SEVEN TO THIRTY-SIX – MAKING OUR MARK

Each soul . . . has a definite job to do. But ye alone may find and do that job!
Edgar Cayce Reading 2823-1

Then let us all do what is right, strive with all our might toward the unattainable, develop as fully as we can the gifts God has given us, and never stop learning.
Ludwig van Beethoven

When my father was young, it was the norm for men to have made up their minds about their path in life well before the age of twenty-seven, and by that age to be established in a profession even if they were still in training. As for women, their 'career' was expected to be in the home, and if they were not married by the age of twenty-eight, they were labeled 'on the shelf', and 'spinsterdom' was written across their foreheads like a death sentence. Fortunately times have changed! I say "fortunately" because, whereas my father regarded mid-life career change or an inability to make up one's mind at an early age about what one wanted to do, as a sign of severe instability, I see this is as very often an important part of our Life Plan and the lessons we have chosen beforehand.

But I want to begin with a couple of people whose paths <u>were</u> clear from early on. The first is a friend from the Geneva Sai Baba group, whom I will call Priya. Priya, who is in her thirties, is Sri Lankan but has lived in Geneva since the age of five. Her parents discovered Baba when she and her younger brother were both young, and for a number of years the family made biennial trips to India to see Him. From the age of twelve to fifteen she attended classes which used the *Bal Vikas* education program for children that originated in Baba's ashram. There, as well as singing *bhajans* (devotional songs), which she was used to doing at home, she learnt Indian Scriptures and Baba's Human Values. Now she helps the Swiss woman in Geneva who teaches children to sing *bhajans*.

Priya gives evidence for a theory that I would like to prove but may never be able to: that people who are brought up to believe in Sai Baba have a big advantage over those who never come to hear of Him. She comes from a very musical family, and her career as a musician was obvious from an early age (as was that of her brother, who is now teaching music in Brazil). I mentioned that it was common in France to go to university in one's home town. Well, the same is true of Geneva, and Priya, who is an excellent violinist, studied at the Conservatoire there. It would have been difficult financially for her to move away from home, and her parents, whose attitudes are open-minded, have always been very supportive and encouraging of her independence. Now she teaches the violin both in schools and privately, as well as playing in orchestras and chamber music groups; and in recent years she has been excessively busy because she has also been studying for a B.A. General Arts degree at the University of Geneva.

Priya only shares her spiritual life with her family and the Baba circle and group meetings. She has friends outside those circles, and meets many people through her work, but with none of them does she feel able to talk about Baba or her spiritual interests. However, this is not a major problem for her, as her intimate 'inner' connection to Baba and her parents' devotion to Him give her all that she needs in the spiritual domain. Her brother is still close to Baba as well and, although they used to fight over little things as all young siblings do, they nevertheless always pulled together, and nowadays Priya feels a very strong connection to him.

The years twenty-seven to thirty-six are very much a time for consolidating career and family, and are often the best time for 'making our mark'. In the childhood years we are getting to grips with being in a physical body again, and in the years of early youth, when we are first spreading our wings and learning to stand on our own feet, we tend to experiment with our new-found freedom, sometimes with undesirable consequences. In our late twenties and early thirties, when we have learnt the lessons from our experiments, we are in a better position to take responsibility both for our own actions and for other people.

Priya says that she has always found her knowledge about karma and her understanding that her life has a plan very useful, but that it is nevertheless not always easy to be sure that you are making the right decision. However, she is aware of Baba's perpetual guidance, and confident that so long as she keeps on following His teachings and handing any difficulties she might have over to Him, she will not go too far wrong.

This is also a period in which we can develop discrimination. The exercise of discrimination is vital in all walks of life, for it affects our own welfare, that of others and that of the planet itself. If our priority in choosing a career is making a lot of money, or if our priority in making relationships is sexual grati-fication, we will never find happiness. People in this age group normally have the energy to be active in various fields and, if they dedicate at least part of their time to working for the common good, it can have a big impact and really help to improve the state of our planet. So it is tremendously important at this stage of life not to become engrossed in acquiring material possessions. Sai Baba says that when someone identifies something as his, he develops attachment, and from that attachment he begins to experience through that object. If, for instance, you own a car, you feel bad when the car gets a dent. If the car is hit, you will say "I" was hit! This is absurd because you are not the car; in reality there is no connection between you and the car. What you are doing in such an instance is expanding your consciousness out on one level and taking on the identity of the car. If someone else's car is dented, your feelings about it are much less strong, so this identification is clearly false.

Sai Baba uses this analogy of false identification for our attitude towards our physical body. He says that we are not the body, but because we possess it, we have identified with the external covering and have become attached to it. Consequently, when we look in the mirror, we think we are the object we see reflected in it, but in fact what we see in the glass is no more us than the car we drive or the clothes we wear - they are all coverings on different layers. Education in the West falls short on conveying this truth, but being aware of it while we are becoming fully established in the world will lead to a much more worthwhile life.

My friend Lawrence was born in Malawi. He says that he is interested in both the place and the time of his birth, as he believes their particular energies and influences to be "relevant to one's purpose and mission in life." The Rift Valley, which extends into Lake Malawi, is sometimes referred to as the 'womb of the Earth', and Lawrence's work as a natural healer and therapist enables people to connect to their essence – the true nature with which they first came to Earth, and which they must again recognize before being finally able to leave her for return to the Source. Also, he comments that the mid-fifties when he was born was the time of the call to independence in Malawi, and Lawrence has throughout his life been a very independent thinker. The people of Malawi, like those of other African countries, have a reputation for being most friendly and hospitable, and these are also essential characteristics for a successful therapist.

Lawrence says that for him the period eighteen to twenty-seven was about getting established in the world, rather than experimentation. By age twenty-five he had a stepson and also his first son to take care of, and he had just started work as an osteopath, all of which made it very important for him to develop discrimination at an early age. Lawrence says that Bennett, at whose Academy he studied after leaving school, was very interested in community and in getting people to have reverence for nature and find new ways of worship - that his Academy was really a school of the future, "versing one in the workings of groups and communities". He feels fortunate in having been given this opportunity of a spiritual ground from which to establish himself in the world.

After starting work very satisfactorily at this comparatively early age, Lawrence went on to obtain an arsenal of further qualifications, at the same time as supporting a growing family. So that by the age of about thirty, he can be said to have already reached the 'pinnacle of success'. This may seem unusual, but then look at the child prodigy Mozart, who died at the age of thirty-five, Henry Purcell, who only lasted one year longer, or Schubert, who only lived to thirty-one. These are exceptions, it must be admitted, and Lawrence says that "most spiritual seekers working in the kind of way I did, and still do to some extent, seem to be middle-aged and beyond". His own stepson, who is now in his thirties, is more interested in politics, community building in existing social situations (rather than creating alternatives) and in anti-nuclear and anti-global protests.

One of the advantages that both Lawrence and Priya had over many of us in the West was learning about karma at an early age. Priya commented that this was an important factor for her in the development of discrimination. Sai Baba says "every activity we do creates a reaction which binds us to either good or bad results", and that "due to reactions to our activities in previous lives (karma), we either enjoy or suffer in various circumstances in the present life, while our present activities create reactions for the next lives. As we experience these results (suffering and enjoying) we burn up our good and bad reactions. As such, in the next life, we will no longer have to suffer these same difficulties." The period twenty-seven to thirty-six seems to me to be the ideal time for working on the realization that (again in Baba's words) "We must learn to rise above the dualities of happiness and distress and be situated beyond the bodily identification".

Someone who has been exercising a great deal of discrimination in recent years is my friend and fellow Woolger graduate, Josephine, who at thirty-five was very busy establishing herself both career-wise and family-wise. She comes from a close knit family, but her childhood and youth were full of difficulties. Her parents had a tempestuous relationship and her father, who is very charismatic and sociable and drinks a great deal, was frequently verbally abusive and violent. His violence was not directed towards anyone in particular, but he would sometimes break things or smash up the house. Living with him was immensely hard for Josephine's mother, who has low self-esteem despite being extremely attractive physically, and her difficulties were compounded by having four children in six years and having to bring them up with very little money. These difficulties rubbed off on Josephine, who was named after her and also looks extremely like her.

A further immense difficulty for both mother and daughter was caused by the fact that Josephine was conceived before the marriage. They are a Catholic family and, even though her parents do not practice their religion, Josephine feels that her mother harbored resentment at being branded as a 'certain type' on account of her 'premature' pregnancy. To this day her mother maintains the lie that she has been married a few years longer than is really the case! Josephine's birth itself was – in her mother's own words – "horrific", and she repeatedly screamed at the midwives to leave Josephine inside because she did not want her!

As the eldest of four born within six years, Josephine had a great deal of responsibility. She was a very creative child, and she says that her pattern as she grew was to spend most of the time completely in her own creative world. This she describes as a safe world where she was in control of events. Her mother was extremely strict, and the children would be punished physically for any misbehavior. So Josephine used to live in a dream world as a way of escaping from a very volatile environment.

But the biggest difficulty of all came when Josephine's youngest brother, Donald, died at the age of seven after being ill for a long time with cancer. Josephine was only thirteen at the time, but was not allowed to show any emotion. When the headmistress came round to see her mother just after the death, all she said to Josephine was "Make sure you look after your mother"! Donald was not talked about any more, and emotions were simply not acceptable in the family. This not unnaturally caused Josephine to become extremely depressed, and her most severe feeling was one of guilt at still being alive. Her only help came from books, and she started reading psychology books when she was in her early teens. Her brother's death was thus the first trigger for her discovering her Life Plan and in due course becoming a successful therapist.

Soon after her brother died, Josephine's aunt fell ill, and when she also died, Josephine could not see any point in anything. Although she is very intelligent, she left school, where no-one understood about her problems, halfway through her Advanced Level course, and then she did what she describes as "crappy jobs" until she was nineteen. Things began to look up for her, however, when she started work with an American computer company, and she stayed with them for twelve years. She had only done a little bit of secretarial training, but the company was a new one for which personalities mattered more than qualifications, and, although it was very hard work, Josephine soon found herself able to develop her abilities and earn a good salary while at the same time thoroughly enjoying herself. She worked for the manager, whose personality was similar to that of her father, but she felt safe with him because he was good to her, and she also made many friends. She started to buy a house jointly with a couple of friends, but by the time she was twenty-four she was earning enough to be able to buy a house of her own.

This period of life sees a major astrological landmark in the form of the First Saturn Return, which occurs at around twenty-eight to thirty. Saturn's keynote is change, and twenty-eight is the age at which unmarried women used to begin to regard themselves as being 'on the shelf'. Certainly it was at precisely this age that I gave up hope of getting married! I went to work abroad a year later, and Carmen also moved (to England) just at the time of her first Saturn Return.

Josephine says that for her, age twenty-eight marked a major shift to a spiritual path. At this point she felt herself creeping towards thirty, which made her start asking herself the question "What am I doing with my life?" She is a Six Metal in the Nine Star Ki system of astrology, and career is always important for Six Metals. Though she had been enjoying her work, she could not see it as a long-term career, and in any case her boss was very controlling and she now realized that her work situation was simply a repetition of her home one. She decided to do some developmental training, and initially the company sponsored her to do that in America for two weeks at a time. She trained in bio-energetics with Sandy Cotter, and had already set up her own practice when she decided to do Roger Woolger's training as well. Often getting on track involves a great deal of trust, and since giving up her well-paid job, Josephine has had a bigger struggle than she anticipated making ends meet. She feels, however, that weathering over three years of struggle is proof enough that she is doing the right thing. Sometimes such struggle entails sacrifice as well. In Josephine's case the change in her financial situation forced her to sell her house, but she feels that the benefits of her training have extended to her whole family as well as to herself.

In any case, sacrifices are frequently rewarded within a short space of time, and at the time that we talked Josephine had entered into a relationship which looked likely to fulfill the other aspect of her Life Plan: the desire for a family of her own. Karmic marriages are an important feature of this period of life, and Josephine wisely resisted the pressure from her family who were concerned about her not being married by the time she was thirty. She did have one possible chance to marry, but realized in time that it would not have worked well. She feels that something karmic was worked out in that relationship, but in her new relationship she became aware of a very strong bond from previous lifetimes.

A very strong bond, however, does not necessarily make a relationship easy or straightforward. Sam, Josephine's partner, has been married twice already, and suffered enormously with his last wife having numerous affairs. The attraction when he and Josephine first met was instant and, though they are both people who find it hard to be with someone else all the time, Josephine says that they felt very comfortable together right from the start. Sam, however, was naturally very cautious, and Josephine was wise enough to let him go at his own pace and not push things at all. They met through Josephine's brother, who is very psychic and had a dream in which Sam was marrying his sister. He told Josephine about the dream before Sam's second marriage had come to an end, but when she first met him, she was determined not to be influenced by it. Rather, she gave Sam time to work on the difficulties he had been through and to make the most of having his own space for the first time. She says that he is a very deep thinker and very sensitive and, although his own career is much more conventional than Josephine's, he is interested in her work and open-minded about spiritual issues.

As far as having a family is concerned, Josephine not unnaturally feels that there is a limited window of opportunity for a woman and that it is best to have your first child by the age of thirty-six. This makes her feel that time is already running out for her and, now that she and Sam have been committed to each other for over a year, they are both ready to think seriously about having a baby. They are at present looking for a house to buy together, and she would like to get married, but Sam has real difficulty over this on account of both his previous marriages having been unsuccessful. Josephine is very conscious of her parents' disapproval of her doing things 'the wrong way round'. This is a common problem even among strong-minded people who firmly believe that commitment does not need formal recognition. The Church's centuries-old habit of instilling guilt is dying hard!

At the same time as looking for a house to buy and thinking about having a baby, Josephine is also very busy successfully setting up a new practice. Six Metals tend to be very good leaders and organizers as well as attaching importance to their career. Josephine sees her career as a therapist as something she could fit round children more easily than most other professions.

I mentioned before that 'getting into the body' was difficult for people who had for one reason or another become cut off from their feelings and emotions. This is a subject very dear to the heart of our mentor Roger Woolger, and Josephine explains, from her studies of bio-energetics, that the early patterning of being 'out of the body'/'in the head' generally happens within the first six months of life and often during the birth transition. Josephine's own birth was traumatic in the extreme, and she adds, "As a very young baby my world would have been absolutely terrifying, which fits perfectly with my bio-energetic profile. The natural reaction of course, when presented with such terror, is to withdraw as far as possible, as the world is not perceived to be safe. I have been told that on several occasions as a very young baby I stopped breathing and turned blue, which prompted my parents to shake me in order to force me to breathe and that would only have compounded the fear!" The result of this was that being 'out of her body' continued to be the safest place for Josephine.

It was through her bio-energetic work with Sandy Cotter that Josephine began to realize what she calls the dysfunction within her upbringing. She says that "Sandy described me as looking like a transparent angel when we first met. I had so little 'body' to me. I had a particularly frail build up until very recently, for most of my twenties weighing under eight stone (112 lbs), which is very little for someone whose height is 5ft 5in. During times of stress I would always lose weight although I would eat huge amounts of food, which I interpret as literally not wanting to be here. At the end of my training, Sandy felt that I looked far more 'substantial'."

In Roger Woolger's work the body is key, and Josephine says that through the training she has done with him "I have gained a far greater sense of my own body and the feelings it generates. Often in the beginning when asked what my body was feeling, I wouldn't have a clue. Gradually it is becoming more natural to be in the body, although I have to be conscious during traumatic times, as I am still very quick to leave! At the most traumatic time of my adult life, when my cousin Stan had a major psychotic breakdown and killed his mother, I could actually feel myself way above the earth, with my legs and feet frantically running. Sandy, and I shall be eternally grateful to her, gently held on to me, over a period of time brought me back down, and also intro-duced me to a fabulous homeopath (Ambika Wauters), as she felt I was likely to become very ill due to the shock. I believe Sandy literally saved my life, and in turn greatly helped the rest of my family."

Another important aspect of Woolger's work is 'spirit releasement'. One of the reasons that Josephine was so very profoundly affected by Stan's psychotic episode and its appalling consequence is that "he is immensely special to me, and we have certainly been twins many times in the past. I feel he and I have a joint role here this time around." Thanks to Roger, Josephine found out that she had taken on the 'spirit' that had had a hold on Stan during the psychotic episode, "when I felt so connected to him and so desperately wanted to help him." She recounts: "Roger, on my very first workshop, worked on me, the result being the most amazing release of this spirit, and great healing for Stan also in the process. This has been shown to be true in that he has made the most amazing recovery – truly miraculous in fact. In January he was almost killed in a car crash, and we were called down to say 'goodbye' to him as he was on the life support machine. I went again to St David's [where she had done a Woolger workshop] and prayed for him, and he has again come back to us."

Few of us (fortunately!) have to go through quite so much trauma as Josephine did in thirty odd years, but the Rev. Dr. Donal McKeown, the Bishop of Belfast, said during a service broadcast on Radio Four on Sunday 7 July 2002, that someone had said that "the longest thirty centimeters in the world was that from the head to the heart". I do not suppose that the bishop was thinking in exactly the same way as we therapists do, but he was certainly on the right track! Suppressed emotion is regarded by alternative practitioners (for want of a better term) as one of the classic causes of cancer; but even if we do not actually become seriously diseased in that way, emotions, as Lawrence comments, "have to go somewhere", and often the result is unexplained aches and pains. Many people find, as Josephine did, that either embarking on therapist's training or going into therapy themselves makes them realize the devastating effect that fleeing the body can have. While we Deep Memory Process therapists are trained to get our clients to focus on bodily sensations as a lead into a past life story, this often proves difficult in cases of clients who have detached themselves from their feelings as a means of protection from deep pain. I always have much sympathy with such clients, having started out myself as just one such 'difficult subject', and one advantage of doing one's training in workshops such as those of Roger Woolger is the opportunity they give for a great deal of practice.

When clients have coped for a long time with their pain by cutting off from it (making those thirty centimeters extra long!), it tends to take a great deal of hard work on the part of the therapist to use the body as a starting-off point. In such cases one can always work initially in other ways, and then gradually, as the client begins to feel safer, the body awareness comes and the deep pain can surface and be dealt with. Josephine found bio-energetics to be very useful for her grounding, just as Yann did. Also, as she did more and more regressions, her body awareness increased, and this in turn encouraged the release of the emotions which she had not been allowed to show as a child. This detachment even affected the way she walked. She is very pretty and 'fairy like', and her training gradually made her aware that she walked "like a fairy", almost on tiptoe, and so – since we do come to Earth as actors in, not as audience to, the drama – she needed to start putting her feet much more firmly on the ground.

Someone else in this age group who, though not a Six Metal, is very career minded, is my friend Angela. Angela is a Three/Eight (Tree/Soil), which indicates firstly enormous energy and creativity and secondly a very good intellect and an immensely strong caring side. It also indicates a choppy transition to adulthood, and Angela, as we saw, took on at an early age the entire upbringing of her younger half sister. All the difficulties she had weathered so well finally took their toll when she had just begun to make her mark as a social worker, but then she was temporarily struck down by a depressive illness. One of the contributing factors to this was unhappiness in her job with the local authority, and there is an irony here: it is Angela's immensely strong caring nature that made social work the obvious profession for her, but the problem with working in this way for the local authority was the lack of caring that she found in her work place. (This sad state of affairs is alas not unusual!)

Angela's illness occurred round about the time of her First Saturn Return, and Saturn is well-known for causing depression as well as for encouraging one to take life seriously. After a period of sick leave, she wisely decided to quit her job and, being in financial difficulties, she also decided, like Josephine, to sell her house. Thanks to having a good circle of friends who practice various alternative therapies, Angela was able to try them all in turn rather than relying on her doctor for anti-depressants. Then, when in due course she found a new, much more satisfactory job, that also made a big contribution to her recovery. The First Saturn Return tends to bring major life changes, and at twenty-nine Angela met a new partner who gave her some happiness. This relationship lasted until she realized that she had paid her karmic debt to him – a lifetime in which they had been together as soldiers and she had deserted him in his hour of need.

Now she is finding it difficult to meet a man who shares her spiritual interests, so is concentrating on her career and trusting that her future will be taken care of. She is at present employed in a deprived area, and one of the tasks that she has set herself is to find and foster the spirituality which is there already but which, under less accomplished hands than hers, would be given little chance to shine its light. She set up a group which had monthly evening meetings with speakers on alternative therapies, and this gave the people of the area an unprecedented opportunity to discuss spiritual matters and learn from each other as well as from the professional healers. Venus, the planet of love, is strong in Angela's chart, and she was told by an astrologer that everything she was doing at that moment was exactly in accordance with her chart.

Astrologers say that our Ascendant is every bit as important as our Sun sign, and I have also heard it said that, just as in the Nine Star Ki system we move into our personality number from our driving force as we grow into adulthood, so the First Saturn Return marks the point when our Ascendant really begins to come into play. Angela is a Leo, which makes her very sociable, but her Ascendant is Scorpio, and interest in spirituality and such things as astrology is a strong characteristic of Scorpios. Scorpios are also very good psychologists, and Angela is very intuitive and quick at summing people up. The position of Mercury in her chart gives her a quick mind and the ability to talk her way out of a tight spot, while Mars conjunct to her Sun gave her a quick temper. She says, however, that she has now learnt to deal with that, and so the days when her partner used to joke about "the scary woman coming out" are more or less over. This is one of the instances where astrology can be so very useful: it helps us to understand our innate tendencies and thus overcome our weaknesses and develop our natural strengths.

In sport, people tend to make their mark very early in life. Physical fitness is of course of paramount importance in any sporting profession, and here is an instance where the First Saturn Return is likely to herald deterioration rather than a change for the better. But this does not mean that stardom is uncommon in the age group we are looking at here. When first Sampras and second Agassi were defeated at Wimbledon, there were actually three big surprises in a single day because Safin, the number two seed, fell as well. My reaction at the time was to think to myself that these defeats were very likely part of their Life Plans rather than being real 'tragedies' for them. Pete Sampras in particular, who was well into his thirties and a seven times Wimbledon champion, had surely long since more than made his mark, and I strongly suspect that his Higher Self was telling him that it was time to hand over and give some of the younger ones a chance.

One of the most memorable events in recent Wimbledon history was the winning of the 2001 championship by Goran Ivanisevic. A 'wild card' entrant up against some of the biggest names in history, many laughed when he talked so sincerely and earnestly about his "destiny". I, however, was not among those who laughed, believing him to be in tune with his Life Plan. Goran crossed himself before matches, and prayed "Please God, don't be out to lunch", which again many laughed at, but no-one could deny the fact that his prayers were answered. And after defeating Tim Henman, he said "I felt sorry for Tim because of all the pressure he has been put through, but this was destiny. God wants me to win. He sent the rain on Friday." (That was the rain that stopped play at the point when Tim Henman was in the lead, and which was considered to have been responsible for swinging the match against Henman.) Probably both his age and his shoulder, which he knew required an operation, made Goran regard that summer as his one and only chance at Wimbledon, and he gave it his all, giving the world incredible excitement and suspense, before finishing with a well-earned victory. In contrast to Sampras, he seems content to be a one-timer, and why not? He certainly made his mark, and now maybe he has found other satisfying things to move on to.

As for Tim Henman, who also stated (though with less convincing fervor than Goran) that it was his destiny to win Wimbledon, one's natural instinct on seeing him defeated by Leighton Hewitt in the 2002 semi-final was to feel desperately sorry for him. He put up such a valiant struggle against the world Number One, and had been defeated at the same stage in three previous years, so that it would have been lovely to see him make it to the final at least once, even if he did not win the championship. However, he was seeded number four, so realistically what more should he have been expected to do than get into the top four, which as a fourth time semi-finalist he did?

My only reason for hoping Henman would win that particular

match was a feeling that it was his turn. (I would like to see all these talented players have a turn at winning, and was consequently glad when Serena Williams won in 2002 after her sister Venus had won two years in succession.) It would be easy to say that it was incredibly bad luck because, had the draw gone otherwise and Henman had faced a less formidable opponent than Hewitt, his chances of making it to the final would have been that much greater, but when we study karma we realize that there is no such thing as 'bad luck'. Although the draw appears to be 'pure chance', there are higher forces at work controlling it. I would say that part of Tim's lesson for this lifetime was to accept disappointment. Rather than wanting them all to have a turn at winning, I should accept the players' defeats as part of their karma. Henman may well have had enough 'wins' in previous lives, but in any case, at twenty-seven, he had really made his mark already. He retired in 2007, but will still go down in history as a truly great player, and in any case all these players I have mentioned have since been outshone by Roger Federer, who, when asked whether his talent was due to genius or hard work, replied "I had to work on my genius." Federer is more modest than boastful yet at the same time completely realistic about his unique ability, and he is my personal favorite not only because his artistry (the best word I can find for it!) is so beautiful to watch, but also because of his generous nature.

Had Henman not happened to be British, not nearly so much pressure would have been put on him by people to whom a 'long overdue British win' seemed so important. If being a Wimbledon champion were really in his Life Plan, I have no doubt that it would have happened, and I hope that he is now content in the knowledge that he truly did his very best and that all the criticism he received was quite unfair. Now his role as a potential British champion has been passed on to Andy Murray, and it remains to be seen whether or not defeating Federer at

Wimbledon or the US Open is in <u>his</u> Life Plan!

Tennis, and other skills such as playing a musical instrument, are instances which to my mind come as near as anything can to 'proving' reincarnation. How could Yehudi Menuhin have been able to play the violin so well at such an incredibly early age if he had not already had a great deal of practice in previous lifetimes? My own son Christopher, who has had a successful career in basketball, learnt to play Pelota as a Mayan, and he certainly would not have picked up any ball game in his present very unsporting family. Sometimes apparent disasters are the trigger for discovering the blueprint. In Christopher's case, a misdemeanor when he was fifteen forced a change of school, but it was the new school which brought his introduction to basketball.

Many people's paths are not nearly as clear as Christopher's. One example is Andrew, who had, as you may remember, an exceptionally difficult childhood with no love at all, but whose innate spirituality and love of learning pulled him through to adulthood. Although he did a couple of regressions with me before he went abroad and we lost touch, Andrew has not yet, as far as I know, found out about his previous links with Tessa, the mother of his children, but I strongly suspect them to be karmic soulmates[1]. I also suspect that he is the one who is indebted to her. Tessa also comes from a very difficult background. In her case it was a strict Church one, and she suffered sexual abuse at the hands of one its members. Andrew regards this as the main reason why she has had many sexual partners besides himself. He says that she is extraordinarily attractive physically, but that it is mainly a desire to look after her that has drawn him repeatedly back to her. Their third child was completely unplanned, and after finding out about the pregnancy, Andrew tried really hard to make a go of living with Tessa again, but found it impossible. So he opted instead for living nearby and making frequent visits.

Sai Baba makes Himself known to people through

innumerable different ways, and Andrew's story is a particularly remarkable one. He had never heard of Baba but, having at the age of about thirty begun to take a real interest in spiritual things and in healing, he attended a *Reiki* healing day. During a meditation he saw a picture of both Sai Baba of Shirdi[2] and Sathya Sai in his third eye, which he described to the *Reiki* Master who was leading the day. She happened to be a follower of Baba's and so she explained to Andrew who they were. He then went off and read some books on Him and subsequently attended a few of the meetings of the Baba group in Hull.

In places such as India and Africa, profound spiritual experiences are taken for granted, but this is sadly no longer the case in Europe. When Andrew had been reading about Baba and studying His teachings for a few months, he found himself filled with such intense feelings of love both for Him and for humanity in general that he tried to share what he was experiencing with those around him. The effect, however, was very different from what he had anticipated. Tessa, who, despite having rejected the Church of her upbringing, was still very much under the influence of her vicar father, simply could not understand Andrew's experiences at all. So the result was that Andrew, under pressure from all those around him, was forced to spend a short time in a mental hospital. Soon after that, he made his first visit to Puttaparthi, and I actually ran into him in Baba's ashram, where I found him much more intent on pursuing his spiritual journey than on finding himself a career. I have not seen him since, and a telephone call to Tessa alas brought only a tirade of anxiety about his mental health having been "destroyed by this guru" and the information that her last news from him had been from Thailand. I feel sad about his young sons growing up without a father, but that is obviously their destiny too, and when I asked Baba inwardly about Andrew, He assured me that he was fine. I can imagine him now making his mark as a Buddhist monk or something equivalent.

In previous chapters I have mentioned the *chakras*, and this now seems an appropriate moment to come on to the fourth one – the heart. It is not for nothing that Valentine cards always have pictures of hearts on them, because the heart *chakra* is indeed the *chakra* of love. What percentage of the world's population is lucky in love the very first time? For most of us heartbreak is a necessary step in the opening up of the fourth *chakra*, and so we can take this perhaps somewhat cliché-ed word quite literally. When my older son suffered his first big heartbreak at twenty-eight, while I shared his pain (as every mother does), a little bit of me was glad at the same time. Up until that time Paul had had it almost too easy, being someone who always seemed to land on his feet in every situation (a fruit of good karma no doubt!). I knew that a bad time had to come at some point as part of his learning experience. When we talk of 'karmic marriages' (or partnerships, which can of course include homosexual ones), we must always remember that karma works in more ways than one. Karma is always at the root of both successful and unsuccessful partnerships.

I have a very vivid memory from my university days of a young couple with whom I was friendly, who got engaged during their first year and married as soon as she graduated. They were regarded by all their friends as 'the perfect couple', but I remember her saying to me one day "We've been so lucky that we feel we'll have to pay for it later." They both came from large families and wanted to have a large family of their own, and they lost no time in having four children and then adopting another two. Everything carried on seemingly like roses until they were in their thirties and then, although I had lost touch with them myself, I heard from a mutual friend that Benjamin, who was a doctor, had left Adrienne for one of his patients. More recently, however, I learnt that, after the initial shock, Adrienne had coped well and also had a new partner. So it may simply be that their mutual karma was complete and that it was time for them both to work out other things with other people (Baba's "floating logs which come together and then drift apart again").

On the subject of the *chakras*, I previously quoted Dr. Sam Sandweiss[3], and he in turn has gained his knowledge firstly from Leadbeater[4] and secondly from Ken Wilber[5]. Sandweiss says that by the time the fourth *chakra* begins to awaken, the mental body has become one's predominant force, which suggests that we are likely to be into this age group at this point. What better awakening could there be for a heart than to be 'broken'? And real experience of love is also vital for this development. Sandweiss mentions the *kundalini* - our spiritual energy that is stored coiled at the base of the spine. As we develop spiritually it rises, clearing through all the *chakras* in turn. Sandweiss quotes Leadbeater as saying that the root, heart and brow centers each contain a *granthi* (knot) that the *kundalini* has to break in the course of the journey, and that the second knot (in the heart) is known as that of *Vishnu*. He says that "the *granthi* or knot associated with the heart center represents a major challenge to contemporary psychology. It obstructs the evolution of consciousness to the next level, and to pass through it requires a whole new orientation to inner and outer reality." According to Sandweiss, the nature of this obstruction is "the ignorance and fears that hold us to duality" (i.e. the belief that we are separate from God). He goes on to say that the dynamics of its transcendence lead us to "a marvelous leap in consciousness and our capacity for intuition, creativity and empathy...", and that Ken Wilber is one of the few contemporary writers who are aware of the dynamics of this kind of transcendence.

So, once we have been through a heartbreak or two and experienced real love in relationships, we are ready to work through (in Sandweiss' words) "the challenge of the knot of the fourth *chakra*, which entails giving up our reliance on mind and the security provided by a false sense of a strong independent (and separate) self. Then, when our heart center is fully opened, we can move on to the fifth *chakra* – the throat – which is the *chakra* of communication. Sandweiss says that the awakening of the fourth *chakra* is Piaget's stage of "formal operations, with the capacity for deductive reasoning and the manipulation of abstract ideas", and – covering the fifth *chakra* too – he says that "with our marvelous minds we can now accomplish through thought experiments which took great energy to discover by the action of trial and error". By this Sandweiss surely means that, while trial and error are the prerogative of early years, in later adulthood we can depend on these much less, and he comments that "increased depth and complexity of social communications, an enhanced capacity for gratifying one's needs and drives and gaining mastery of the outer world, all lead to great reliance on and respect for this advanced stage of evolution".

My friend Marina (yet another person that I met on a Roger Woolger course) has two sons, six years apart, who are both in this age group and both making their mark successfully. Adam, the older one, who was in his mid-thirties when we talked a few years ago, writes and directs plays for the theatre, and has always been "extraordinary". Marina says that she has always felt that he was her teacher and that he has been her father in a previous life. They are very strongly connected and have what she describes as "amazing discussions". He often prefaces things he tells her with the words "Other people wouldn't understand this…" When Marina was pregnant with her younger son, Nathan, she was very prone to headaches, and Adam always had a headache whenever she did.

When Adam was only eight, Marina went off on a *kundalini* weekend, and on her return he commented that she had changed. He said: "You look as though you're not afraid of death any more." Marina was thirty at the time, and the weekend (again, round about the time of her First Saturn Return) was a life-changing experience for her. Before that time she tended to have mild attacks of tonsillitis about every six months, but after the weekend she had her worst attack ever. She could not even open her mouth, was hallucinating and seeing Indian gods and goddesses that she did not know about, and was really very ill indeed. The *kundalini* arousal obviously did the trick, however, as she has never had tonsillitis since. Another thing that the initiation did was to cause her to become vegetarian: after that illness she found that she just could not eat meat any more. And very shortly afterwards too, Adam went on a school trip to a factory farm and returned saying that he would never eat meat again.

Marina says that this decision of Adam's was the trigger for her looking into cooking more healthily. He ate everything she cooked quite happily (how many mothers can say that of their youngsters?), and gradually her husband came round to being vegetarian as well. But this was only one aspect of the changes that occurred at that time. Up until the age of thirty Marina had always been extremely shy, but the *kundalini* weekend made her realize that her path was working with groups. She is Trinidadian, lived there until her parents brought her to England when she was thirteen, and was brought up Catholic. She went to a convent secondary school, and practiced her religion (going to church twice on Sundays, even though her family did not) until the age of fifteen. But then she became aware of what she describes as "the hypocrisy of the Church" and so gave up. She returned to a spiritual path, but not the Church, when Adam was born, and she says that later she was guided at the right time to someone who could deal with the *kundalini*. Since then she has never looked back, making her mark by working with groups, bringing people to increased spiritual awareness, and feeling herself to be on track with her Life Plan.

Marina and her husband separated when Adam was fourteen and Nathan was eight. She says that he is a good man, but that they grew apart. For instance, he had not wanted her to go away on the *kundalini* weekend and, despite following her into vegetarianism, he did not follow her spiritual interests. Both of them are Nine Fires, but whereas she is a double Nine and consequently had a smooth transition to adulthood, he is a Nine/Seven (Fire/Metal), which is more difficult. The boys were given a choice of which parent to go with and both chose to stay with her. There was no animosity, and Adam coped reasonably well with the break up. Nathan, who is more emotional, coped less well, however, and Marina had quite a difficult time with him through his teenage years, when he was "slopping around the house" and she thought he should be getting a job. But he had no behavioral problems in school and did not take drugs. Both boys went to university, but whereas Adam went away and cut the ties quite easily, Nathan stayed with Marina until he was twenty-five. For a while she was afraid of being stuck with him, but at twenty-eight he became a graphic designer and well set up on his own.

On the question of karmic relationships, Marina says that both her boys had other long-term relationships before their present ones, and Marina always got on very well with their partners, so it seems likely that they had all known each other before and had something to complete. Now they are both in relationships that Marina is very happy about. Unlike the children of many people who are deeply into spiritual matters, both Adam and Nathan are in sympathy with what she does, and she feels that she gains different things from each of them. While Adam feels like a former father to her, she thinks that Nathan has been her brother. All his life he has never hesitated to correct her, but he does it in a kindly and authoritative manner without making her feel stupid. She says that whereas Adam (a Five/Two – double Soil, and Soils are the carers) is protective and empathetic, Nathan will push her without being authoritarian; (Nathan is an Eight/Seven, which is Soil/Metal, so both of them had smooth transitions to adulthood).

Though many people in this age group succeed in making some sort of mark in the world without having any real understanding of their own true natures, the most successful in spiritual terms are those who achieve at the same time what Sai Baba calls "spiritual intelligence". Part of this intelligence means understanding that there are many levels of covering for the soul. Though there is much consensus in esoteric writing, esoteric science can never be as precise as the science of physical matter, and varying descriptions of these levels can always be found. Sai Baba says that the lowest level is that of physical matter – what we refer to as the body. He further says that the body is basically made up of various senses, which transmit information through the brain to the mind, which is situated within the heart. The mind is higher than the physical body, yet it is also an external covering of the soul. Baba reminds us that the physical body is unique to this life, whereas our mind is carried through every body we have inhabited over a countless span of incarnations. Higher than the mind, He says, is the discriminating factor of the intelligence, which is a reflection of our original consciousness; and higher than the intelligence is the self – an eternal spiritual entity constitutionally situated beyond matter. The problem is that our association with matter from time immemorial has given us illusions which make us identify ourselves as either the body, the mind or the intelligence, forgetting that our true identity is as an eternal spirit soul.

The Upanishads (part of the earliest Indian scriptures and among the very oldest scriptures in the world) give a rather nice analogy: "The body is like a chariot. The senses are like five horses which pull the chariot. The reins which control the horses are like the mind. The driver who holds the reins is like the intelligence. And the passenger who instructs the driver is the spirit soul (the actual self). If the driver (the intelligence) holds the reins (the mind) tightly and controls the five horses (the senses), then it is possible to attain one's proper destination. But if the driver (the intelligence) lets go of the reins (the mind) then each of the five horses (the senses) will run off in a different direction pulling the reins (the mind) with them, causing the chariot to be broken into many pieces." Sai Baba explains that "if one's identification is only on the level of the body, then the imperfections of the body will limit one. If one's identification is on the level of the mind, then the body's limitations will not affect one, but the mental limitations will limit one. If one's identification is on the level of intelligence, then the mental limitations will not affect one. But if one's identification is on the level of the pure spirit soul situated beyond matter, there are no limitations. Such a state is known technically as *jivan-mukta*."[6] This is the goal of human life, and it means that we can be liberated from material existence while still living within the body.

So that is our ultimate aim, whether we achieve it in this lifetime or five hundred lifetimes hence. Those who, like Priya, Angela and others I have mentioned, are aware of this during this twenty-seven to thirty-six period, are likely to weather the next – the 'Mid-life Crisis' period – much better than those who are not. But now the next question is: is there really any such thing as a mid-life crisis?

Notes

1   See my book *SOULS UNITED – The Power of Divine Connection*, Llewellyn, 2009.

2   Sai Baba of Shirdi, who died in 1918, is the previous incarnation of Sathya Sai Baba. He said before he died that he would return eight years later, and Sathya Sai Baba was born in 1926. The latter said that this was a triple incarnation and that He would return as Prema Sai.

3   *Spirit and the Mind*, Samuel H. Sandweiss, M.D., Sri Sathya Sai Publications Trust, India, 1985 (reprinted 2001).

4   *The Chakras*, C. W. Leadbeater, The Theosophical Publishing House, London, 1969.

5   *Odyssey: A Personal Inquiry into Humanistic and Transpersonal Psychology*, Ken Wilber, Journal of Humanistic Psychology, Volume 22 #1.

6   *Jiva* is the Sanskrit word for the individual soul, which, as opposed to the *atma*, the universal soul (Higher Self), is not immortal; and *Mukthi* (or *Moksha)* means Liberation from all kinds of bondage, especially the one to the cycle of birth and death.

EXERCISES

1   Are you at present in the age group with which the above chapter is concerned? Are you doing what you really love to do, or are you simply working in order to make ends meet? Or not working at all and really struggling to make ends meet? If you are not finding fulfillment in your life, have you thought seriously about making a change? <u>Right now</u> is a really important time to be finding out what you have come to do this time round, and when you <u>have</u> found out you can be assured that your life will seem happier and more worth while. A DMP, or other well-qualified regression therapist, could help you to get into your Life Plan, which in turn might suggest a good change of direction you could consider making.

2   Have you discovered what your real talents are and are you making full use of them? Do you not believe that you have any real talents? If so, please believe me when I tell you that you are WRONG! Everyone on Earth has some sort of talent and, if you are having difficulty in discovering yours, again a good past-life regression therapist could help you by taking you back to a previous life (or lives) in which you exercised certain skills. You might well find something that you fancy developing again. (I once had a client whose partner was about to retire and they were going off to sail the Mediterranean for several months. She was anxious to find something with which to occupy herself on board and regression to previous lives in which she had been skilled in certain crafts inspired her to try her hand at them again.)

3   Are you in this age group, but very busy as a parent? If so, always remember that you are doing the most important job there is, but also that complete self-sacrifice is not a good thing. Continuing with/developing a special skill of your own will (a) bring you much satisfaction and (b) inspire your children on their own path in life.

4   Are you the parent of anyone in this age group? If so, do you feel that they are realizing their full potential? Do you give them your full support and encouragement, or do you worry constantly about them? As a loving parent it is never easy not to worry about one's offspring, whatever their age, but "letting go and letting God" is of the utmost importance here! Remember too that they have their own karma to work out and their own Life Plans, which may differ in every possible way from your own. Prayer can also be the most useful thing we can offer them.

CHAPTER SEVEN

THIRTY-SIX TO FORTY EIGHT - THE 'MID-LIFE CRISIS'

Out of suffering arises learning; out of learning, knowledge. And just as in respect of much else, we may say of pain that we have grasped it only when we know it not only in itself but in what proceeds from it. As to many other things, pain is known only by its fruits.
Rudolf Steiner[1]

"What mid-life crisis?" asked Arun as we sat at the dining table on his verandah in Grand Saconnex, watching the setting sun sink slowly behind the Jura mountains, whose outline stood out so clearly now against the darkening sky. It had been one of those August weekends that I had come through the years to expect in Geneva: the temperature building up over several days, the atmosphere getting heavier and heavier, working and getting about becoming more and more of an effort. Then, after the thermometer had risen to the mid thirties, you felt you could hardly move another inch, and the fresh milk had turned sour in the refrigerator, the storm had suddenly burst. You did not mind being kept awake half the night by the thunder and torrential rain, for such was the relief at knowing that the next morning would be clear, bright and cool, and your energy and enthusiasm for life would have returned.

Nita smiled serenely as she put the delectable dishes down in front of us. When we had each filled our plate, she set off with hers back to the kitchen, and Arun explained that she was offering it to Baba before we could say Grace and start eating. She took the sample of food to the tiny shrine that the family have erected in the kitchen next to where they normally eat, the verandah dining table being kept for meals with guests. Arun had already shown us the basement of his newly built house, where the large shrine to Baba holds pride of place in the beautiful, spacious prayer and meditation room.

Grandmother, eleven-year-old Niraj and nine-year-old Anisha joined in the recitation of the Gujarati Grace, and when that was done and we had started enjoying the meal, I asked Nita whether she too had been a follower of Baba for most of her life. "No," she replied, "it was Arun who introduced me to Him when we got engaged. I took quite a long time to be converted, but now it's wonderful because I know that He's looking after us all the time. A few months ago Niraj went off on a scout camp and it rained the entire week, but I wasn't the slightest bit worried. I just knew that all would go well."

"And they had a great time, I suppose?"

"Yes! They got a bit muddy, but really enjoyed it, and Niraj said himself that Baba had been taking care of him."

The sky above the Jura was now a glorious pink and the aeroplanes setting off from nearby Cointrin airport glinted in the last shreds of light, but the house was so well sound-proofed that we were not disturbed at all by any noise. "What a perfect place to live!" I thought to myself slightly enviously, but then hastily reminded myself that we all get in life what we want and need. In Geneva accommodation is very expensive and, apart from the few who have inherited family houses, almost everybody lives in rented flats. A small proportion of the population are able to buy their own flats; a smaller proportion still buy houses. Arun, who in mid life is so content with his family, his house and his work, has obviously accrued some very good karma. He also seems to be evidence for my as yet unproven theory that people brought up to believe in Sai Baba have fewer problems and bigger advantages than the average.

But Arun was not born with a silver spoon in his mouth. He

has worked hard, and continues to work hard, for every Franc that goes out on his mortgage; and Nita and his mother help too by running a little Indian take-away catering service from home. Arun's father was a Hindu from Gujarat, who, at the age of fifteen, before the Second World War, left home for Tanganyika (now Tanzania) at a time when Britain was encouraging Indians to move to some of her other colonies. After trying his hand at a number of different jobs, he eventually set up a shop in Dar es Salaam, where Arun's older sister and he himself were born. When they were both very young, their mother took them on a trip to India by boat, reluctantly leaving her husband behind to mind the shop. While they were in Gujarat they noticed a number of statues and pictures of Sai Baba of Shirdi, and Arun's aunt explained to them that He was the local god, which they found rather odd. On the return journey Arun's mother was feeling rather apprehensive traveling without her husband, but she nevertheless failed to appreciate the attentions of an Indian gentleman about her own age, who at the time also lived in Tanganyika. After a few days on the boat, they noticed this man with a crowd around him apparently performing a conjuring trick. He had a small, empty box in his hand, which he shut, rubbed, reopened, and then showed his audience that it had filled with grey ash. Both children dismissed the performance as some trivial sleight of hand, and it was only some years later that they learnt that they had been in the presence of Dr. Gadia, now deceased but still well-known to Baba devotees in many countries for his wonderful lectures on this avatar. Far from wanting to take advantage of a woman on her own, he had simply been following Baba's injunction to give service to others at all times; and the box was one that had been given to him by Baba Himself with the promise that the *vibhuti* (healing ash)[2] it contained would never run out.

All this was the prelude to Arun's family's full introduction to Baba, which came through a cousin who had moved to Uganda.

When, on a return visit to Dar-es-Salaam, she recounted tales of Baba miracles, Arun's mother and both the children believed her instantly. She taught them to perform *bhajans* (devotional songs) every Thursday – a practice they continued after the cousin's return to Uganda. When Baba made his only journey outside India – to Uganda just before the advent of Amin – the three of them longed to go there to see Him, but could not afford it. The cousin and her husband heeded Baba's warning and returned to India, whence she has continued to play an important role in Arun's spiritual life.

So Arun has had the certainty of being cared for by Sai Baba ever since he was eight years old. When it was time for him to move to secondary school, he wrote Baba a letter asking for His help in getting to the school he wanted. This prayer was answered, and Arun feels sure too that Baba helped him throughout his studies. He had much ability, but also worked hard and always got good grades. However, when it came to the time he was due to leave school, his desire to get into Dar es Salaam University was thwarted by the government policy of giving preference to Africans over Indians. Now in retrospect he sees Baba's hand in that too, as he won a scholarship to Cairo University, and while he was doing his chemistry degree there, an opportunity came up for a student visit to Geneva. So that is how his link with Switzerland was made.

But before Arun had reached university age, the family were feeling rather alone until his mother discovered that there was a Sai Baba group in Dar es Salaam, which had between thirty-five and forty members. This group met twice a week, and Arun thoroughly enjoyed joining in the *bhajans* until the day when he was asked to sing alone. Feeling tremendously self-conscious, he felt sure that he would never be asked again as he sang "so badly", but the group leader was inexorable. Week after week Arun was made to sing again. He hated it so much that he almost gave up going to the meetings, yet some strange force kept pulling him there. "This guy is destroying my peace," he said to himself as he was told: "You must put ornaments into your voice, just as you put ornaments on to a woman to enhance her beauty…You have to play with your voice and make the *bhajans* interesting." This man obviously recognized Arun's potential, for now he sings quite beautifully, with his own percussion accompaniment, and is one of the chief leaders in the large *bhajan* group in Geneva. (Sometimes an outsider is given the role of forcing us into realizing our potential and finding part at least of our Life Plan.) Arun now also teaches his own children to lead *bhajans* and when, after the first Geneva meeting I had attended, I expressed my admiration of their performance, he replied, "I tell them that Swami is perfect so they have to be perfect".

So, far from having a crisis in mid life, Arun is very much aware that, since so few people in Geneva are able to buy their own houses, some of his acquaintances are jealous of him. This bothers him at times, but on the other hand he knows both that he has earned his present good fortune in previous lives and that he has worked, and is still working, hard for it in this life. His job is very demanding, and the little spare time that he has he devotes mainly to his family and to the Sai Baba group. He brought his mother to live with him in Geneva after his father had died, and when he invited us for a meal at his house he was leading the group, which is active in such things as care of people with Alzheimer's as well as the weekly *bhajan* singing meetings. He has mastered French very well, and is useful to the group as an interpreter as well as a lead singer.

Dr. Harry Moody, in his inspired book *The Five Stages of the Soul*[3], argues that there is really no such thing as a 'mid-life crisis'. He says that research has shown that crises are equally likely to occur at any stage of life, which I am sure is a very valid point. But I am equally sure that everyone would agree that this phase of life is characterized both by very particular difficulties and by unusual opportunities. Jung said that the way of wholeness was "full of fateful detours and wrong turnings", but he also said that some time between about the ages of thirty-five and forty an "inexorable inner process" would begin more or less automatically. And the great American psychoanalyst Erik Erikson described mid-life as a "choice between stagnation and regenerativity" – a time when people would either deny change or embark on new ventures. In *Childhood and Society*[4] he has an eight-stage view of the life cycle, and he says that each stage culminates in a "psychological crisis" or turning point, which is in fact a moment both of increased vulnerability and of heightened potential. Passing well through each of these turning points facilitates success in the subsequent stages, but on the other hand, each crisis also mobilizes new energy and affords an opportunity to rework previously unresolved issues. The key factor of adolescence, for instance, is identity versus identity confusion, and Erikson maintains that those who do not resolve that issue during their adolescence will have the problems resurface in mid life. How many marriages does one see breaking down during this period, and how many people decide on career changes?

My friend Kitty explained to me that this period is a particularly active one from an astrological point of view. Age thirty-six brings the Third Jupiter Return, which tends to be a fairly buoyant moment, when many people are in a position to entertain new possibilities and more options. Those who are at this point relaxed in their jobs, with time and income on their hands, might well start attending night classes in something new; others might choose this moment to have another child, or even a first one.

At about thirty-eight, on the other hand, when Pluto squares Pluto, life-changing transformations can occur to those who want them or not. This is a crucial moment from the point of view of the blueprint, because those who have not been following the right path will find that Pluto can obliterate absolutely everything. My astrologer friend Gertrude had already split up from the man she had espoused at seventeen, in what Gail Sheehy[5] describes as a "jail-breaking marriage" (which was in this case to escape from her domineering family), when Hubert walked into her life at the precise moment of her Pluto Square. Gertrude describes Hubert, her second husband, as the most powerful influence of her adult life. Undoubtedly a 'karmic soul mate'[6], he was simultaneously the greatest teacher and the greatest cause of suffering of her sixty-seven years. Having children at a very early age deprived Gertrude of the opportunity to develop her academic potential at what is generally regarded as the normal age and, while the children were young, financial constraints forced her to take jobs which were beneath her intellectual abilities. Being a very strong character, however, she managed at the same time as bringing up her family to qualify first in nursing and then in health visiting, and she was doing the latter when she married Hubert. (The first marriage had died a natural death, as the two of them had little in common.)

Hubert was a very angry man, and right from the beginning of their relationship he hated such things as astrology, which had for long already been a great interest of Gertrude's, and her intuitive gifts, which are also very strong. The more she asserted her independence, the more punitive he became, and this anger and resentment were also taken out on Gertrude's middle child, whom he regarded as not fitting in and with whom he had a total incompatibility. Gertrude wonders in retrospect how she endured this painful relationship for so many years, but she says that she was still in love with Hubert even when she left him. It proved, however, to be the main trigger for Gertrude asserting the immense independence that appears to be one of the strongest characteristics of her current Life Plan. But before being able to reach that stage, she went through a "three-year darkness" which began with a suicide attempt. She took an overdose, which was more than a cry for help, but fortunately her middle child found her just in time. Forced to give up her health visiting, Gertrude probably only carried on living for the next three years for the sake of her children. But eventually the light did begin to penetrate through the other end of the tunnel. She took a holiday in the Maldives, which was so healing that it gave her the strength to break free from Hubert, and on her recovery she went into private nursing.

Gertrude is very much aware that she deliberately chose a difficult life this time both for her learning and to work out a large amount of karma, and she is almost grateful to Hubert for his contribution in both those things. Although they still live in the same area, she had lost contact with him completely until comparatively recently, when she suddenly bumped into him in a park while walking her dogs. He, who has remarried success-fully, invited her back to his house for a coffee, and she says that an extraordinary healing of the relationship took place in the space of just an hour. This would appear to confirm my hunch that the original attraction was caused by a karmic debt which Gertrude has now paid off, and that they are therefore both able to get on with their lives after having learnt the lessons that they needed from their time spent together.

Pluto is the planet both of death and of transformation. Many people at about thirty-eight (the time of their Pluto Square) find themselves faced with death for the first time. Indeed I was thirty-eight myself when my father died, and up until that point death was a thing from which I had been overprotected. Gertrude had a real brush with death when Hubert was making her life intolerable, and in her astrology generally she is very much under the influence of Pluto. That partly explains the fact of her life being one of transformation. Though she has never left the area in which she was born, she has moved house many times, and a third marriage also ended in divorce (though on that occasion much more amicably).

For my good friend Carmen death had even more prominence

during her 'mid-life crisis' period. First of all her father, with whom she had always been extremely close, died when she was forty. Two years later, before she had got over that, her husband committed suicide. Then, six months after her husband's death, she lost all the staff of their business in a lorry accident, and finally her mother died before that year was out! She says that it was only having the most wonderful neighbors that pulled her through; (she lives in a small cul-de-sac in which everyone is close in both senses).

Carmen describes thirty-three (when she got married) to forty-two as her "materialistic phase". She never wanted children – even before coming to believe in reincarnation she used to joke that she must have had a surfeit of them in previous lives! – and, always wanting to travel and do many things, she had never felt a strong wish to marry. David and she, however, hit it off from the word 'go', and she says that he came at the right time, when she had given up hoping for the perfect job. They met at the end of a year in which she had gone to work as an *au pair* in London in order to learn English. On her return to Spain she started working for a Spanish travel agent, and this made frequent meetings financially possible. After a three-year courtship, Carmen settled in London extraordinarily quickly, and she feels her karmic links with England to be very strong, as she is so at home there. David was nominally Church of England, but not at all interested in anything spiritual, so the years of her marriage were mainly a time of socializing. Now she wonders what might have happened if he had not died, because she feels that a return to her innate spiritual nature was inevitable and that David would probably have been unable to follow her in that direction.

Carmen was the stronger of the pair, having come from such a stable family background, while David's childhood had been traumatic. She says that contact with her well-adjusted, happy family was a real education for him, but alas in spite of that, depression eventually got the better of him. The first two or three years following his death were naturally Carmen's period of most intense crisis. Although she never actually blamed herself for what happened, her main thought during that time was "if my plan in life was to help David to overcome his problems, I failed". She says that she believes too strongly in individual choice to feel responsible herself for what he did, but she did during that initial period often chide herself for not having said the right thing at the right moment, for their arguments, and for not having told him more often that she loved him. During the initial period after his death, the worst time of the day used to be between five and six o'clock, when everyone else's husbands were coming home from work. But her salvation was the empathetic neighbors, who never left her alone at that time, often, for instance, sending their children round to visit her.

Up until the time of her father's death, though her links with the Church had at times been tenuous, Carmen had always been a believer. However, losing this man who had meant so much to her, seemed suddenly like the end of everything. The prelude to the death was weeks and weeks of suffering in hospital with lung cancer. Watching her first teacher – the father who had taught her at such an early age to appreciate the wonders of nature in their beloved Pyrenees – suffering so much, simply tore Carmen apart. She yearned with all her being to help him, and yet felt powerless. For the funeral she wrote a moving little poem in her own language (Catalan), and after she had read it, all her friends and relatives asked for copies of it.

Que trist es veure al pare morir
Que trist es veure a un pare sofrir.
El cor se'ns esqueixa a bocins…
Bocins fets d'amor

(How sad it is to see one's father die. How sad it is to see a father suffer. My heart breaks into pieces...Pieces made of love.) The poem continues with a plea to her father to take one of these pieces of her heart with him, and asks whether she had ever told him quite how much she loved him. "A love which, over the years, takes root ever more deeply. A love which can be compared only with the love of the Mother, Mary."

Despite the apparent faith of the last line of her funeral poem, Carmen says that after this death she felt an incredible emptiness. She really believed that her father had gone to "nothing", and found herself totally unable to communicate with him. She was still not over this when suddenly, two years later, her dear husband was gone too. Anyone who has not in this lifetime suffered so much loss, will probably find it hard to imagine the full impact of such a tragedy. Besides her neighbors, it was only the parish priest, who had made good friends with her husband on account of a mutual interest in trees, who got her through it. The neighbors surrounded her with so much love and companionship that she was hardly given a spare moment to brood. Much though she loved her house with its beautiful big garden, she spoke of selling it because it was so much work. Then she would wake up in the morning to find a neighbor already out working in her garden!

The loss of David, however, stimulated in Carmen a real need to believe that death was not the end, and so began an intense spiritual search that she was still pursuing when we spoke, nineteen years later. Not finding the answers she required in the Church of her upbringing, she went to the College of Psychic Studies in London and started voraciously to read books on the Afterlife. This reading gradually led her, very naturally, to a belief in reincarnation and in due course she went for a regression to Judy Hall[7]. It was this regression that gave Carmen the biggest piece of the jigsaw in her current Life Plan. She found that in a previous life she had also been married to a man who had killed himself, and that on that occasion she had never got over it, but had died a bitter and resentful old woman. She then saw that part of her Plan for her present life had been to redeem this piece of karma, not merely by coping admirably with the loss, but even by getting over it completely. <u>What</u> a challenge!

But Carmen is not a woman to duck challenges. While her husband was alive she had always occupied herself both with little bits of Spanish teaching and with giving a hand in his business. Now she suddenly found herself landed with keeping the business going more or less single-handedly, and this challenge was of course intensified six months later when the staff got killed in a lorry accident. Somehow she managed simultaneously to recruit new staff and get the business properly on its feet again, to continue with her Spanish teaching, to pursue her studies with the London College of Psychic Studies, <u>and</u> to get involved with the local Buddhist Centre. All this in addition to looking after her house, her garden, four cats and a neighbor's dog when the latter was out at work!

Carmen says now that, whereas she previously believed that her task had been to help David, later she began to wonder whether the reality was not more the reverse. For she is quite sure that if he had not died, she would never have started her serious spiritual quest. She says that the struggle with the business was a real help to her, and that friends she has seen left money when their partners died have not been happier than she has. Carmen, however, agrees with me that karma is very often two-way. Whether one of this couple had a debt to the other is not clear, but the mutual benefit of their coming together is surely very clear. She helped him during the time of their marriage by giving him the affection of which he had been deprived as a child and by showing him what good family life could be like, and she is doubtless still helping him now with her continuing prayers and concern for him. He helped her by being the main trigger for her spiritual path, and by enabling her to shine in her community as an example of how a tragic death need not be the end for the surviving partner.

Mystics and spiritual teachers normally tell us that suicide can never be part of a Life Plan. Human life is a sacred gift from God, and (though I accept that there may be the occasional exception) the Higher Self will as a rule only withdraw a soul from its physical body when the latter can no longer serve any purpose on Earth and has completed the span of working out its pre-selected karma. (This is why I cannot agree that euthanasia could be right even in cases where the physical body is doing apparently nothing except cause its owner suffering. That very suffering must surely be part of the karma.) So what happens when someone's mental or physical pain on Earth becomes so intense that they take steps to curtail it? Well, all the books on the Afterlife or on regression therapy that I have read make it very clear that there is in fact no escape from the problems that one has. This of course makes perfect sense once we appreciate that the only problems we ever encounter are those of our own creation. The quotation from Rudolf Steiner at the start of this chapter is appropriate here. Difficult though this may seem to most of us, suffering is best seen as a golden opportunity for growth, and when we opt out of such an opportunity (which, please note, we had ourselves chosen before coming in to a given life), the only solution is a repeat performance. Consequently suicide victims will, more often than not, in due course find themselves thrust into another life in which the very same problems which triggered their opting out are not only repeated but actually intensified.

I do not doubt that we have most, if not all, voluntarily brought to a premature end at least one of our previous lives. But fortunately we have eternity on our side! Prayers for the dead are invaluable, and what greater use can they ever have than in cases of suicide? If someone has been so weakened by the life circumstances that drove them to put an 'end' to their suffering, they will not be forced to go through it all again before they are ready.

Resting incarnations to build up their strength once more are always an option before the time is considered ripe for the 'biggie', and here there is plenty of advice available on the other side. Carmen is undoubtedly helping her husband now with her prayers - and, who knows?, he might even be back on Earth already!

In *Light Beyond the Darkness - the Healing of a Suicide Across the Threshold of Death*[8], Doré Deverell tells a moving tale of how, despite her own acute suffering, she was able to help her son Richard after he had drowned himself at the age of thirty-six (the beginning of our 'mid-life crisis' period!). Doré had had a very tortured life herself, and Richard's epilepsy and his inability to relate to people reinforced her own sense of inadequacy as a mother. A spiritual search, however, led her to train as a Steiner teacher, and it was this that gave her the idea of reading to her dead son. Richard had always been a great seeker of Truth, and Doré read to him daily – for instance the philosophical works of Steiner, which she felt would have been a real help to him if he had discovered them during his lifetime. She was in due course rewarded by Richard appearing to her just as she was waking up one morning, and making it clear to her that the reading was helping. Some time after that Richard further indicated to her that he had moved on to a place of light, and she came fully to appreciate that no suffering was without meaning. In their case the fruit of it was that the two of them were working together on the spiritual plane.

Not more than nine years after Richard's death, Doré saw that he had reincarnated as daughter to a young couple she had got to know and regarded as perfect parents. When the thought "that baby was Richard" first flashed through her head, she dismissed it, but three clairvoyants subsequently told her independently that this was the case. Also, when the young couple (to whom she never breathed a word about it) obtained a clairvoyant reading for their new baby, they were told that in the child's last life she had committed suicide and that part of their task as parents would be to help her through problems arising from that. The couple later moved away to another part of the US, but Doré felt happy about the baby Maria's future. Her spiritual quest further equipped her to give love, and when her grandson Adam was born, she found some of the joys of motherhood that she had previously failed to experience.

But suicide, as my fellow Deep Memory Process therapist friend George comments, can be committed in more ways than one. George and his older brother both had very difficult child-hoods, as their father was physically violent towards them, and George suffered also in that the brother, two and half years his senior and very big (he grew to be six foot five eventually), always dominated him. Both trained to be doctors on leaving school, and both had failed first marriages, but there the similar-ities end. George weathered his marriage break-up bravely, has always been an excellent father to his two children as well as an excellent doctor, and is now married to a delightful woman who shares his interests in spirituality and healing. His brother, on the other hand, despite his medical knowledge of the conse-quences of heavy smoking and drinking, fell victim to both and died at the height of his 'mid-life crisis' period.

George, like myself, took a Diploma with the College of Past Life Regression Studies, and also like myself he subsequently decided to undertake further training in the subject with Dr. Roger Woolger. On the first course, under Dr. Keith Hearne, he had learnt a great deal about 'spirit attachment', but it was only in 1999 – about eleven years after his brother's death – that he came to appreciate the full implications of this from personal experience. In a regression that George underwent on one of his Woolger training weeks, it became clear that his brother's spirit had attached itself to him when he had kissed his brow in the coffin immediately before the funeral. People who die are not always ready immediately to leave the Earth's plane, and this is often particularly true of those who suffer from an addiction. Cravings do not die with our physical bodies any more than do our other imperfections, and so the obvious solution for an addict is to attach him or herself to someone who is still incarnate and thus to endeavor to satisfy their craving vicariously. George, who is a strong character, has never drunk excessively, and he had never previously smoked either, but, as I said, his brother had always tried to dominate him. So, what did he find a few months after his brother's death? He had started smoking cigars! He began with just the occasional one, but it gradually increased to about five a day. It may well be that many more people than we realize who suddenly start smoking, drinking or taking drugs, do so under the influence of an Earthbound discarnate entity. Fortunately George's brother did not succeed in getting him to drink excessively.

None of this was apparent to George until a workshop when one of Roger Woolger's colleagues performed a successful 'spirit releasement' operation on him. One of the reasons he knows it to be successful is that only about a month afterwards (on his brother's birthday!) he suddenly decided to give up smoking and has not touched another cigar since. An important element of this therapy is not only releasing the Earthbound spirits and dispatching them to the light, but also strengthening the 'victim' in order to help them to avoid falling prey to further attachments. George says that, had he had the knowledge that he has now at the time of his brother's death, he would have protected himself. Different people suggest different ways of doing this, but George's habit, when he visits hospitals, for instance, (obviously a veritable hive of newly departed spirits!), is to imagine the divinity within himself as a little golden light, and then to visualize that light expanding until it entirely fills his aura. Dr. Roger Woolger nevertheless, who runs regular workshops on ancestral spirit healing, believes it to be very difficult to avoid acquiring attachments of this nature all together. He comments that people such as therapists tend to wear a label saying "Helper", which inevitably draws lost spirits to them. His own solution is, when he has finished his day's therapy, to shut the door firmly behind him and mentally turn the "Helper" label over until he is ready to return to work the next day.

It has been found that spirit attachments rarely come singly. Once a person has become vulnerable, further entities are likely to attach themselves as well. In past life regression therapy jargon these are known as 'nested attachments', and in a subsequent Roger Woolger workshop, George's mother and paternal grandmother were both released from him. But George points out that these two must have been with him since long before his mid-life period, as they both died earlier than his brother. While on Earth, the two of them had a long standing love/hate relationship (with greater emphasis on the hate), so the chances are that the grandmother attached herself on death to her daughter-in-law, in a desire to continue exercising control over her – a not uncommon phenomenon – and that George's mother brought the grandmother's spirit with her when she attached herself to him after she died. The practice of spirit releasement (pioneered very much by the Baldwins[9]) is "last in, first out", which explains why George's brother's spirit was the first to leave George.

'Victim' is certainly not the word that I would use for my friend Marie, another Roger Woolger graduate, although she is someone who suffered a great deal during the early stages of her mid-life period. In fact Marie's physical suffering began much earlier than that, with the onset of severe arthritis when she was only eighteen. An avid reader from an early age, Marie discovered two books on Phrenology and Palmistry in the house of a family friend, and then started reading palms successfully herself.

Marie took up dancing when she was six or seven and never really wanted to do anything else. She continued with dancing lessons until she was seventeen, and performed in a number of shows and exhibitions in the North of England. At nineteen she had a battle with her father because she wanted to leave home, and she ended up doing a secretarial course locally. Her father, who had been orphaned at ten, lived on the edge of fear. Whenever Marie was going off anywhere on holiday, he would always say "You'll be killed!".

Marie feels sure that, if her father had not won the battle over her leaving home at eighteen, she would not have got the arthritis, and she also believes that carrying on with her dancing would have enabled her to escape it. A regression undertaken during her training, however, made it clear to her that before coming into her present life she chose to experience pain in order to write about it for the benefit of others – a brave woman! So it would appear that everything has been part of her Plan, however difficult.

After successfully completing her secretarial course, Marie went to Newcastle and did the first year of a degree. She then did secretarial work for a while before returning to College and completing a degree. On this course she met her first partner, Douglas, and they were together for fifteen years. The mid-life crisis period began, however, with this relationship coming to an end. Even though Marie and Douglas were not destined to remain together, she sees the experience as an important part of her Life Plan. For Marie discovered on a Roger Woolger course strong karmic links from Egypt with both her father and Douglas. A friend of Douglas' (of both that life and this) was a priest in Egypt, who engineered Marie's father to believe lies about her before he died. Douglas was then a soldier who saved her life, and in their present life too it was he who, after she had moved to Newcastle, succeeded in getting her away from her overbearing father.

Those who are involved in Deep Memory Process therapy never cease to be amazed at the power of it. In that regression

Marie saw that her father (of both lives) was still bound by ties to four Egyptian priests. At the precise moment when she (in Wales) cut him free from all of them, he (at home with of course no conscious knowledge of what she was doing) fell over for no apparent reason. He landed on top of Marie's mother, who then (although it was midnight) telephoned Marie in alarm to tell her what had happened.

Setting out on a new life on her own, Marie bought the house where she still lives. An added difficulty for her at that point was that the hips she had had to have replaced on account of her arthritis caved in, and she had to have two operations. So at thirty-six (again at the beginning of our 'mid-life crisis' period!) Marie found herself flat on her back in a Birmingham hospital for three months. She says: "Suddenly I didn't know who I was any more. I had completely lost my own power and truth."

So often does the blueprint seem to involve one's being hurled into the deepest depths so that one can find new strength through struggling up again and making a completely fresh start. Marie, who all her adult life had weathered tremendous physical problems with enormous courage, regards her 'identity crisis' as the greatest challenge she has ever had to overcome. Thirty-six marked the end of a phase which had been very comfortable materially, but the beginning of a life which is deeply spiritual. She says that it took a full ten years to reclaim her lost power, but that she has "more than got it back now". She now works as a writer as well as a therapist, and feels herself to be once again on her Life Path.

As Gail Sheehy[5] says, a crisis appears to be necessary for the achievement of identity. They are very painful at the time, but everything that happens to us does so for a reason, and often crises seem to be the trigger for either getting us on to the right path or getting us to do something valuable (such as get into therapy) that we would not have been persuaded to do otherwise.

Part of this achievement of identity, which from my perspective includes full recognition of one's blueprint, is often helped by exploration of one's previous lives. Though some start earlier and others later, the mid-life period is frequently a peak one for this. On one of my courses with Roger Woolger I met a delightful German woman of forty-one, who expressed to me her desire to understand how the soul expresses itself through the body. The eldest of three girls, she feels that the name her father gave her – Hildegund – was an unfortunate choice. This is because he chose the name of a woman he had always been attracted to, and the girl was expected to live up to her namesake, who even her mother regarded as a wonderful person. She was always close to her mother (who, unlike her father, appreciated her), but she sadly died of a kidney disease in 1990. My friend, who was supposed to "be successful like the first Hildegund", found that nothing she did was ever worthy of praise from her father. She trained as a translator, but even that was not good enough, and when she changed career to become an assistant to a homeopath, that was regarded as really going downhill. She settled in England in 1998 after meeting her present partner at Findhorn, but the onset of a back disease caused her father to cut her off completely!

When Hildegund first arrived in England, her name suddenly became an even greater burden to her. English people found it difficult and always wanted to abbreviate it, but she did not like "Hilda" anyway. After a while, an English friend suggested that she change her name, which would never have occurred to her as such an act is frowned upon in Germany. So she chose the name Joy, which she rightly believed to well describe her character, and now she is busy establishing her identity completely independently of her family, and finding a new path in spiritual work through which she can fully realize her joyful potential.

Pluto is the planet of transformation, and under Pluto's influence Joy took the transformation to the extreme by changing her name. The Pluto Square period lasts generally from about age thirty-eight to the mid forties, and Pluto is very important to this book since he represents Soul Purpose – the alignment of the ego self with the Higher Self (or soul with spirit if you like). During this period everything is tested – relationships, career etc., and Pluto can cause a total realignment. Dealing with death has been a strong factor for both Carmen and Marie particularly, but another characteristic of Pluto is that he causes the resurgence of latent talents. Survival of a crisis (a common phenomenon also written about extensively by Gail Sheehy[5] and a little less extensively by John Clay[10]), sometimes has the bonus – as it did with Marie – of enabling people to come into their own power. Phoenix rising from the ashes!

Indeed it is not uncommon for people finally to discover their life purpose during this period. Sometimes even those whose talent is obvious at an early age can be deflected from their Plan by, for instance, a critical teacher or unappreciative parents. My friend Polly, who has a truly wonderful voice and remembers singing to herself for company and comfort even in her cot, was turned out of the school choir after she had got into folk singing, because her voice was deemed to be "no longer suitable"! She nevertheless became a professional singer for a while after completing her college studies, but was later put off by further criticism and decided to try her hand at other things, none of which proved to be truly fulfilling for her. Then, when she was about forty, she suddenly saw an advertisement for a workshop that was being given by a very well-known folk singer whom she greatly admired, and so she plucked up the courage to enroll for it.

That workshop proved to be a sudden real turning point for Polly. To her surprise she found herself by the end of the day thinking "I could do that!". So, little by little, she began to develop ideas of her own and to advertize various singing events locally. Now, as well as running regular workshops, she directs a flourishing community choir, which gives popular performances of a wide variety of music in a number of different places, and for which she also composes songs of her own. She makes particular efforts to encourage people who have never sung before to come along, and finds that many of them had been told in their youth that they could not sing yet under her direction develop great talent. Polly has a particular interest in singing for health, and so – now that she is fully in tune with her Life Plan – her role is a unique one in the area in which she lives and beneficial to very many people. How many of us have to contend with having been told when we were young that we were no good at something? Yet, once we <u>have</u> got over that challenge, it makes us stronger and clearer in our life's purpose. Sometimes we need a trigger to get us on track, and often it can be something just as simple as Polly noticing an advertisement for a workshop.

I have talked quite a lot about talents, and obviously some people have these to a greater extent than others. We cannot all be geniuses (not in every lifetime anyway!), and that is surely something to be thankful for. Sofia Tolstoy says in her Diaries[11] "All great people are alike: their genius is a deformity, an infirmity, because it is exceptional. There is no harmony in people of genius, and their unbalanced characters are a torment to others." Few women would be able to endure the sufferings that Sofia survived, as well as doing all the work that she did (regularly copying out her husband's manuscripts until the early hours of the morning!), and she did in fact seriously contemplate suicide on a number of occasions. Yet, as the lives of many of the world's greatest artists bear witness (Beethoven, Brahms, Van Gogh, to name but three more), personal torment and anguish are so often a vital ingredient of the most powerful, enduring and moving works. Those, like Sofia Tolstoy, who were close to these men must have incarnated with difficult Life Plans that they had fully agreed to beforehand. (Alas such geniuses do mostly seem to be men, but that may well change now that we are achieving greater equality. Felix Mendelssohn's sister Fanny appears to have been at least as gifted musically as he was, but was not permitted to make it her career!)

Thinking about the role of a life of torment in great art (used of course in the widest sense of the word), I asked myself why the life and music of J. S. Bach seemed to be an exception. The only answer I could think of was that, rather than working out incredible anguish, as did Beethoven for instance, through his music, Bach was a very highly evolved soul and thus able to receive the purest and most spiritually perfect music direct from the highest realms. My personal belief is that he came in as a healer – for what can be more healing and spiritually uplifting than listening to truly wonderful music? For Sofia Tolstoy, who was clearly a gifted pianist as well as a gifted writer, I believe it was her salvation. She says in her Diaries[11] "Music has a strange effect on me; even when I play myself it suddenly makes every-thing clear, fills me with peaceful joy and enables me to see all life's worries in a new light, calmly and lucidly."

But now to return to more ordinary mortals! Another astro-logical feature of the mid-forties is the second major life transition (the first being the First Saturn Return at about twenty-nine): the Uranus Opposition. For Barbara Hand Clow[12], Uranus is the planet of illumination and "kundalini break-through". The kundalini rises as we develop spiritually, clearing in turn through all the chakras. When it reaches the crown, we are ready for reunification with God. It is seen as being akin to sexual energy, but (though the two can of course be intertwined), for true spiritual development to occur, the red/orange energy of the base chakras needs to be transmuted into the violet/white of the spiritual, higher chakras. The kundalini can be aroused at more or less any age, but this mid-life period is typical for it. Though problems can sometimes occur when the arousal is aborted, in normal circumstances there is no need for this to happen, and as often as not the kundalini arousal produces no physical sensations at all. For further information on the *kundalini*, I recommend David Tansley's book on the subtle body[13].

My astrologer friend Kitty describes the Uranus Opposition as "very liberating", for Uranus gives universal permission to totally reinvent oneself. A symptom of this can be seen with men who do crazy things such as buying flashy cars or going out with much younger women, and women who – particularly if their children have left home – celebrate their new freedom by, for instance, dying their hair or taking up belly dancing. "What's got into her?" is a question often voiced at this time. As Barbara Hand Clow[12] points out, each new incarnation gives us a chance to clear past-life blocks and become whole. Sometimes this involves doing apparently crazy things.

In contrast to the Uranus Opposition, but occurring at about the same time (though this varies between generations because of changes in the elliptic) is Neptune squaring Neptune. Neptune represents illusion, fantasy and spiritual things, so, while this mid-life period can be a time of disappointment and disillusionment, it can also be a moment of great spiritual yearning. It is at this point in their lives that people often take up, say, meditation or yoga, and it is Neptune who encourages the realization that we are all connected. There are two sides to the Neptune coin: when it goes well, we grow spiritually; when it goes sour, we escape (like George's older brother) into drugs or alcohol.

This period gets rounded off at forty-eight by another Jupiter Return. Jupiter is the planet of philosophy, encouraging us to find the meaning of things, and if we do not start to do that in earnest at this point, we may fail to discover our blueprint. This discovery is, as I have already mentioned, often helped by an exploration of past lives. My sister did this during her mid-life period, when she was coming to the end of a horrendous marriage. I always wonder how she endured living with Jeremy for sixteen years, but it is amazing what a woman will put up with when there are both children and her own sense of security involved. When she looked into it, she found out not, as she had feared, that she had a karmic debt to Jeremy, but that she had got trapped in a repeated pattern of abuse. She had fallen in love with and married him on several previous occasions, and in the past he had abused her physically as well as mentally. This discovery gave her the courage to cut ties with Jeremy for ever, and she is now happily married to her twin soul.

The subconscious is a curious thing: often it causes us to remember one aspect of the past such as my sister's attraction to Jeremy, but not the consequences of it, and this is one of many instances where DMP therapy can be so useful. In my first book[14] I wrote about a man whom I called Ambrose, who I discovered had fallen madly in love with me in Israel at the time of Christ. At the time I was a widow with four young children, which made physically following Jesus impossible, and so he was faced with the dilemma of having to choose between us. He chose me, but, after learning of the crucifixion, he regretted the choice he had made and blamed both himself and me for not preventing Jesus' death. He is dead now, but was still clearly carrying this blame in his most recent life, and so, although when we first met he clearly immediately remembered the attraction, that memory was quickly supplanted by a feeling of hatred. He consequently took every opportunity to take it out on me, never, for instance, allowing me to have a say during meetings we were both attending. Not understanding what I had done – and indeed in reality I had not done him any wrong either in Israel or in our present life – I reacted with anger, which I later greatly regretted. If when we first met I had had the knowledge of the karma between us that I subsequently acquired, I would no doubt have handled the situation rather differently. On the other hand, that relationship was clearly a crucial one in my Life Plan, for more than one reason. Firstly, it gave me an outlet for the anger against my father that I had been holding in for too long, (the man in question was over twenty years my senior); secondly it gave me a long overdue incentive to learn to speak up for myself; thirdly it was one of the triggers for my research into reincarnation; and fourthly it helped me to learn forgiveness.

On the subject of karmic relationships: another challenge that people are often faced with during the mid-life period is coping with ageing parents. When I met Arun's family in Geneva, having his mother living with them did not appear to be a major problem, but for many people ageing parents can be quite a burden. One such was a client of mine: in her case it appears that her adoptive mother greatly exaggerated in her subconscious mind a very small karmic debt that her daughter incurred to her a long time ago as her older brother. Her attitude gave my client problems which seemed to be totally unfair but, thanks to having therapy and working on herself, she overcame them wonderfully. My client Anil, on the other hand, whose career has been severely affected by having to look after his widowed mother, really believed himself to have a huge karmic debt to her. Being a Hindu Indian, she took such things as karmic debt for granted and played on it to Anil's detriment. So when we eventually discovered exactly what the debt was, Anil and I were both surprised by its insignificance. This discovery helped Anil to cut ties with his mother and to be more firm and 'selfish' in his dealings with her, while still giving her the care that she really needed. Such a problem is of course less likely to occur in Western society, where so few people are aware of karma, but the fact remains that – whether or not we are aware of it – many of us do have debts to pay to our parents, even if it is only from when they cared for us as children, and mid life is the period when this is most likely to occur.

Death, too, whether it be that of parents, other relatives, or friends, is often faced seriously for the first time during this mid-life period. Coming up against it tends to increase our awareness of our own mortality, and the way in which we handle both this and the realization of our departing youth will greatly affect the way in which we live the years remaining to us. Towards the end of 1998 I saw a television program which saddened me immensely. It was the first of a short series, and I do not remember the title, but the subject matter was this very question of coping with getting older. The people portrayed in it had to my mind a total misconception of what life was about and a total misunderstanding of beauty. "I felt that my life had come to an end when I found I could no longer wear a bikini", was one woman's lament, while others were shown rushing off to have face lifts. As for the men, some went to the most extreme lengths to combat their 'beer bellies', while others were dating a long series of young women in an effort to convince themselves that they were still attractive. It is of course always a good idea for the health to keep one's body in as good shape as possible, but is attractiveness really dependent upon an absence of wrinkles? I kept the program on waiting for someone to put the other side, but no-one did, and when I briefly put on the next episode the following week, it seemed to be showing nothing but pictures of ageing bodies.

When one sees life as a continuum, with souls regularly leaving the reality of Home and dipping into the illusion of matter in order to gain more learning experience, growing older yet again need hold no fear for us. On the contrary, it can be very exciting – especially when we realize that we have outgrown so many of the problems of our youth. Love that is given mainly because of physical appearance is not real love at all, and is therefore not worth the money needed for a face lift. Mid-life, with the big upheavals it can bring when children grow up and leave home, or marriages come to an end because people in finding their true identity are no longer compatible with one another, is undoubtedly often a period of great challenge. But that should not prevent it from being regarded as a time for unique and immense opportunity. Dispensing with the bikini can be, rather than the end, the prelude to something much, much better!

Notes

1   *The Origin of Suffering, the Origin of Evil, Illness and Death,* Rudolf Steiner.

2   *Vibhuti* is the sacred, healing ash, which Sai Baba manifests constantly for His devotees, and which also often forms on His portraits in their houses.

3   *The Five Stages of the Soul,* Dr. Harry Moody and David Carroll, Doubleday, USA, 1997.

4   *Childhood and Society,* Erik Erikson.

5   *Passages,* Gail Sheehy, Bantam Books, USA and Canada, 1977.

6   See *SOULS UNITED – The Power of Divine Connection,* Ann Merivale, Llewellyn, USA, 2009.

7   Judy Hall is the author of many books, including *Déjà Who? – A New Look at Past Lives,* Findhorn Press, Scotland, 1998.

8   *Light Beyond the Darkness – the Healing of a Suicide Across the Threshold of Death,* Doré Deverell, Temple Lodge, London.

9   *Regression Therapy: Spirit Releasement,* William Baldwin, 1992.

10 *Men in Mid Life – The Facts, the Fantasies, the Future,* John Clay, Sidgwick and Jackson, London ,1989.

11 From *The Diaries of Sofia Tolstoy,* Alma Books Ltd., England, 2009.

12 *Chiron: Rainbow Bridge between the Inner and Outer Planets,* Barbara Hand Clow, Llewellyn Publications, St. Paul, Minnesota, 1990.

13 *SUBTLE BODY – Essence and Shadow,* David V. Tansley, Thames and Hudson, London.

14 *KARMIC RELEASE – Journeying Back to the Self,* Ann Merivale, Sai Towers Publishing, Bangalore, India, 2006.

EXERCISES

1   Are you in this mid-life period at the moment? If so, do you see it mainly as a time of 'crisis', or as one of growth? If the latter, give yourself a pat on the back and enjoy it. If the former, I hope that this chapter may have given you some ideas as to how you might be able to turn the crisis into growth. If it hasn't, then I strongly advise you to look seriously for a good therapist. Believe me: it is never too late to turn one's life around, and there is nothing shameful about seeking help. Most of us who are now successful therapists started off by doing precisely that!

2   Have you always loved music, or are you tone deaf? If the latter, then music as therapy is perhaps not for you, but the vast majority of people in the world do find great pleasure in one or another type of music, and sound healing has been gaining in popularity in recent years. So, if you are in crisis or feeling very depressed, I strongly recommend looking for some of your favorite music and making time to just let yourself go listening to it. Choose carefully, though! In my previous book[6] I wrote about a client of mine who in her youth, when she had been very depressed, had got hooked on Tchaikovsky. Listening to him, however, amplified her feelings of depression, and it was only when she had discovered Bach that she began to find real healing in music.

3   If you are not musical, think about which of the arts does give you real pleasure and a feeling of upliftment. Do you enjoy looking at paintings, or find solace in poetry? Whatever it is that can give you pleasure, seek it out and let some of the beauty of our amazing world seep into your being through the eyes of the great painter or poet. Or simply allow the Greatest Painter of all to speak to you through the ravishing beauty of Nature. Even in the heart of a big city it is always possible to find a tree or a flower whose beauty you can contemplate!

4   Have you got a family member or a friend who is going through a 'mid-life crisis' and whom you would dearly like to help? You might consider lending him or her this book, or simply putting some of the above suggestions into your own words. Love and intuition, combined with prayer for the person concerned, can work wonders!

CHAPTER EIGHT

FORTY-EIGHT TO FIFTY-SIX - THE SEARCH FOR SPIRITUAL MATURITY

I realised for the first time... the unity of all manifestation and that all existence – the material world, the spiritual realm, the aspiring disciple, the evolving animal and the beauty of the vegetable and mineral kingdoms – constituted one divine and living being which was moving on to the demonstration of the glory of the Lord.
Alice Bailey (The Unfinished Autobiography)[1]

The notion of life being divided into distinct phases is universal. "And one man in his time plays many parts, his acts being seven ages," wrote Shakespeare, and Seven has always been regarded as <u>the</u> spiritual number. In Chinese astrology life is divided into seven-year cycles. Yet for Erik Erikson there are eight stages, and in Hindu tradition the number is just four: Youth, when children study and learn (usually under the eye of an elderly guru), Young Adulthood, in which people work to earn a living and raise families, the Later Adult Years, in which married couples spend more time together in prayer and contemplation, and finally Old Age, when they return to the community in order to impart to the young the wisdom and learning that they have gained during their lifetime.

In the Petit Palais in Geneva there hangs a painting by Georges Lacombe entitled *Les Ages de la Vie*. As its name implies, the characters in the picture represent each stage of life from babyhood to old age and, though the scenes it depicts are in a sense distinct, the painting presents a unified, harmonious whole. Thomas Cole, on the other hand, painted his view of the life cycle in four separate pictures (entitled *The Voyage of Life*), which now hang side by side in the Art Gallery of Utica in New York State. Born in England, it was Cole who introduced landscape painting into American art, and this series was begun in 1842. Robert Hughes describes these paintings thus: "To a modern eye, they are unalloyed Victorian kitsch: four stages in the progress of the soul, from childhood through youth to manhood and thence to old age. Under the watchful eye of his guardian angel, the soul rides in a sort of canoe, heavily ornamented with other, gilded angels, down the river of life. As the soul enters the dangerous rapids of manhood, one of the angels on the prow seems to be squawking with alarm; and once the canoe is into the peaceful waters of old age, the angelic heads have broken off altogether, leaving gilded stumps behind."[2] In this book I am aiming to give a more optimistic view than Cole's!

So now we come to the third of Hinduism's four stages, the Later Adult Years, and it could be argued that it is the most important phase of all. In *Discipleship in the New Age*[3] Alice Bailey maintains that, if one has not found one's spiritual path in life by the age of fifty-six, afterwards it will be too late. My good friend Agnes of the Sai Baba group in Geneva read this passage of Alice Bailey's on Christmas day 1995, just three days before leaving for her second visit to India. Since her fifty-sixth birthday was on the 5th March 1996, she felt that the timing of the book's arrival into her hands was very significant, and her saying to herself "I've just got time!" was one of the major turning points of her life. Although she was born into an agnostic family in Sweden, as a child Agnes was probably never far distanced from her blueprint. For as long as she can remember, she was always searching for "something else" – for that which she describes as "the reality behind what is visible, visible objects being in actual fact mere shadows". The search of her early years ended (she thought!) in her early twenties, when, on a holiday in Scotland, she met a Swiss man whom she in due course married, and who introduced her to Catholicism. She describes her first mass most movingly:

"All my trivial worries about how I should conduct myself – for instance whether or not I should receive communion – just melted away as I felt God open his arms to me and say 'just come'. I seemed to be caught up in a cosmic smile, which was enveloping my whole being with love." At the end of the holiday she returned to Sweden to finish her degree and qualify as a teacher. In Agnes' small university town there were no indigenous Catholics, but she was accepted into a wonderful little community led by two French monks. It was made up of expatriates, many of whom were Italian, and for a time it satisfied the spiritual hunger that she had felt throughout her childhood and adolescence. When she married and settled in Switzerland, this fervent community was replaced for a while by one in Einsiedeln, where her husband had been educated, and to which he still returned regularly for spiritual renewal. In Geneva, however, where they both worked, there was no equivalent, and Agnes' strong feeling of connection with Catholicism gradually waned.

After twelve years of marriage, Agnes realized that she needed to break free from her relationship in order to find herself, although both her teaching and her daughter kept her in Geneva. Her 'mid-life crisis' period saw firstly the tragic end to a second marriage, and secondly an intensified spiritual search. Agnes feels that the fact that her second husband took his own life perhaps indicates that he had strayed impossibly far from his Life Plan, and that the only solution was a completely fresh start - something that she claims does happen occasionally. (An alternative solution is what Ruth Montgomery calls a "walk-in": the taking over of a body by an advanced soul who firstly feels up to getting out of the fix the person has got themselves into, and secondly is glad of the opportunity of a lifetime which skips childhood. I personally find the Montgomery book on walk-ins[4] very convincing.)

Agnes' husband's tragic death stimulated, just as it did for

Carmen, an intensified spiritual search. She also started to attend classes given by a Western Buddhist monk. These she found extremely useful and interesting despite the fact that (also like Carmen) she did not feel a strong affinity with Buddhism. She began to put some of the techniques into practice in her daily life, and then she started studying Krishnamurti. She even had the good fortune of being able to attend one of the last teachings that Krishnamurti gave shortly before his death, as it happened to be in Switzerland. Agnes says that her initial impression of him was of someone very austere, but that she saw a different side to his character when a little girl presented him with a bunch of flowers. After that she went every year until 1995 to Krishnamurti group discussions in Saanen, which used videos made during his lifetime and which she found excellent; but from there Agnes' next step was to the Theosophists. This induced a conflict within her, since Krishnamurti had defected from the Theosophists, who consequently regarded him as a traitor. In her youth Agnes had loved reading romantic novels, but later on her dream of 'perfection' as portrayed in such love stories had been replaced through her spiritual reading by the ideal of the pupil-guru relationship. Krishnamurti, whom she admired, had moved right away from the 'guru' concept, claiming that the only guru was to be found within, while the Theosophist philosophy corresponded with her own deep-seated feelings, and she realized that her innate devotional side could not express itself in a Krishnamurti group. God, however, always responds to those who call on Him from the depths of their being, and in Agnes' case the dilemma was resolved by Sathya Sai Baba.

Agnes first heard of Sai Baba on a visit to India in 1989. She had gone there on account of her interest in Indian culture and religion, and people at the ashram she was visiting talked about Baba, but what they said failed to arouse her interest at that point. She did, however, fall in love with India, and shortly before her second visit, her daughter received a letter from a friend (Yves), who spoke ecstatically about having found all he was looking for at Sai Baba's ashram in Puttaparthi. This letter coincided with Agnes' reading of Alice Bailey, and it struck another deep chord within her. Though she herself still felt little interest in Sai Baba, she was truly delighted for Yves, who had been on a spiritual search for quite some time, and she decided to go to Puttaparthi simply to see him.

She arrived at the ashram very shortly before *Darshan*, and Yves suggested that she go into the hall straight away while he went to the accommodation office on her behalf. Despite having travelled to Puttaparthi as a complete skeptic, Agnes nevertheless did as Yves had suggested and entered the hall only a few minutes before Baba appeared. She says that all she saw was a sort of orange blur in the distance, and immediately her heart leapt inside her and became intensely warm. When *Darshan* was over and she met Yves again, he told her that she would have to go and look for a room outside as the only space available in the ashram was in the sheds, which are each shared by about sixty women. She insisted, however, that she would be all right in a shed, where she in fact stayed for several nights until she met a woman who invited her to share her room. On that first night Agnes had the most powerful dream of her life. In it Baba appeared to her as the all-powerful God Shiva, and since that moment she has dedicated a very large part of her life to working for Baba.

Something else that Agnes had read in Alice Bailey books was that auras of great masters or gurus tend to be visible to those whose spiritual development has attuned them sufficiently. Experts have found Sai Baba's aura to be immeasurable (extending more or less to infinity), but to Agnes on one of the first sights she had of Him, it appeared as a thick gold band, just like a halo, around His entire body. This further convinced her that she had found what she had been seeking all her life. Sai Baba combined what was for Agnes the best of both

Krishnamurti and the Theosophists, giving her at the same time the external authority and the focus for devotion that satisfied her emotional needs. If we had not strayed so far over the eons from our divine origins, Krishnamurti would no doubt be right in maintaining that everything can be found inside. But my own view is that if, when the world is in a sorry state, a major avatar descends to help put it right, it is well worth paying attention to what He has to tell us.

The mid-life period tends to be one in which people, if they have not done so earlier, are finding their true identity, becoming aware – often for the first time – of the blueprint they had made for themselves prior to their current incarnation. This discovery is by no means strictly limited to that period; it can continue well into the fifties – particularly for those who change careers and/or partners. But by the time of the Second Saturn Return, which occurs somewhere between the ages of fifty-six and sixty, a person's spiritual direction will normally be clear. Agnes claims to have found hers "just in time". For someone who has chosen a path of materialism, believing possessions and a successful career in worldly terms to define their identity, it will probably be more difficult to cope with the challenges that getting older inevitably brings, and to focus on its rewards rather than mourning the loss of youth. The way we live our lives is important not only for our immediate happiness and that of those close to us, but also for its effect upon our long-term future. An American lawyer called Randall is quoted in Robert Crooke's book on death[5] as saying that "thoughts are things and every act and thought functions around us and about us in the aura…Every act and thought is photographed in this psychic ether and, in dissolution [i.e. after death, when the etheric counterpart of the physical body disintegrates] becomes visible". In other words, everything that we think and do moulds us and, far from being shed with the physical body, it goes forward with us into the interlife and into our next incarnation.

Obviously some people take much longer than others to define their identity. In an ideal world parents would help, as did Ann and Ken Evans, but there are also many instances in which parents are more of a hindrance. I needed to leave the country, which I did at the age of twenty-nine, before being able to break free from the oppressive weight of a family in which I had always been a misfit and criticized for it. I took a job in Geneva and I shall never forget the sudden wonderful feeling of liberation that gazing at the lake Léman first gave me. I would probably have remained there to this day had marriage not intervened and been the first trigger for getting me on track with my Life Plan.

During those five years, which were infinitely happier than the previous twenty-nine, I thought that I had found out who I was, and it is only now, in retrospect, that I am aware of the extent of my error. For now I can see clearly that at that point in my life I was in fact defining myself as nothing more than someone who lived in Geneva. Consequently, when, for the sake both of my husband's work and of the upbringing of the children we were planning, we moved to the north of England, the identity that I thought I had was suddenly shattered. It had to be replaced, but since I was still unaware of my blueprint, all I had at my disposal as a replacement was the identity of a wife and mother. Both of those being true, that was not difficult, but my difficulty in defining myself as a wife and mother resident in the north of England was compounded by the fact that my husband was fairly regularly invited back to work at the University of Geneva in the summer. With its wonderful parks and open air pools, Geneva was an ideal place for spending the summer with young children, but the trouble was that returning to England each time was again a terrible wrench for me. Despite knowing that we had made the right decision, I somehow felt cheated by life, and it was many years before I came to appreciate all the reasons why the move had been a necessary part of my Plan.

Though there are people I have known for years who hardly seem to change one iota, I also know that many others feel as I do that they have had several different incarnations within the one. The identity I have now bears no resemblance to the one whereby I used to define myself over thirty years ago. But finding one's purpose in life in spiritual terms is only the first stage. Jesus said "Ye are gods", and all the great sages tell us that we cannot truly know ourselves (or anyone else for that matter) until we have become aware of the full implications of that astounding statement. Whatever name one gives this understanding – enlightenment, God-realization, self-realization, 'One Taste' – it is absolutely fundamental to the "Perennial Philosophy" which, as the great American philosopher Ken Wilber points out, "shows up in virtually all cultures across the globe and across the ages."[6] Wilber picks out seven of the most important points of this philosophy thus: "One, Spirit exists. Two, Spirit is found within. Three, most of us don't realize this Spirit within, however, because we are living in a world of sin, separation and duality – that is, we are living in a fallen or illusory state. Four, there is a way out of this fallen state of sin and illusion, there is a Path to our Liberation. Five, if we follow this Path to its conclusion, the result is a Rebirth or Enlightenment, a <u>direct experience</u> of Spirit within, a Supreme Liberation, which – Six – marks the end of sin and suffering, and then – Seven – issues in social acts of mercy and compassion on behalf of all sentient beings."

Though I like Wilber's summary, I must point out that the seventh point is not entirely dependent upon the preceding six. Returning to Earth <u>purely</u> to work on behalf of others without simultaneously having to deal with one's own karma can only be done after one has progressed through the previous six stages, but helping others is also an essential ingredient for progress. In fact Dr. Harold Moody[7] describes a fascinating experiment carried out by the Harvard psychologist, Professor David McClelland, which shows that caring for others actually has a positive effect on the immune system. (See also Dr. David Hamilton's book *Why Kindness is Good for You*[8].) Not that that is the best reason for doing it! I mention this merely as interesting information. If by the age of forty-eight one has managed to extricate oneself from the 'rat race', then care for others – whether it be ageing relatives or other members of one's local community – can be interwoven naturally with the steps being taken towards spiritual maturity.

This period of life is also marked by some major astrological turning points, and these are very relevant to the search for spiritual maturity. The Chiron Return occurs at about age fifty or fifty-one. Chiron, which was not discovered until 1977, is a planetoid with a diameter of only about eighty miles, and it orbits the sun between the courses of Saturn and Uranus. This timing, however, is viewed by astrologers as appropriate, as it coincided with an upsurge of awareness in the domain of healing. For Chiron is the 'wounded healer', the centaur accepted as neither man nor horse, wounded in the thigh by Hercules' poisoned arrow. Through the struggle to heal our own wounds we, like Chiron, can learn to help others who are suffering in similar ways. Chiron also encourages us to look at our own mortality, and to come to terms with things that we might like to alter but in fact have to accept as part of our life pattern. Weaving into a cohesive whole the parts of our blueprint that we might wish we had not chosen beforehand can help the healing process. The result is not only a lessening of the impact of the pain, but also an increased understanding of the similar pain of others.

My client Miriam, who spent a large part of her childhood in an orphanage, was in her fifties before she found out who her father had been. Since by this time both her parents were dead, she had to do the work of finding out who she really was entirely on her own. Her anger with her mother, who only took her back home from the orphanage when she needed help with bringing up five younger children, and had these other children regard her as a cousin rather than a half sister, was confused with feelings of both empathy and compassion. The reason for her confused feelings about her mother became clear when Miriam was regressed to a previous life in which she had had the very same parents. In the earlier life the parents, who were very much in love but too young to marry, had Miriam adopted, and then the father was killed and the mother died not long afterwards. When she met them in the Bardo at the end of the earlier life, Miriam's compassion for her parents far outweighed her anger towards them. This new vision of them enabled her to forgive the very great error they had made in her present life by concealing her true identity. While still suffering from the pain of not having been brought up in a 'normal family', Miriam is now aware of the role she chose before coming in of a healer for three generations of her family. Her own daughters suffered from her divorce when they were quite young, but she is now working hard to integrate them and their children into her newly found father's family.

By fifty or fifty-one we are likely to be ready and eager for a fresh start. Melanie Reinhart[9] describes the tone of the Chiron cycle as one of "awakening, rebalancing and intensification of our commitment to life". She says that it "represents a series of opportunities to realign inwardly with our deeper nature, and perhaps also a realization of how this seeks to manifest itself in the outer world. In this way we may often catch hold of a thread of personal meaning running through the Chiron cycle, which, *deo gratias*, culminates at about the age of fifty in a sense of rebirth, new life and wider purpose at the Chiron Return." Miriam, who works as a nurse, is clearly benefiting from this Chiron activity, and was when in therapy with me well on the road to a spiritual maturity whose seeds were firmly planted in the Christian orphanage of her childhood.

Miriam's case is particularly interesting to me as a Deep Memory Process therapist, because she is a practicing Christian who did not believe in reincarnation when she first came for therapy. Belief is not necessary for the therapy to work, but the relevance to her present life of the past lives that her subconscious brought up was immediately apparent to me. I watched with fascination as this relevance slowly dawned on Miriam herself, and as her comments progressed from "Perhaps it was my great grandmother" to "Perhaps I should start studying natural remedies, since I was a herbalist before". Here too Chiron has played his part, for Miriam's evolution was from a rejected child to a woman with a clear purpose.

Therapy can of course be started at any age (it is never too late!), and it often has a big role to play in our attainment of spiritual maturity. The well-known American therapist John Bradshaw, author of *HOME COMING – Reclaiming and Championing your Inner Child*[10], discusses how we mask our pain by addictions, making the important point that unless we really work through the pain we simply replace one addiction by another. Dr. Roger Woolger talks similarly about "filling a hole" – another way of putting the same thing. Bradshaw says that he himself replaced his alcohol addiction by an addiction to work, and I am aware that I myself am <u>still</u> working on the latter addiction even after many years of therapy.

It is said that no-one who has had less than two hundred hours of therapy themselves should attempt to set themselves up as a therapist, and I know someone who has never yet been persuaded to deal with her childhood pain. This person has done various trainings, yet her attempts to establish herself as a healer/therapist have been in vain. It does take courage to do 'inner child work' when it involves reliving the pain, but Bradshaw insists that "the only way out is through", and I can personally vouch for the rewards being immeasurable. Addictions to alcohol, drugs, smoking or food are well known and easily recognized, but there are probably even more of us who are just as seriously addicted to work or general activity as a means of "filling our hole". Someone else of my acquaintance, who has had a very difficult life, does not suffer from any of the above, but she is addicted to people. I often feel that she must still be in touch with more or less everyone that she has ever known, and whenever or wherever she travels she makes use of a friend or acquaintance in place of a hotel. An admirable trait of course, but still an obvious way of filling a hole from the outside rather than the inside!

We have seen how a 'mid-life crisis' can be a trigger for the most important part of our spiritual development, and Carmen and Gertrude are good examples of what Harry Moody describes as a "successful Return". (This follows his previous stages: The Call, The Search, The Struggle and The Breakthrough.) Carmen was helped through the loss of her husband by supportive and incredibly inventive neighbors. Her students were also tremendously supportive, ferrying her to and from the Spanish classes until she had obtained her English driving license. Even through what she describes as her materialistic phase, Carmen had never given up talking to God, but it was the knowledge she gained through the London College of Psychic Studies that enabled her to strengthen the connection with her Higher Self and to come to her present very strong belief in what she calls Destiny – for me the Life Plan. Although the support that Carmen found was not within the Church of her birth, in her early fifties she did start again to go regularly to her local parish church, encouraged initially by an Alpha course, which gave a good general introduction to Christianity. Thanks to that, she made a group of new friends. She has always felt very close to Jesus, and a sense of community, which she believes to be what Jesus wanted, is important to her now. She says that, if she had she been involved in the arguments in the early Church (well, very likely she was!), she would have followed James the brother of Jesus, who created a Jerusalem Church, rather than Paul, who wanted a universal one.

In recent years, and helped by her involvement with the local Buddhist Centre, Carmen has come to regard meditation as much more important than prayer. She explains that prayer is about asking, and that what one is asking for might not be in God's plan, whereas in meditation she is trying to get in touch with the inner truth. She describes her life as a long series of WHYs?, to many of which she has already been given the answers, and she cited an instance several years previously (when she was about fifty-one and therefore probably in the throes of her Chiron Return) when someone had let her down around Christmas time. She is always affected very deeply by people letting her down, and so she used to wonder whether a karmic debt was a factor in that. On this occasion she was feeling so low that – unusually, as she is an exceedingly sociable person – she was not in a mood for partying, and so for the first time in her life she spent New Year's Eve alone. Sitting on her own in her house on the verge of tears, asking "WHY?" really strongly, Carmen suddenly had a very clear flashback to a previous life. In this life she had been a lady in court interested mainly in leisure and pleasure, and had let many people down, even destroying families with her love affairs. The scenes of that life unfurled before her quite naturally like a film and, although it did not make her feel any better about the situation she was in at that moment, she found the understanding useful.

Carmen has not gone in depth into many of her previous lives, but a regression that she did with me gave her insight into possible causes of a way of being for which she has always tended to have little sympathy. In that regression she found herself as a young boy who was forced through poverty into being a jester – something he found extremely difficult. After eventually fleeing, he rather wasted the rest of his life, drinking excessively. Carmen finds it hard to tolerate people who lack her own strong sense of purpose, and a personality more different from her present one would be hard to imagine. This is a good example of how we learn through our many lifetimes by going from one extreme to another.

Whatever Carmen's remaining lessons may be, she is endeavoring to learn them now not only through meditation, but also by changing the course of her life in the direction of healing. She has given up Spanish teaching, which she finds less fulfilling than seeking answers to the big questions of life, sold the business with which she coped so well following the first fifteen years after David's death, and, besides becoming a *Reiki* Master, has qualified in Indian Head Massage and Aromatherapy. She used to find the business very stressful, and now she wants to have the freedom to do things that she really enjoys.

Carmen has no worries about her future, firmly believing that the rest of her Life Plan will reveal itself in due course, but she has recently purchased an apartment in her home town in Spain and is thinking of ultimately dividing her life between the two countries. This is partly because she feels that her spiritual quest would diminish if she lived permanently in Spain, where family life tends to take over; but on the other hand she says that she has never feared growing old, as old people are never lonely in Spain. She used to be afraid of dying, but now her conviction about the afterlife has quite removed that fear.

The same can be said of Gertrude, whose years from forty-eight to fifty-six were also strongly characterized by spiritual search. After recovering from the trauma of her years with Hubert, she left private nursing for a teaching post in Health Studies in an Adult Education college. This enabled her to develop more latent talents, and at the same time she began to explore various spiritual paths. She had long since rejected her Puritanical upbringing, and a spell with the Mormons had ended with her being excommunicated when she got divorced, but in her mid-fifties she found her home in Quakerism, which was totally compatible with her long-held interests in pacifism and animal rights. She also became interested in healing, and it was through *Reiki* training that she and I met.

One evening when we were giving *Reiki* to each other, Gertrude had a flashback to an early mediaeval lifetime in which we had been nuns in France together. Separate regressions to that life revealed a remarkable amount of coincidence in what we saw, but a difference between us was that, whereas I now saw that very tranquil, prayerful life as rather boring, she felt quite a hankering to return to something similar. I later found a slightly more recent life in which we were French Dominican itinerant preachers together. Though Gertrude may hanker after the peaceful nun's life, her recent years have in fact borne more resemblance to the Dominican one, for she is an exceedingly active person, involved in many things besides disarmament and animal rights campaigning. She also greatly enjoys her grand-children – often a particular boon of this phase of life.

It was thanks to the Geneva Sai Baba group that I made friends with Agnes. Like her, my discovery of Sai Baba ensured that the direction of my spiritual path had become quite clear by my fifty-sixth birthday. When I lived in Geneva in my thirties, I used to feel that I almost <u>was</u> the lake, the big fountain, the Rhône and the mountains, while in more recent years I have seen them all simply as aids in my search for God. This is perhaps reminiscent of descriptions one reads of flashes of 'God-realization' experienced by advanced souls, so I must hasten to add that I have not yet come anywhere near that point! Enlightenment involves a feeling of being totally at one with all that there is – becoming completely and utterly 'egoless' – but the paradox is that it is not possible to transcend the ego until one has an ego to transcend. When I identified myself so strongly with the lake Léman, the Alps and the Jura mountains, it was because I did not really know who I was. There was a certain possessiveness in my relationship with it all, and it was that which made returning to England so hard for me. Now, however, I see myself as a writer and therapist on a long journey back to

God, and I simply find spending time in such beautiful surroundings a useful stepping stone on that journey. (Since my husband retired from the University, work trips back to Geneva have ceased, but we have the good fortune of having moved to one of the most beautiful parts of England, where we are surrounded by excellent hill walking country.)

Hopefully most of us will have found out who we are at least by the end of the mid-life period, and can consequently spend a lot of this next period on our true spiritual search. There are as many paths up the spiritual mountain as there are people to climb it and, while the different religions can be of help, the last bit always has to be scaled for oneself. Nowadays, with the Churches' authority sinking into oblivion, I find that almost everyone I make friends with has moved beyond the Church of their upbringing, if they had one, seeking the answers to their deeper questions elsewhere. Agnes told me that, when she first got excited about the idea of finding one's guru, she imagined that it would entail "tremendous sacrifices", since one had to shed worldly things. But once she had firmly started on the path, it was "even more wonderful than you could have dreamt, because you find that your desires for transient pleasure simply fall away of their own accord". As Parahamansa Yogananda says, "Surrender yourself to God and you will find that your life will become like a beautiful melody."[11]

Ken Wilber makes the interesting point that we all want our "egoless sages" to be "dead from the neck down, without fleshly desires, gently smiling all the time..." In other words, "less than a person", whereas in actual fact, far from meaning "less than personal", egolessness means "more than personal". He points out that all the great yogis, saints and sages were able to accomplish as much as they did because they had very strong egos which were "plugged into a cosmic source", and they were living life to the full. He says that "Soul and spirit include (my underlining) body, emotions and mind; they do not erase them."[6] But of course inclusion does not mean subjection. Full spiritual maturity can never be achieved while we are slaves to our emotions. All the masters of meditation teach not suppression of emotions, but the art of standing aside and witnessing. (Suppressing emotions can firstly cause cancer in one's present life, and secondly create a *samskara* to work out in a future life.) To quote Wilber again, "if we can but watch or witness our distresses, we prove ourselves thereby to be truly 'distress-less', free of the witnessed turmoil. That within which feels pain is itself pain-less; that which feels fear is fear-less; that which perceives tension is tension-less. To witness these states is to transcend them. They no longer seize you from behind because you look at them up front."[11] Much easier said than done of course, but during these particular years it is very useful to have an aim such as this to work towards. I find that so many people in this age group are taking up meditation seriously.

I mentioned in Chapter Six the desirability of getting into the practice of meditation at an early age. Leaving it till later need not be too serious a handicap on the spiritual path, but it is important to appreciate the need for persistence and patience. You cannot expect enlightenment to dawn within the first week of making the decision to meditate daily! Anil Kumar, Sai Baba's translator, summed it up admirably in a lecture he gave in Puttaparthi on 25 March 2001. Talking of miracles, which he said were often the doorway enabling us to "get into the mansion of Divinity", he went on to point out that we cannot expect them to happen throughout our lives, for this would be a contravention of Nature. The Creator would not tamper with His own Divine Law by preventing every calamity. Kumar says "the precious things happen in life slowly, as we follow His teachings...Many people say 'Sir, in the beginning I had a wonderful experience. Now I am not having any.' In the beginning it happened because of His Grace. Later your effort is required. Your effort is expected. Therefore the subsequent happenings and experiences are based upon our effort."

I have personal experience of this. Before my first visit to Sai Baba's ashram, in February 1998, I had read many books about Him and believed totally in His miracles, but was at the same time firmly convinced that I myself could never be the recipient of a miracle. This was because I felt "so much less deserving" than the Baba followers I had read about. I had yet to learn in practice as well as theory that we are all equal in God's eyes. Well, imagine my amazement when, five days prior to my departure for India, Volume One of *Sathya Sai Speaks*, which had been in the briefcase I had had stolen on a train to London the previous year, suddenly reappeared on my bookshelf! When I had recovered from the shock, I interpreted this as Baba's acknowledgement of my forthcoming visit. During the three weeks of my stay He did not once look in my direction, but He further acknowledged my presence by replacing in my seat/bag the pair of knee-length woolly socks that had fallen out of it the previous day somewhere in between my room and the Sai Kulwant Hall. (This happened immediately after I had said in meditation, thinking of the journey home from Heathrow in February, "OK, I accept that there are worse things one can suffer from than cold feet.") On none of my twelve subsequent pilgrimages to Puttaparthi, however, have I experienced anything similar. As a previously rejected child who had had so much difficulty in believing in God's love, Baba must have thought that I needed something the first time to convince me that my existence was acknowledged, but now that I have been 'hooked', He is showing me that I have to continue with the effort unaided – or rather with the aid being less obvious.

Anil Kumar, after elaborating in his above-mentioned lecture on the "spirituality of waiting", endorses other writings by pointing out that enlightenment can come at the most unexpected moment. He quotes a delightful story of a woman who danced for joy when the two pots of water she was carrying both fell and broke. Questioned on her strange reaction, she replied "The two pots broke. That means for me that this pot, my body, will also break…The water has been limited in the pot…Now it is flowing freely in all directions! As the pot of my body breaks, the Supreme Self within me goes freely into the atmosphere. The Supreme Being merges with the entire environment. I am happy, so I am dancing."

This state of consciousness (Baba's *Sath-chith-aanandha* – Being-awareness-bliss) is beautifully described by the Sanskrit word *Samaadhi*, which is also the word used both for 'death' and for 'tomb'. The Glossary of *Sathya Sai Speaks*[12] defines *Samaadhi* thus: "It is the super-conscious state transcending the body, mind and intellect, attained through rigorous and protracted *Saadhana* (spiritual effort). In that state of consciousness, the objective world and the ego vanish and the Reality is perceived or communed with, in utter peace and bliss. When in this state, the aspirant realizes his oneness with God, it is called *Nirvikalpa Samaadhi*." We may from time to time have flashes of it, but we should not despair if they do not last. All the Masters assure us that our ultimate destiny is to return to this state permanently.

Returning to the Ken Wilber quotation about great saints and sages, everyone has his or her own favorite places, where they can best find "living life to the full" a real possibility. In a book on construction[13] by Christopher Alexander and other distinguished architects, there is a section entitled 'Zen View'. It recommends, if there is a beautiful view outside the house, not placing a major window in front of it, because after a while it will simply become "part of the wallpaper" and we will cease to appreciate it. When I lived in Geneva in my youth, it was possible on a clear day to see the Mont Blanc from the window of my studio apartment. The fact, however, of it not being visible every day made it impossible for me ever to get used to the wonder of it, and even when there were several clear days in a row, its appearance would change almost from moment to moment. I could sit down for my evening meal while it was gleaming the purest white before my eyes, then, before I had reached the second course, it would have turned to the most exquisite shade of pink. As I sipped my coffee, it would gradually fade to grey before disappearing all together, only to reappear the next morning shrouded in a haze through which it was distinguishable only to those who knew exactly where to look.

Jill (mentioned earlier on as well as in my previous book, SOULS UNITED[14]) is another friend whose spiritual search culminated with the discovery of Sai Baba at the age of fifty-six. While Agnes describes Krishnamurti as "Baba's ruse to get me to India and find Him", in Jill's case it was Jesus who was responsible. Her mother had had her brought up Catholic, believing it to be the only way for her to be eligible to attend the Catholic school. During the years that elapsed between her childhood and my first getting to know her well, Jill never forsook the Church completely, but she went through several periods in which she found that it did not really meet her spiritual needs. In fact it would probably be more accurate to say that it was only during her two years of teaching in Malta, when she was in her twenties, that she has ever really felt that being a Catholic had done very much for her. In Malta she was surrounded by Catholicism and went to mass most mornings, which helped her to feel close to Christ. After returning to her home town, however, where she took up peripatetic music teaching and felt less content with her life, she started to have serious doubts and consequently stopped going to church at all.

At thirty-six Jill had the good fortune of marrying a wonderful man. Her mid-life years were marked not by crisis as such, but by fitting her piano teaching around bringing up two daughters, and by pursuing a spiritual search to some extent jointly with her husband, who had been brought up as a church-goer but was now more interested in finding God within. When their older daughter was born, however, Jill started going to a Catholic church again because she felt it was important for her children to have a religious education. She had always been an avid reader, and her questioning gradually led her to a wide variety of spiritual books, including those of Doris Stokes and one or two on Edgar Cayce. She and I had been acquainted through our local parish for some years before we discovered a mutual interest in such things as reincarnation, and we then started lending one another books regularly.

It was in 1993 that Jill first asked me whether the name Sai Baba meant anything to me and I replied negatively. She had seen Him mentioned in a book by the well-known healer Betty Shine, which I had read too, but the relevant section had slipped from my memory. This was very shortly after Jill had, unbeknown to me (and round about her fifty-sixth birthday!) made a very earnest prayer to Christ to show her the way. Within less than three months of making this prayer, she was in the local library, when two books on Sai Baba more or less fell off the shelf on to her head. She in due course encouraged me to read these as well and, though my conversion took longer than hers, she founded the Hull Sai Baba group in plenty of time for me to catch up before my fifty-sixth birthday.

It is not normally easy for anyone whose parents had difficulty in showing love to their children to feel very close to God. One can believe in His love intellectually but, without direct experience, God may seem horribly remote. Avatars (divine incarnations) come to Earth to serve more than one purpose, not the least of which is the visible spreading of divine love. Jesus of course did that, as well as showing the way Home to many who had forgotten it, but another two thousand years have since passed – enough time for people to forget again. At the moment we are particularly fortunate because – presumably since the need is greater than ever – there are several avatars on Earth. I have been to see both Mother Meera and Amma (the hugging one!), but in this book I am focusing mainly on Sai Baba since I believe Him to be <u>the</u> major avatar; and another of His declared tasks is to remind us of who we really are. (He says that the only difference between Him and us is that He knows that He is God whereas we have forgotten.)

We repeat patterns in lifetime after lifetime, and I mentioned in *SOULS UNITED*[14] that when Jill became a follower of Jesus in his lifetime, he tested her sorely because her husband, who is consequently a karmic soul mate and again her husband now, threw her out for believing in him. Sai Baba has not given her quite as severe a test as that, as her present family are all very loyal to her even though they have not completely followed her on the path to Him, but He has certainly not made things easy for her. Her big reward was the total faith in the existence of God for which she had been searching for a long time, and now she finds herself more comfortable in Hinduism than in Catholicism.

Jill's upbringing so sapped her confidence that she did not start to regain it until the latter part of the period with which this chapter is concerned. She prayed for two years to Baba for a group to be started in her area before it finally dawned on her that He wanted her to start one herself. Even after she had taken the decision, she still felt in need of confirmation that it was right for her to be doing it, and this confirmation came in a most interesting way, not directly from Baba Himself, but from our mutually favorite composer, Johann Sebastian Bach. After the first meeting, which was attended by about half a dozen people including our friend Angela, I had my first dream in which Baba figured. In it I first met Baba Himself and then Bach, and I invited the latter to attend the next meeting, knowing that he was not incarnate. When I told Jill about the dream, she was delighted, but when the second meeting came round a month later, I had momentarily forgotten about it. Angela had not met either of us before the first meeting, when there had been no time for us to become acquainted, so she knew nothing of our musical interests. After the meditation, however, Angela said: "All I could see during the meditation was a man playing a keyboard instrument. He was wearing a red velvet jacket and a shirt with those ruffles like they used to wear a couple of centuries ago." So then I instantly remembered about the dream, everyone present was delighted that Bach had obviously accepted my invitation, and Jill took it as Baba's confirmation that He wanted her to carry on leading the group.

In great contrast to Jill and myself, someone who has always been fully in touch with his blueprint is our mutual friend Ivar Hafskjold. Ivar, who was fifty-five when I studied under him, was born into the Norwegian nobility and more particularly a family which is unique in having resisted the efforts of the medieval Church to stamp out everything that it viewed as 'Pagan practice'. He is heir to a fascinating tradition known as Stav (pronounced *starve*), which his family can trace back fifteen hundred years and forty-four generations. It is based on the Runes, which were originally a form of semaphore, and it covers every aspect of health, both physical and mental. It is in fact a whole way of life, which I find quite fascinating. Ivar was brought up and educated in Norway, but his wife is Japanese, and he studied for fourteen years in Japan before settling in England with the aim of spreading the Stav philosophy in the West. (He was the only Hafskjold man in his generation sufficiently interested in Stav to study it in depth.) He does this not only by teaching himself, but also by training others to teach, and through his web site. His son took a year out before going to university in order to study the Stav system in greater depth, so there seems now to be no risk of it dying out.

The Hafskjold family at one time owned a great deal of land, but when an act of parliament made landowners give land to the tenant farmers, they were left with just a thousand acres. Ivar's great grandfather later started to sell off parcels of land whenever money was needed, and Ivar himself was brought up in a small town which was a very close-knit community. His father inherited the job of chief of the fire department, which was in the family, but after doing his degree in psychology, Ivar felt no desire to pursue any career other than teaching and counseling. His father had in any case always expected him to teach Stav and, as reincarnation within the family is an integral part of the Stav belief system, Ivar was aware even as a very young child of what he had come to Earth for. Inherited wealth has given him the freedom not to live a life of luxury (something he does not believe in), but to devote himself totally to study and to helping others. He is aware that the family money will not last for ever, and has handed over financial management to his wife, who makes sure that they keep within the budget that he allots to them annually. During their fourteen years in Japan, the family did without a car, and the two children were given a choice between a television and a horse. They chose the latter, and later their daughter decided to train as a vet.

As Sai Baba says, there is only one race, the race of humanity, and the more one studies different world philosophies, the more common ground one tends to find. It is so sad that the Christian Churches have made a habit of regarding traditions that preceded them as 'inferior' and of stamping them out, for I am quite sure this is one of the last things that Jesus wanted. Indeed much has been written in recent years about the evidence that Jesus himself travelled to India during the 'seventeen lost years', and studied under oriental sages before beginning his mission[15]. But in the East of course these long-held spiritual and healing traditions have never been lost, and fortunately, as we all know, there is now a big revival of them in the West also. While in Japan, Ivar made an in-depth study of oriental philosophy as well as of his own family tradition, and he found an enormous amount of overlap. To the uninitiated, Stav could be described as 'Norwegian T'ai Chi', but it is in fact older than the T'ai Chi so widely taught in England.

The word 'Stav' actually means a "staff", and it refers both to the staff used in martial arts and to the Runes. There are sixteen Runes, and by duplicating them with one's body – in the way that centuries ago people in Norway used semaphore to send messages to one another from mountainside to mountainside – while breathing in the manner taught by a Stav practitioner, one can improve one's physique as well as one's general wellbeing. The Stav equivalent of *Chi* or *Prana* is known as *Megin*, and it is well known that blockages or reductions of the life force flowing through the body can manifest as pain or illness. Practicing the Stav stances daily (which does not take more than about ten minutes) keeps this energy flowing, so it is clear that the health benefits will be great; but it is also a form of meditation. An uncle of Ivar's kept up the daily practice of the stances until he was a hundred (then retired to bed for the four remaining years of his life!). But Stav consists not only of stances and martial arts; it is a whole philosophy of life. Ivar makes use of the Runes in counseling, and he specializes in helping people who are suffering from depression. For anyone interested in learning more, there is a booklet available through the internet[16].

In the Stav system, life is divided into phases of nineteen years each – a figure based on the Runic calendar. (If today is Monday, August 21st, then nineteen years hence August 21st will also be on a Monday.) Stav says that during the first nineteen years you are being taught, and during the subsequent nineteen you learn from what you have been taught. During the second nineteen years too, you tend to find a career, marry and become a part of society; and in the second half of that period in particular, you are settling down. During the next nineteen years (thirty-eight to fifty-seven) you tend to be teaching your own family rather than learning, and also caring for others; you are likely to be at the height of your career, but already thinking of handing over to the next generation. Between the ages of fifty-seven and seventy-six, you no longer have anything to prove; you have made your mark in the world and can collect your pension; your children have taken over and you can teach your grandchildren. During the final nineteen years (or more if you live beyond ninety-five and are still *compos mentis*), you can withdraw from the world and start studying again, going deeper and deeper into what you have learnt already. Ivar says that "at this stage of life you can sit on top of the mountain and let people come to you. You might come up with some great revelation that will be of benefit to the world."

So I hope that I have made clear my reasons for believing the artist Thomas Cole's view of the life cycle to be unduly pessimistic! There can be no 'right' way to reach spiritual maturity, for everyone's path is unique. Ivar is unusual in having had his Life Plan completely clear all along, but the more evolved we become, the more chance there is of that being the case. Everyone is at a different stage of the long journey back to God, and in some lifetimes we progress much more than in others. In some lifetimes of course we do not even reach the age of fifty-six. But for those of us who do, the last lap will be much more rewarding if we are on track with our blueprint by the time it begins.

Notes

1   *The Unfinished Autobiography*, Alice Bailey, Lucis Press, London and New York, first edition 1951.

2   *American Visions – The Epic History of Art in America*, Robert Hughes, Alfred A. Knopf, New York, 1997.

3   *Discipleship in the New Age, Vols. I and II*, Alice Bailey, Lucis Press Ltd., London, 1979.

4   *Strangers Among Us*, Ruth Montgomery, Fawcett Crest, New York.

5   *The Supreme Adventure*, Robert Crooke, James Clarke and Co. Ltd.

6   *The Perennial Philosophy* (from *Grace and Grit*), in *The Essential Ken Wilber - An Introductory Reader*, Shambhala, Boston and London, 1998.

7   *The Five Stages of the Soul,* Dr. Harold Moody and David Carroll, Doubleday, USA, 1997.

8   *Why Kindness is Good for You,* David Hamilton, Ph.D., Hay House.

9   *Chiron and the Healing Journey – An Astrological and Psychological Perspective,* Melanie Reinhart, Arkana, London, 1989.

10   *HOME COMING – Reclaiming and Championing Your Inner Child,* John Bradshaw, Piatkus Books, London, 1991.

11   *Spiritual Diary - An Inspirational Thought for Each Day* (Chiefly selections from the writings of Paramahansa Yogananda), Self-Realization Fellowship, USA, 1996.

12   All the volumes of *Sathya Sai Speaks* are published by Sri Sathya Sai Publications Trust, Prashanti Nilayam, India.

13   *A Pattern Language - Towns, Buildings, Construction,* Christopher Alexander et al, Oxford University Press, New York, 1977.

14   *SOULS UNITED – The Power of Divine Connection,* Ann Merivale, Llewellyn, USA, 2009.

15   See, for instance, *The Lost Years of Jesus,* Elizabeth Clare Prophet, Summit University Press, USA, 1987.

16   *The Principles of Stav* by David Stone based on the teachings of Ivar Hafskjold (www. stavinternational.org).

EXERCISES

1   Are you approaching fifty-six, or have you already reached it? If so, have you already decided which is your path this life time? There is no "best": Hindu, Buddhist, Jewish, Christian, Muslim, Humanist – all are as good as each other – and all the great Masters teach the same things (Peace, Love, and Unity, Service and Right Conduct). But it is normally best to stick to one particular path once you have decided which one suits you. Otherwise one's energies can get dissipated and one can seem to lack focus. (You may

know people who try to have their fingers in too many pies, touching on so many things superficially that their own stance is never clear and they tend consequently to be unable to draw others to them.) If you are in this age group, NOW is the time to consolidate your life and your beliefs and to go all out for them. If this entails a complete swing away from what you were brought up in, then good for you! (Sai Baba, whom I happen to follow, though He doesn't call everyone, which is just as well since the ashram is already overcrowded, says that it is good to be born into a Church but not to die in one.) If you are having trouble deciding on which route to follow, I can only suggest more reading and experimentation. You'll know when you've found what feels comfortable for you.

2   If you feel you do know which path you want to be on but are having difficulty in, say, keeping to a regular discipline of meditation, then join the Club! There is no doubt about the benefits, and classes can be helpful, but intention is the main thing and so long as you keep focusing on God (or your Master) and keep on doing what feels right, you can't go too far wrong.

3   If you haven't yet reached this age group, it's never too soon to start thinking about your personal spiritual path, so the above can apply to you equally.

4   If you're already passed this stage and on to what I am calling the "Last Lap", think back a few years. What did you learn and do you feel that you did reach some sort of 'spiritual maturity'? If so, feel pleased that you can really cash in on it during your final years. If not – whatever Alice Bailey may have said! – I don't believe that it is ever too late to change. One often hears of 'death bed repentances', and you're probably not at that stage yet or you wouldn't be reading this book! So enjoy your reading and seek out lots of the many other excellent spiritual books now on the market.

CHAPTER NINE

THE LAST LAP

You came to earth to accomplish a divine mission [to be reunited with God]. Realize how tremendously important that is! Do not allow the narrow ego to obstruct your attainment of an infinite goal.
Paramahansa Yogananda

So now we come to what is, in some ways, the most important period of all. The years following fifty-six, whether they be but four or forty-four, are those in which we have the chance to bring to fruition all that we have gleaned earlier on, to repair any damage we may have done, either to ourselves, to others or to both, and to prepare for – I will not say "the end", but rather for our forthcoming interlife and next incarnation (if we still need one).

I believe that a radical change of attitude is needed in the West – especially now that longevity is increasing so much and that care for the elderly is commonly regarded as a 'growing problem'. Recent research by the organization Help the Aged in Britain has revealed that housebound people who are lonely in their own homes make up twelve per cent of the population. It is natural for the elderly to want to stay in their own homes for as long as possible, and our system of home helps and meals on wheels is an aid to this, but loneliness can be a real problem, and there does also very often come a time when sufficient care is simply not available within the community.

For many – especially in these days when early retirement is on the increase – the realization of being 'on the last lap' dawns earlier than it did for me. In fact it was in India, when I made a visit to Sai Baba's ashram at the age of sixty-two, that I was made to realize it fully for the first time. Since it was my first trip there on my own, I was delighted to meet on the journey Caroline, a German homoeopathic doctor going to India for the first time, who agreed with pleasure to my suggestion of sharing a room. We got our accommodation fixed up just in time for afternoon *Darshan*, and I had a strong sense of being an 'old hand' showing the way round to a newcomer. On trying to enter the hall, however, I was told that my purse, acceptable on my previous visit, was now deemed too large and should therefore be deposited in the cloakroom round the corner. The same applied to my companion's small bag, and the *Seva Dal* (service person) said to Caroline "She's old. YOU go." I later found out that (although I mounted the stairs more quickly than she did) my new friend was eighteen years younger than myself and, when we returned to our room, a glance in the mirror made me notice, as though for the first time, the wrinkles on my face and the grey hairs which had recently increased from about one dozen to two. At the same time, however, it occurred to me that I should not take the *Seva Dal*'s attitude to me as an insult, because I was aware that in India older people are treated with immense respect.

There is great variation in people's reaction to the realization that they are on the 'last lap'. In countries such as India and those of Africa, where the elderly are respected and valued as a fount of wisdom, I imagine that acceptance generally comes more easily. Also, in societies which take reincarnation for granted (and in Africa it is only Christianity that has in many areas stamped out this belief), fear of old age is alleviated by the knowledge that it is no more than another step in a continuing cycle.

But my Indian experience was 'way back' in 2002, when, if I was buying a ticket for the cinema, the salesperson still needed to ask whether I was entitled to a discount. Nowadays my 'Senior

Citizenship' status is clear to all, which would not bother me in the slightest if everyone talked to me (as do my relatives, friends and acquaintances) as though I still had a well functioning brain, but this is alas no longer always the case. And when my husband goes to the hospital for his regular eye appointments, he finds that, although he knows more about the condition of his eyes than does anyone else (after all, whose eyes are they?!), many of the staff there treat him as though he were an ignoramus. We, and other people we know who are in their seventies, find being 'talked down to' by, for instance, transport staff or dentist's receptionists immensely irritating.

So may I put in a plea to younger readers to appreciate that not everyone over sixty-five is suffering from dementia? Personally I don't believe in talking down to children either. My fifteen-month-old grandson listened most attentively when I told him a bit about the Bach cantatas and seemed to be thoroughly enjoying the CD that we were playing at the time! At the other end of the scale, when Tony Benn (my all time favorite politician) came to give a talk in Ludlow, I found it most encouraging that he was still writing at eighty-four.

I have already mentioned various different philosophies of the stages of life and the fact that in India there are just four – childhood, youth, middle age and old age. Sai Baba describes these as four stages in the acquisition of *jnaana* – knowledge of the Supreme Being – and says that *jnaana* is the ripeness of the fruit, which is the consummation of a long process from the first appearance of the flower. The first is the 'Apprentice' stage, when you are being trained by parents, teachers and elders. During this stage you are led, guided, regulated, warned and repri-manded. The second is the 'Junior Craftsman' stage, when you are eager to establish happiness and justice in society and eager to know the world and its worth and values. The third is the 'Craftsman' stage, when you are pouring out your energies to reform, reconstruct and remake human community. However, once you reach old age, you are in the 'Master' stage, and at this stage you realize that the world is beyond redemption by human effort. The best that we can do is to save ourselves by trying to reform the world, and as our wisdom increases we come to see that "it is all His Will, His Handiwork, His World, Himself".

This period of life differs from all the others in that it is often much more extensive. It can even be like a whole new incarnation, if people embark on new careers or new relationships or on life on their own following separation or widowhood. I have many friends and acquaintances who have entered the healing professions after ending a career in a more conventional field. I have already mentioned my good friend Carmen, for instance, widowed quite young and now in her sixties, who sold the business that her husband left in her hands, became a *Reiki* master and qualified in aromatherapy and Indian head massage. In contrast, I know a retired teacher who has qualified as a walking tour guide and now regularly leads groups in Spain and Italy. Taking measures to keep fit is very important at this time of life, and is of course one of the best weapons against the current pandemic of obesity. I myself have never been at all athletic and, unlike many spiritually minded people, do not even enjoy yoga because of being so stiff, but my husband and I moved to Shropshire partly for the walking; and I have also made a promise to myself still to be swimming a mile two or three times a week when I am eighty.

How one copes with retirement depends upon one's general attitude to life. Those whose life has revolved almost entirely around work without many outside interests will much more easily be bored. When people are made redundant before the age at which they had originally planned to retire – now quite common in the West – there can easily be a feeling of rejection and also 'uselessness'. This seems to me not only sad but also completely unnecessary, and this is where a radical change of attitude is particularly called for.

There are so, so many ways in which people who are still fit can be usefully employed. Of course there is always a danger – and I know people who have fallen into this trap – of becoming even busier after retirement than one ever was before in a nine-to-five job. I would therefore strongly advise anyone who is making plans for their retirement not to start saying "yes" to things too quickly. Discrimination is advisable, and after many years spent putting job and family first, these final years can be seen partly as a time for oneself – perhaps for doing things you have always wanted to do but never managed to make space for previously. According to the Norwegian Stav system, it is during these last years that we can make time for in-depth study. Ivar explains that older people are better at focusing on a single subject. When we are younger our energies tend to be more scattered.

I have two good friends a bit older than myself who are excellent examples of this. Elizabeth was widowed very suddenly while in her early forties. She was a teacher at the time and got called out of school when her husband had a heart attack. She got home just in time to be with Philip while he died at the very moment that the ambulance was arriving. About a month after the death, she had a dream in which she met him and told him about the horrible dream she had just had: "I dreamt that you'd died". Philip replied "It's all right. It was only a dream", but gradually the reality of what had happened dawned on her. Elizabeth has always been naturally spiritually inclined, though never religious in a strict sense, and one day not long after the dream, she suddenly made the most deeply heartfelt prayer "PLEASE take this misery away from me." An answer to the plea came instantly! Elizabeth says that she quite literally felt the burden of pain being lifted off her more or less physically. Then for a while she went around looking at the world as though through a glass wall, "seeing everything but not being part of it", but after a holiday with friends in South Africa and the first anniversary, she began to come to terms with her loss.

Elizabeth stresses that no-one should make any major decisions during the year immediately following such a bereavement. After her first year of widowhood, she went back to college and did a degree, and then she changed her job and bought a new house simultaneously. Thirty years on she was still dreaming about Philip occasionally, but she told me that they were not dreams that appeared to have a great significance. She believes that one should not try to hold on to those who have died, and in Philip's case she feels that the karma between them is complete and that he may well have returned to Earth already. She also comments that it is pointless to ask "Why did he have to die so young?", which she thinks sounds like self-pity.

Up until her bereavement Elizabeth had had a comparatively easy and contented life, and this has apparently been standing her in good stead ever since. I have never met anyone who is more constantly cheerful than she is. "Sadness" or "depression" are words that simply do not exist in her vocabulary. She has an immense zest for life, combined with a tremendous sense of humor, and her gaiety is infectious. Even if she were invisible, her presence in a room could always be detected by the laughter of all around her!

Elizabeth never wanted children of her own, much though she enjoyed teaching other people's, but when she felt that she had done enough teaching, she moved to the Hull area to a post as an inspector of schools. By the time that we made friends she had already taken early retirement and qualified in both aromatherapy and reflexology. She enjoyed practicing these for quite some time through her early sixties, but her clients gradually tailed off naturally as her desire to do other things increased. "Boredom" is another word that is completely outside Elizabeth's vocabulary. She is a talented painter and not only attends art classes locally, but also goes on organized painting trips to attractive areas such as the Lake District. In addition she is a voracious reader, mainly of spiritual books, and has a large circle of friends with whom to share her books and other interests.

Elizabeth says that she has no fear of death. She was close to her mother, but shortly after she died, her grief was alleviated by a very vivid dream which she sincerely believes to have been a real encounter. In the dream her mother appeared to her clad in a yellow summer dress that had been a favorite of hers when she was younger. She was floating through a field of poppies and looked so happy and carefree that Elizabeth woke up quite confident that her mother was doing fine and that she herself had nothing to worry about either. When asked about her thoughts about being on the 'last lap', she replies that, rather than dwelling on anything morbid, she is filled with curiosity and excitement about what is to come next. She says that she has been conscious of the transitory nature of life ever since she first became an adult, and that quality is more important than quantity. For that reason she rather hopes that her remaining years will be twenty rather than thirty, since it would be "Hell for carers if you were senile!" She says that she makes fewer and fewer plans since, though still enjoying life, she is detaching from it already, and she loves having time to read, study and practice reflexology occasionally. Thinking ahead to the Afterlife, she likes the idea of being a "meeter and greeter" – i.e. someone who explains to people who are unaware that they have died what has happened to them.

In the great spiritual classic *The Tibetan Book of Living and Dying*[1], Lama Sogyal Rinpoche deplores the lack of preparation for death that we have generally in the West and stresses that the best possible preparation is the way in which we live our lives. Well, I regard Elizabeth, who is – it goes without saying – extremely unmaterialistic, as more or less a perfect example. (If I were to describe her as "<u>the</u> perfect example", her modesty would no doubt make me edit out that phrase!)

My second 'older' friend, Sally (who never wants to divulge her age after having once been made a victim of ageism, but I do know that she is in her seventies), attended meetings of the local Sai Baba group for a while, but gave it up because she prefers to listen to her own inner guru than to follow an avatar/teacher. This is completely in accordance with Baba's teachings, for He encourages us not only to follow our own inner guidance but also to realize that we are God as much as He is. Sally has been interested in spiritual things all her life, but says that in her youth she had no-one to ask about it. Her parents were not religious, though her mother started going to church in her later years as an "insurance policy" and Sally went with her occasionally, but queried Christianity when the priest said such things as "What Jesus really meant was..." She felt that the teachings ought to be clearer, and personally I believe that they were made clearer in the past by, for instance, the Gnostics (who were of course persecuted). Sally says that basically she has always been a 'Pagan', for she has always seen God in nature and she finds churches oppressive.

As a child Sally could see auras around people's fingers and she assumed that everyone else could too. When she discovered, at about the age of ten or eleven, that this was not the case, she switched that ability off. She has nevertheless remained very sensitive, occasionally experiencing instances of clairaudience; and earthquakes affect her even when they take place on the other side of the world! When she has been near water – in Venice, in Bruges and in the Morecambe Bay area – she has felt "spaced out" for a short time and as though the ground simply was not there when she stepped, and each time that this has happened she has learnt shortly afterwards that an earthquake was occurring somewhere at that precise moment.

Sally, who was also once a teacher, has had to make completely new starts in her life several times, and she feels that her big lesson for this lifetime has been to do with letting go of everything. She lived in Canada for five years, in Zaïre for another five, and then in Belgium for over ten years, and on each occasion she was forced to leave everything behind when she moved. Since reaching the age of seventy she has been living much more simply, in the tiny flat she inherited from her mother, and has been giving away many of her belongings. She says that possessions make her feel oppressed, and often, when she has a sort out, she says to herself "I can't imagine why I bought that!" The only thing that she finds herself unable to give away is books.

Sally also attended the classes in the Norwegian Stav system, and she is a supreme example of someone who is making use of the 'last lap' for in-depth study. Ivar says that during their last nineteen years (or sometimes more of course), people who are less active physically can use their energy to focus in a way that is more concentrated, if narrower, than that of their younger fellows. They can thus be a real source of wisdom and information for the rest of the world. (My husband has a mathematician friend who at over eighty was still making his mark in his own, highly specialized, field and finally stepped down from his connection with the University of Birmingham at the age of eighty-five!) Sally describes herself as a "vacuum cleaner of information", and whenever I have a problem, be it physical or otherwise, I can always be sure that if Elizabeth does not have a remedy to recommend or an answer to it, Sally will!

Sally is, as I said, very sensitive and once, when putting some flowers into a vase in preparation for a visit from her sister, she suddenly saw an aura around them and something like a flame coming from one of the leaves. She interpreted this as a signal to follow her sister in starting to think about higher things, but says that in fact she put it off for a while, until the time of her mother's death. This occurred when she was fifty-nine, round about the time of her Second Saturn Return, and Sally, who had recently left Belgium following the break up of her marriage, took over her mother's flat. One day she clearly heard her mother's voice calling her name, and went into the kitchen to look for her even though she knew quite well that she was dead. She accepted the death and never tried to hold on, but she feels that her mother was keeping a watchful eye over her.

Sally's father died a few years before her mother and, while he was ill, Sally looked after him full time for several months. During his final illness she kept a candle burning for him for a whole year without knowing why. Then later she was told by the well-known clairvoyant Edwin Courtenay that in a previous life in Greece she was a priestess of Vesta, and they always kept the flame going continuously!

In another previous life Sally was put in prison during the time of the Salem witch trials. She says that because of that she always wants to be out of doors now. She would really like to move either to the South of France or to Spain, but accepts that this is not possible for her financially. In fact she has become more accepting of things generally and says that, whereas she used to have a "very low boiling point", this changed once she had got to about sixty, and that now she no longer gets upset about things. This ties in with the point about avoiding accumulating more *samskaras* by acceptance of what IS. Though she claims not to be focused on attaining enlightenment, Sally says nevertheless that "getting off the wheel" is one of her main aims. As soon as she has left this body and gone "through the tunnel into the nice spring day", she says that her first question will be "Where's the library?". The thought of obtaining a ticket for the cosmic library delights her more than anything else! She says that she will browse endlessly, reveling in the thought that all the books that have ever been written are inexhaustible, and that she wants to learn a lot of things that would be useful if she did have to return to Earth.

In the meantime Sally is doing a great deal to keep herself

physically fit. Her studies of aromatherapy and reflexology (a popular combination) taught her a great deal about health and, besides having learnt the Stav postures, she regularly attends T'ai Chi and keep-fit classes. She has no fear of death, and says that becoming decrepit is not a concern of hers either. She expects to die easily and peacefully either sitting on a chair or in bed. Well, the whole thrust of Lama Sogyal Rinpoche's book is that we will die as we have lived, so here is another role model!

My friend Jemima, whom we have not met since Chapter Three, is rather different from Carmen, Gertrude, Elizabeth and Sally in that she has no belief at all in God or an Afterlife. I do not regard her as an unspiritual person – it is simply that her innate spirituality manifests in other ways, such as caring for others. Jemima, you may remember, was born into a well-to-do family, and she has never been short of money. She loves to travel, and she and her husband own a flat in Spain, which they generously share with other people. Jemima takes a great deal of interest in my writing and says that she would dearly love to believe in reincarnation and that death is not the end, but she simply cannot. Since faith is a gift from God, all I can do is to put forward the arguments (which seem so convincing to me) and then leave the rest to Him. I certainly look forward to discussing all these matters again with her on the other side! Jemima is now a proud grandmother, which gives her immense joy, and she sees her 'immortality' as carrying on through her descendants. This is surely preferable to those who build, for instance, great monuments in stone (like the chief of police in Mexico City, who built himself a replica of the Parthenon with money collected from on-the-spot fines!).

Jemima says that as a child she tried hard to be a believer. Her grandmother, who brought her up together with a series of nannies, while her father was fighting in World War II and her mother was in and out of mental hospital, went to church a lot and always told her that it was much better to give than to receive – a teaching she obviously took to heart. But she says that she has always had a "very sharp nose for hypocrisy", and she must have been unlucky in the Church people that she met. Besides loving travel, Jemima has always been very adventurous. She reckons that for her the years between about fifteen and twenty-five were a time for learning what people are like and what can make you happy. She had many relationships, including lovers, and says that at twenty-five she felt that she had "done it all". This makes her smile to herself now that she looks back from nearer seventy, having done her degree in Spanish rather late. Having children, however, which she now sometimes wishes she had done earlier, was something "huge and new", and she recalls looking at herself and her baby daughter in the mirror and thinking "You're the mature one!". She believes that the personality is innate and that only exceptionally bad parenting will make a real mess of anyone. This supports my notion of the Life Plan, though Jemima would no doubt disagree with me on that. Until we can discuss all these questions again on the other side, she is making the very most of the last lap not only in her role as a grandmother but also working hard to improve her excellent Spanish and simply "being there" for friends and neighbors as well as for her family.

The last lap, as I said, is partly a period for giving time to oneself. Well, to my mind, perhaps the most important aspect of this is developing our relationship with God. Even if we do find our spiritual path by the age of fifty-six, finding it is of course only the beginning! Keeping on it afterwards and intensifying our efforts towards achieving self-realization are even more difficult. Sai Baba says that the *atma* is capable of being known only after vast perseverance. One has to divert the mind from its natural habitat – the objective world – and keep it in unwavering equanimity. "Only a hero can succeed in this solitary internal adventure and overcome the monsters of egoism and illusion! That victory alone can remove grief." And Paramahansa

Yogananda says that it takes us on average a million births to attain Liberation. But let us not despair! The Lord who sits at the top of the mountain always holds a bit of rope He can throw down to the exhausted mountaineer who has managed to get very nearly to the top through effort and persistence. Both Yogananda and Sai Baba say that God's grace is always available to those who implore. In *Man's Eternal Quest*, Yogananda says: "The soul is bound to the body by a chain of desires, temptations, troubles and worries, and it is trying to free itself. If you keep tugging at that chain which is holding you to mortal consciousness, some day an invisible Divine Hand will intervene and snap it apart, and you will be free."[2] And in Luke 5 v 17-26 Jesus, by the grace of God with whom he is in such very close contact, is able to remove the sick man's karma, – "Thy sins are forgiven thee" – and so he is healed instantly. Though Jesus subsequently does say "Rise up and walk", he says that it is easier to say that the man's sins are forgiven, which is surely an indication that the karma had to be cleared before the healing could take place.

So what is the best tool for achieving this aim of being liberated from *samsara* (the cycle of births and deaths)? Meditation is important, and Sai Baba adds to this two other things: *namasmarana* (repeating the name of God, which my French lama friend, Ngawang, also explains is the only way to remove all the little grains of karma) and selfless service. Carmen and Elizabeth go to Jyothi for the weekly meditation sittings I described. Lawrence finds that it is mainly older people that attend his meditation courses. He has formulated various successful meditation practices and has kindly summarized some of them for me. He says: "Meditation is a word that covers a very wide range of practices, and anything I can say is a gener-alization which may not fit specific people or situations, and there are usually exceptions to these generalizations. As with most spiritual practices, I think that it is preferable to be drawn to it at the right time and to approach it gently and without force, but with a steady persistence. Look for certain features in a meditation practice and see what it is that is needed and helpful. For instance, most practices involve some use of voluntary attention, i.e. focusing the mind gently on some theme, image, mantra, and returning to this focus whenever you become aware of your mind wandering. So here we have the gentle practice of voluntary attention, or holding the mind, as one aspect of the practice. This can be thought of as the 'active' part of the practice. Secondly, there is the question of what to choose as the object of your focus. One study on the health benefits of meditation compared a group of meditators who focused on traditional sacred mantra with another group who used everyday words such as 'banana' as their mantra. Both groups were found to have equal health benefits, but the group who used traditional sacred mantra were able to sustain their practice, whilst the other group fairly quickly lost interest. In most traditions the focus is considered crucial, and a sacred image, mantra, or being is chosen in the belief that there is a two-way flow between meditator and that which is the focus of the meditation. There is the idea that we draw to ourselves and are affected by that which our mind dwells upon. One way to approach this choice is to consider what one's aim is. I, for instance, associate Christ with love and forgiveness, and when wishing to contact or strengthen these qualities in and for myself, I might focus on Christ and use the Jesus prayer as my mantra. On the other hand, I associate Mohammed with submission to the Will of God, and I might use the words *La Illaha il Allah* to try and contact a sense of acceptance and faith. If, however, you want to avoid religious or sacred imagery, then you can choose something inspirational or uplifting such as a poem, a flower or an experience or image from nature.

This then brings out the next feature of meditation practice: receptivity and openness. We are becoming receptive and open to the influence of that which we focus on. In order to be receptive we need relaxation, safety and a sense of trust. There is a kind of letting go and release of our habitual tension, pain and anxiety. It follows then that, although it is possible to meditate anywhere and at any time, it is best to practice in a safe and sacred space where you feel at home and inspired. It is also important to be comfortable and in a healthy posture so that the body is taken care of and can relax. The body is our vehicle and is a wonderful place to start any meditation practice. Much of modern life separates us from the body and takes us into 'virtual experience', and we experience many things second hand through the media and through sedentary occupations. The body suffers from this lack of attention, and our bodies are needed for soul experience. So I will usually begin meditation with relaxing and sensing my physical body, acknowledging its presence and asking it to let go of tension and allow me to open into the meditation. We may then lose sense of the body in a deep meditation, but we lose the body via the body, and in this relaxed state it is able to rest and recuperate. Not all meditation will be comfortable, and another feature in practice is to contact our inner 'witness'. Two birds sitting in a tree; one eats of the fruit whilst the other looks on. We may find that when we quieten our bodies we become aware of thoughts, feelings, memories and sensations which are uncomfortable, painful or unpleasant. This may need individual help or guidance, but in general it is helpful to allow whatever arises to come and go without interference or attachment. Try to observe and let go. In this way we may also be given new insight into our nature and our problems. Meditation can also be done alone or in groups. In general, as with any skill or practice, it is best learnt from an experienced practitioner with whom you can discuss individual requirements and personal experiences."

Not everyone who has gone well beyond the realms of materialism is consciously seeking Liberation. Many very spiritually-minded people are not consciously aware that Liberation is the goal. I have many friends and acquaintances who still have strong Church affiliations, and I believe that to be the right path for them in their present lives. One such was Ursula, who – reluctantly at first but she came to terms with it well – had to spend her last few months in a residential home for the elderly. I visited her fairly regularly while she was there, and we had some very interesting discussions about her life and her faith, which she felt had sustained her throughout times which had sometimes been difficult. For instance, she was interned in France during the war, after having gone there at the age of nineteen to work as an *au pair*, and her father's death from a heart attack at the age of only sixty-seven was a very big shock for the whole family. Ursula was the third of six children and the last to survive, which she found quite hard, especially since her last home was one she had shared with her mother and one of her younger sisters. She had never felt any desire to marry, and her many nephews and nieces ensured that she was never lonely after her sister Clare's death, but she said "it means there's no-one you can ring up who understands you intimately". To her many friends, however, she always appeared cheerful, and no complaint was ever heard to pass her lips until the very last few weeks, when she was really ill and in a great deal of pain. Only when I pushed her to review her life did she express some regret at never having learnt to drive and at not having taken her studies of the violin a bit further.

After Ursula's release from France at the end of the War, she worked firstly in Harrogate at the Air Ministry and then at the Tax Office in Hull, and in her retirement her life was always filled by worthwhile voluntary activities. She was the sort of person who could always be relied upon to turn up to a meeting. She kept up her French until the very end of her life, always appreciating the loan of books in that language, especially spiritual ones. When she was either too tired or too ill to read, she would occupy her mind with deep philosophical questions such as "If there really is life on other planets, why did Christ come here to save us rather than those other races?", and, thinking about evolution, she loved Teilhard de Chardin's answer to the question "When did Man become Man?" ("When he knew that he knew.")

Ursula was always realistic about her approaching death, and even when she was in her eighties and in poor health, she made every effort to clear the house and leave it in good condition so that her relatives would not have trouble selling it. She told me that the headmistress at her Catholic secondary school had always warned her pupils about the dire consequences for those who were not prepared for death, and so Ursula made her will in good time and gave the power of attorney to a cousin and a friend in case she herself became incapable. Though I never made any attempt to talk to her about reincarnation, she expressed interest when I spoke of my reading about the work one did in Heaven, agreeing with me that the 'life of eternal bliss' she had previously always imagined sounded boring!

It is perhaps obvious that the last lap will be easier for those who have fulfilled their Life Plan, as I feel sure Ursula did. Another example of a Catholic who has dedicated a long life to selfless service is Dominic, who at eighty-four, when we talked, had not so far noticed any of the possible 'disruption' caused by the Uranus Return that I shall come on to shortly, but his (much younger) wife fell ill very shortly after that and died only a few months later, so that must have brought major changes in his life.

While in the air force in his youth, Dominic made friends with some Dutch Franciscan friars, and even thought seriously at one point of joining the order. Instead, at thirty-one, he joined the Franciscan Third Order, which is for lay people, and religiously kept up their daily discipline of some form of office ever since. After leaving the air force, he attended meetings of the Third Order in two different locations but, not being made welcome at either, he struggled on his own for some time, reading the breviary, saying the morning and evening prayer of the Church, or meditating on the Passion, for instance. When he retired at fifty-five from British Airways and moved to a different area, he was made very welcome by the local Franciscan Fraternity, and their monthly meetings have been a great support to him ever since. Dominic is very musical, used to sing in a good choir, and fell in love with Chant on a one-week summer school. He carried on attending these summer schools for fifteen years, and it was there that he met the ex-nun whom he married at forty-five. The two of them were always pillars of their local Catholic parish church, and also deeply involved in the St. Vincent de Paul Society, whose members visit the sick, lonely and housebound. We lost touch when I left the area, but I have heard from one of his fellow parishioners that he still gets to daily mass in his electric wheelchair; (he always walked to church until he was over eighty).

The only thing that Dominic wanted from his three daughters on his eighty-fourth birthday was three little books – on Leonardo da Vinci, Rodin and Le Corbusier. He was thankful still to have both his sight and his hearing, since reading and listening to music were his greatest pleasures. Until his death last year, he regularly visited a friend about ten years his senior, who had lost both his sight and his hearing, and Dominic said that this made him appreciate his own good fortune. He said that he was still the same mentally apart from a deterioration in his short-term memory – surely more or less a universal phenomenon in the elderly – but that he only ever worried about things that he could do something about! Here is an example of someone who is accepting getting older gracefully and peacefully, and he is still always ready to be of service – for instance in repairing the church railings, which get vandalized regularly.

However, when people have not realized their potential, have not found any happiness in life, or – worse still – sunk into drugs or alcohol, these years will be the most difficult of all, since it will seem 'too late' for change. Such people are a real challenge to our society, and I feel that we will not have the right to call ourselves 'civilized' until means have been found to give hope to everybody. Of course a certain amount is being done already – soup kitchens, shelters for the homeless and so on – but it is not yet nearly enough, and this is surely an area where retired people who do have time on their hands could be gainfully employed. Organizing such activity would only take a little bit of imagination combined with some of the money currently spent on, for instance, arms.

For those of us who are too busy with our own work to make time for such activities, the challenge is surely to do our little bit wherever we can and to see the divine even in the most wretched specimens of humanity. In the area where I used to live, "Joe", who I would guess to have been in his sixties and was homeless, turned up regularly at the Catholic church and asked the priest for shelter and money for food. The latter responded generously on many occasions, but, not surprisingly, his patience tended to wear thin when he knew that Joe had recently been offered accommodation by the Council. Something – who but God can know what – always drove Joe back on to the streets even when he had been found a place in a hostel, and something else – could it be that tiny spark within him that still knew that he was divine? – drove him back over and over to sit for hours on end outside the church. Sometimes, when I was walking the dog, I used to pop into the church to say a prayer or two, and if Joe was there, I tied the dog to the bench beside him. To Merlin everyone was a friend, and it always warmed my heart to see what those few minutes of real soul communication did for both of them. According to some of my reading, Joe could possibly be an evolved soul who had chosen this lifestyle in order to help others work off some of their karma by caring about him.

The final years of the fifties are very important astrologically, as they see the Second Saturn Return that I mentioned in connection with Sally. This can occur anywhere between the ages of fifty-six and sixty. Under Saturn we tend to release a great deal of karma, and I am told that it can even be possible to clear it by the time we reach sixty. Saturn has a reverence for limitations and gives structure and necessary boundaries, but at the same time our whole life structure can change at this point. For Gertrude, Carmen and Agnes, it brought early retirement, and in Agnes' case the Second Saturn Return also entailed the purchase of a studio apartment in Puttaparthi, India. This enables her to spend more time than before at Sai Baba's ashram, and the only thing that is still tying her to Geneva is her daughter and two young granddaughters. She believes in living in the moment and is making no plans for the future, but is trusting Baba to guide her on how to divide her time between the two. The valuable work that she does – for instance translating His discourses into French – can of course be done in either place. I also have a widowed English friend, Eileen, who bought a studio in Puttaparthi at the time of her Second Saturn Return, but she used to feel a need to spend most of her time there and only return about once a year to see her children and grandchildren. She was never idle, as there is always work to do in the ashram such as chopping vegetables, serving meals, washing up or sitting at the cash desk in the cafeteria, and at one point her family accepted the fact that she was hoping to end her days in the ashram. However, a couple of years ago, she suddenly felt that Baba was sending her back to England, and she returned to her home town, where she soon found herself being grandmother to an unexpected new arrival in the family. This goes to show how we can never be a hundred per cent aware of our entire Life Plan!

My own Second Saturn Return started when I was fifty-six, and it was in the following year that I started my training in Regression Therapy. Elizabeth gave up working for the Education Authority and studied aromatherapy and reflexology at the time of this Return, and Carmen, who sold her business in order to devote herself to healing in various forms and to have more freedom, felt that her Second Saturn Return was changing her radically. When she re-read my two previous chapters, she told me that she found it strange as "it all seems a really long time ago now. I feel detached from how I was then because I've changed in so many ways." She says that, whereas before she was always searching outside, now her searching is more inside. I see this as part of her natural development towards maturity, because do not all the sages say that we have all the answers inside ourselves? *The Prophet* says "And seek not the depths of your knowledge with staff or sounding line. For self is a sea boundless and measureless."[3] Carmen says that not having a family of her own gives her fewer distractions from her daily meditation practice.

Those who live to eighty-four will experience a Uranus Return. The Uranus cycle is the longest of all, and Gertrude tells me that the outer planets are more powerful than those which are closer to us, and that they are felt more strongly by society as they affect whole generations more than they do individuals. Uranus is a planet of disruption. During the mid-life period, when it is in opposition to our Sun sign, it challenges us to look at our whole life. It is all about breaking free and not accepting the norms of society, and so makes us want to go out there and do something different. This, however, can cause internal conflict, since middle-aged women taking up belly dancing and older men having affairs with young girls are obviously not always viewed as acceptable. At the time of the Return, however, Uranus sitting conjunct with one's Sun is likely to feel more companionable than when it is in opposition. So – if you are still sufficiently fit physically– doing something completely new may well feel acceptable and exciting. Also, by the time we are eighty-four we will probably care much less about what other people think!

Ursula was eighty-four when she died, and my own feeling is that she had been constrained by her Catholic middle-class environment. Our environment can restrain us from expressing what is inside, and things that are not expressed will often manifest as illness. Well, maybe Ursula could have been spared some of her final intense discomfort if only she had been encouraged to break free. As it was, I feel she chose to break free by dying, which she was extremely ready for. On the other hand, a Catholic priest I know, who died in May 2007 at the age of eighty-nine after having been something of a rebel all his life, devoted some of his very last years to the serious study of other religions – a thing normally frowned upon in the circles in which he had moved all his life.

My friend Molly is someone who <u>was</u> aware of her Uranus Return at eighty-four, and she is now eighty-six. A mother of four, with many grandchildren and three great grandchildren, Molly has led a very busy and fulfilled life. She coped extraordinarily well with being widowed at sixty, but even before that she was very independent, and she comments that she has always disliked authority. Despite being short-sighted and needing spectacles to drive, she has very good eye sight, which used to be invaluable when she was a silversmith. Even now, although she has been told that she needs an operation for a cataract, she can still read perfectly and for long periods without her eyes getting tired. She says that she can mend <u>anything</u> – a talent that proved very useful during the five years in which she worked as a volunteer in an OXFAM shop, where many of the items that people donated were broken. She is also, like most of her family, very musical, and she is a gifted pianist and organist.

Molly told me that she once read in an astrology book that you should become wise at eighty-four, and she reads a lot of philosophy, which she feels, together with much life experience, has helped her finally to come to the realization that "everything is perfect all of the time". But she regards her Uranus Return point as the stroke that she had when she was eighty-four. This, though fortunately not as serious as strokes sometimes are, has forced her to slow down – something she is not finding easy. She appreciates, however, that it is an important lesson in acceptance and, while finding it frustrating not being able to play the piano as well as she used to, she says that she is learning to obtain even more enjoyment from listening to other people play. Her great granddaughter, who is already fifteen, is very musical, and on a recent visit it gave Molly great satisfaction to listen to her playing. She is also busy learning to accept help – something that I think most mothers find difficult – and having sometimes to ask for help is harder still for her, but she claims to be working on it.

Like Elizabeth and Sally, Molly has lost interest in material possessions and is now endeavoring to get rid of as many of hers as she can. Though her daughter and son-in-law who live nearby are discouraging it, she is even coming to terms with the idea of going into a home. This is partly because she hates the idea of being a burden to anyone, but on the other hand the high cost of such a home is a big deterrent and, for the time being at least, she prefers to carry on paying someone to come in to assist her when she has a shower. One of her present aims is to be of help to people of her own age who feel less positive than she does about this stage of life, and she has recently been of use to an eighty-eight-year-old neighbor who has had to have her thyroid removed. This neighbor used to be a pillar of her local church, but has lost her faith, and Molly, who has recently been reading books on the Afterlife such as that of Dion Fortune, would dearly like to be able to share her convictions on the subject with this neighbor.

Molly's mother was psychic and she used to tell her when someone that they knew was going to die; and after her husband's death Molly felt much better when she had had a dream in which he put his arms round her and assured her that he was looking after her. All this, combined with her reading, has helped her to regard death as even more interesting than scary.

Her only reservation is that, having occasionally had some horrid chest pains recently, she dreads dying in such intense pain. However, she says that her motto is "Cast thy burden upon the Lord", and she also loves to quote St. Teresa of Avila: "Let nothing disturb you". So Molly is another wonderful example of someone who believes the secret of life and health to be Love and Trust!

A belief shared, I am sure, by ninety-year-old Joy (very different from either of the two Joys we have met already), with whom I have had a couple of interesting telephone conversations since a mutual friend put us in touch on account of the fact that she is currently on a Rudolf Steiner biography course and doing research into the three seven-year periods of life that can follow age eighty-four. Steiner divided the whole of life into seven-year periods and detailed the planetary influences that people are under up to the age of sixty-three, claiming that these became less strong between sixty-three and eighty-four. But his research stopped there and Joy feels that, now that so many people are living longer, there is a lacuna to be filled in this last lap. Though she is at present in the early days of her project, she has a particular interest in somehow linking the years eighty-four to a hundred and five firstly with the three days after death, before the etheric body detaches itself completely from the physical body, and secondly the first three years of life, when little ones are first learning to walk, speak, and so on.

When I made my first visit to Sai Baba's ashram, another member of the group I was in was an eighty-four-year-old who was going to India for the first time, but Joy marked her Uranus Return by going to visit her daughter in New Zealand entirely on her own! Her husband had died three years earlier, and she did not feel that that should in any way curtail her activities.

Joy thinks it important for those who are at her time of life not to live in a sort of 'ghetto', but rather to endeavor to mix with people of all ages. She herself does this not only with her own family, but also the in groups to which she belongs: for instance a singing group which sounds to be very similar to my friend Polly's community choir that I mentioned in Chapter Seven. Joy says that there was never very much music in her family and that she always felt herself unable to sing in tune, but this group, just like Polly's, encourages people to overcome the inhibitions instilled by their upbringing and brings together people of all ages to sing for fun.

Although she never felt able to share this type of interest with her family, Joy started reading the works of Rudolf Steiner when she was still at school, and she says that she has been a student of his ever since. She saw herself as a writer from the age of about seventeen, and she graduated in English from London University in 1939 and married immediately after that. Neither the war nor bringing up three children curtailed her literary activities, and she worked for a while as a reader for a publisher's agent. One regret she has had in her life is that her aspirations as a novelist were never fulfilled, but she has over the years had various articles published in magazines and was for some time the editor of the Anthroposophical Review. Her most recent project was a book on Rudolf Steiner in Britain, but failing eyesight forced her to abandon that and the book was completed by someone else. This was hard for Joy as the second author had rather different ideas from her own about how the book should be written, but she came to terms with it.

Joy is of the opinion that too many people of her age get caught up in looking backwards excessively, which prevents them from making the most of the present and still enjoying life to the full. She says that from the age of eighty-four one should look forwards rather than backwards – forwards to death, which, like Molly, she sees as both scary and interesting. She appreciates that it can be difficult for people suffering from the sort of afflictions that tend to be an inevitable part of old age to be positive, but she stresses the importance not only of acceptance but also of finding meaning in things which others might view negatively. Her own macular degeneration means that she is now registered blind, but she continues to read with a CCT magnifier, and in fact when we spoke she asked for a copy of my first book. Also, besides being on the Steiner biography course and a member of a singing group, she does clay modeling and art therapy!

When I asked Joy whether a belief in karma had helped her to cope with the disappointment of having the manuscripts of her novels rejected and "never having broken through the barrier of getting published", she replied affirmatively, saying too that she had stopped minding about it. However, she felt 'belief' to be not quite the right word as it suggests something too static, and 'knowing' seemed to her too strong a term for what she prefers to think of as her "explorations" into spirituality and working with the philosophy of people like Steiner. So here is yet another wonderful role model for all of us!

Sight is of course only one of the faculties that can so easily deteriorate during the 'last lap', and people vary immensely in the way that they handle such deterioration. My husband has for a while been having problems with his right eye and has consequently lost his driving license. He never complains, but during a recent appointment with Lawrence they had an interesting conversation about the fact that the loss or deterioration of an 'outer faculty' can stimulate the improvement of an 'inner' one. When David told me about this conversation, it suddenly occurred to me that when on a shamanic 'Death and Dying' workshop I had received an order from spirit to carry on doing soul rescue work on my own at home, I was already on the waiting list for my first hearing aid. I then asked my sister Philippa whether her acquisition of hearing aids had coincided with the messages from Archangel Metatron that had started her off on bringing through a new form of healing[4] and she replied affirmatively. Lawrence says, however, that "I do not think that the deterioration of physical sense 'automatically' results in improved inner faculties, but it may give the potential for such." He also points out that it could alternatively be a signal that one needs to start working on the inner faculty, or that it may release energy that could be used for sensory input. He told me that my examples were exactly the kind of thing that he had seen happen quite often, but that in certain people "some of that energy might be wasted on frustration or annoyance, while in others the frustration might be used to stimulate inner work." He concluded by commenting that "there are many possibilities and it is good to be aware of them." And when I continued this discussion with Sascha, our Ayurvedic practitioner, his comment was that in his experience the loss of something such as sight often reflected a loss of direction or purpose in life.

Sai Baba, who delights in being a punster, says that we do not need to go to university in order to acquire an MBA, since we are all MBA holders already. M is for the Mind, B for the Body and A for the *Athma* (which also signifies Awareness). All basic sciences deal with the body, while the spiritual sciences deal with the mind. However, in order to be in our True Self we have to know what is beyond both body and mind. In a lecture at Prashanthi Nilayam (the Puttaparthi ashram), Anil Kumar, Baba's translator, summed up the twenty characteristics that Baba gives of the person who is in her/his True Self. I feel that these are worth listing as a goal for us all to aim at.

The first is Humility. Such a person is never proud or egoistic, and as examples Kumar mentioned Jesus, Buddha, Mohammed and Socrates (who said "I know only one thing: that I do not know"). The second characteristic is Unpretentiousness. This person will never appear any different from what he or she really is. The third is *Ahimsa* (Non-violence) – one of the five Human Values in Baba's coat of arms – which Kumar translated as non-injury and simplicity. Fourthly comes *Shanti* (Peace) – another of the five Human Values – translated in this case as Forbearance. The fifth characteristic is Uprightness or straightforwardness (which is equivalent to *Dharma* (Right Conduct), another of the five Human Values), and this means an absence of manipulation or strategy. Next we have the Spirit of Service – the service of the teacher – and Kumar commented that the real teacher teaches spiritual things. Seventh we have Purity, and this has to be both within and without; and eighth comes Steadiness, which means that we should always be uniform. Number nine is Self-Control. It is necessary to control the body, the senses and the intellect, so that the Self will manifest, will start expressing itself. Tenthly we have Dispassion, and this involves detachment both from objects which give pleasure to the senses and from a desire for publicity. The eleventh characteristic is Egolessness, and here Kumar said that the egoless person commands respect, whereas the egotist is like a blown up ball that gets kicked around until all the air has come out of it.

Characteristic number twelve is the essence of this book, for its possessor understands and accepts the pain of birth and death, sickness and old age. Kumar said that in life we pass through certain cyclic changes: the new born baby cries at being born again and if it does not, the doctors make it cry; sickness is expensive, and in old age (when the ears refuse to hear and the mind refuses to think and forgets everything) we are totally dependent. Birth itself is a cause for worry, and both birth and old age are painful, yet they are all important parts of life and have to be accepted. Kumar said that "having been born in tears, we should leave the world with a smile". Thirteen is Non-Attachment to family, because relationships are incidental and have nothing to do with the True Self. Spouses were not spouses before marriage, and in your previous life your children were not the children you have now. Fourteen is *Asakthi*, which means non-attachment to worldly things, and fifteen is Non-Identification of the self with persons and things. The sixteenth characteristic is unswerving devotion to the Lord, and the seventeenth is resorting to solitary places. Number eighteen goes hand in hand with seventeen, since it is Distaste for Society (and by that I think is meant ordinary society rather than that of other holy people). Number nineteen is Constancy of Self-Knowledge - constant integrated awareness. *Satchitananda* (Being-Awareness-Bliss) is our true nature and, once we are able to return to that, we will always have equal-mindedness, will ever be in a state of equanimity. The twentieth and final characteristic is perception of the True End of Knowledge.

Baba summarizes spirituality with just three things: killing the animal in us, improving our human qualities such as compassion, and being at one with the God in us. Once you attain your True Self, you will speak, because God is the speech in you, yet beyond your speech, sight and so on. "Once you feel Him in you, around you, above you, below you, then you know that He is everywhere. If you cannot see Him, you are in *Maya* (Illusion), so remove the *Maya*".

Number seventeen jumps out at me as I write this, because I find that as I get older solitary places appeal to me more and more, and I always want to avoid crowds, especially noisy ones. Returning, however, to a slightly more mundane level, one of the important features of these later years for many people is the fact of being grandparents. I appreciate the well-worn joke "Grandchildren are a very good idea. If we'd known beforehand, we would have had them first." On the whole grandparents can have the enjoyment of the young children without the twenty-four hour responsibility that parents have. But there are always exceptions, and in some cases, for instance with mothers who have full-time jobs, grandparents do partially take on this responsibility for their offspring. This is obviously only possible when families are not separated by distance – a thing that is happening less and less with increasing job mobility. Nowadays, with more longevity, some people are even living, like Molly, to be great grandparents. This must be very exciting and rewarding!

However, another common feature of these final years is bereavement. This can happen at any time in life, but it is obviously most likely during this last stage, and feelings of loneliness are liable gradually to increase as more and more friends and siblings die. Widowhood must as a general rule be the hardest of all to cope with, and the adjustments that it entails are difficult for any of us who have not experienced it to imagine. However, something positive can always be drawn from the most difficult of experiences and, in my friend Alan's case, contact with the local hospice, where his beloved wife was cared for through her final illness, inspired him to train as a bereavement counselor. I also know someone whose father died when she was only thirteen and who in adulthood worked as a bereavement counselor for children.

Alan is in fact an excellent example of someone who has for long been very much in touch with his Life Plan. He was in business all his working life, and he explained to me that his personal philosophy had <u>always</u> been one of turning negative events into positive ones. This attitude had invariably been useful both to himself and to those with whom he worked and so, when his beloved wife was diagnosed with terminal brain tumors, his immediate reaction was to look for the positive side of what was happening. It is perhaps hard to imagine how this could be possible for someone whose early retirement was initially largely taken up by care of his wife, but Alan's salvation was a deep inner 'knowing' that this was not the end for <u>him</u> and that he had work to do. Within not more than six months of Rosalind's death he attended an open evening organized by the Samaritans and then went for an interview. He was, however, turned down for work with the Samaritans when he told them that his wife had died only the previous year. Undeterred, he then went to see the woman at the local hospice who had given him bereavement counseling and she leapt at the suggestion of his training with them.

Alan has now been working with the hospice for three years and is much sought after not only for his natural aptitude and skill but also because most of the other counselors (not to mention 'counselees', to coin a horrible word!) are women. Since it had often been a question in my mind, I asked him whether or not he had found that religious belief, or belief in an Afterlife, tended to help people to cope with bereavement, and I found his reply most interesting. He told me that he had come to the conclusion that "religion often doesn't help at all". As an example he quoted a man who had been a churchgoer all his life but who, now faced with the reality of his beloved Ruth having died, found himself quite unable to believe that she was still around. Even Alan telling this man that he could personally feel Ruth's presence in the room did nothing to help him.

At the other extreme, Alan has counseled one or two declared agnostics or even atheists to whom he has given tremendous reassurance and help. All the work that he does for the hospice is entirely voluntary and he finds it extraordinarily rewarding. He also appreciates the extent to which he and Rosalind had planned their life together beforehand. Her brain tumors took a long time to be diagnosed, and they caused her character to change in ways which were very difficult for Alan to cope with. For instance, they had both always been very keen gardeners and used to do it together, but towards the end of her life Rosalind 'took over' to such an extent that Alan felt forced to find new interests for himself. He then took up photography among other things, and gradually their previously very united lives became much more separate. When, after Rosalind's death, a clairvoyant explained to Alan that this had been "her gift" to him, so that he would learn to stand on his own prior to being widowed, it made a great deal of sense to him.

Alan further told me that, whereas men are generally more reluctant to seek bereavement counseling than women are, people around them tend to offer help more readily than they do to women. This is because, while women often feel that they should be able to cope, men tend to be seen as more vulnerable and to have fewer friends. (Certainly, when my husband retired and we moved to a new part of the country, I often felt that he would not have got to know anyone if it had not been for me!) Alan's experience is that men on the whole miss the companionship of a spouse even more than women do, and that women tend to go through the grieving process and come out the other side better than men do.

But of course bereavement is not confined to the loss of a partner. Alan has found on occasion that some people cope even less well with the loss of a parent. Obviously circumstances vary as much as do individuals, but he explained to me that sometimes a deceased parent had been the mainstay of a family even in later life and the 'child' will consequently feel totally unsupported and unable to cope any longer. Often too, if someone has had a particularly difficult life, bereavement can be, as it were, the last straw that causes them to fold up completely. Alan says that not being able to help everybody has been one of the difficult lessons that he has had to learn, but he also appreciates that there is learning for all concerned in whatever happens, whether or not the person in difficulty realizes it at the time. Both he and another bereavement counselor I met recently (but did not talk to about my writing because her orthodox Christianity would have conflicted with most of it) comment that "when people are really struggling with grief, much of it relates to what had been going on <u>prior</u> to the death. The death simply causes everything to bubble up to the surface and is the trigger for them to seek the counseling that they should have had years ago."

My friend Olive's husband Daniel was twelve years older than she was, so that throughout her happy years of married life she always knew that she would probably one day have to face widowhood, but she says that that did not make it any easier when it happened, when she was seventy-three. Alan echoed

Olive's words when he remarked that "even when one is fully aware of the loss having been part of one's agreed Life Plan, NOTHING can take away the grief. It's something that we all have to go through at some point in our lives – a vital ingredient of our emotional development." But he always tells people, whether or not they are willing to believe it, that "time is a great healer". This no doubt sounds like a cliché, but that does not prevent it from being true. Alan also stresses the importance of letting go of the lost loved one, explaining that this is equally important for both parties. People who have died can remain trapped on the Earth's plane while their families or friends are hanging on to them, but Alan also finds that he often has to explain to people that "letting go doesn't mean forgetting." Speaking in a heartfelt way from the depths of his own experience, he says that "you have to lock them up in your heart, knowing that they will always remain there even after you have given them permission to move on."

This Olive had clearly already done with Daniel well before the time that I met her. He remained mobile and reasonably fit until very near the end, and she knows that he knew he was dying even though they never talked about it a great deal. He was of a generation in which it was not the done thing to talk about such difficult subjects, or even to show one's affections, but Olive always knew how much he loved and needed her.

As a compromise between their respective, rather rigid, Churches, they decided to have their three children baptized in the Scottish Episcopal Church. However, since Daniel had been brought up Catholic, Olive and the children decided after his death to contact the local priest. He was extremely sympathetic and helpful, and he suggested that she could bury Daniel's ashes in the church garden. This was a comfort to her, even though she felt quite unable to be sure that there was an Afterlife and that she would ever see Daniel again. Soon after that, as a result of the encouragement of her daughter who was living in Singapore and had attended an Alpha course there, Olive joined one that started up at the local Catholic church. There not only did the priest continue to be sympathetic and helpful to her, but also (like Carmen when she started going to the same church) she made a very good group of new friends, whom she describes now as part of a loving family. Her own family are all very supportive but none of them lives close by, and so, when we were talking three years on, thanks to the love shown to her by these new friends, she felt at peace with herself and said that she had begun to live again. After attending a couple of the Alpha courses she decided to be received into the Church, partly in order to feel herself belonging more, and partly through a desire for a better understanding of where Daniel, with his Catholic upbringing, had been coming from. Alan also has given counseling to someone who has been greatly helped in bereavement by joining a church community.

Olive, like Joy, has never shown any sign of losing her zest for living, and she gives a great deal of help to her family on her regular visits to her children and grandchildren. She has even joined a team at the church who provide a monthly luncheon for the elderly, though some of the people to whom she serves the food are younger than she is! Olive is open to the idea of reincarnation, and she feels sure that her life does have a Plan, that she is still here for a reason, and that she will go when it's her time. In the meantime she told me that she was winding up her life, and she coped amazingly well with a minor heart attack which forced her to cancel a pilgrimage to Rome and Assisi.

Sometimes of course people who are bereaved have the good fortune of making a new relationship. Although I know that this can often bring great joy and consolation to both parties, there must be many possible pitfalls and, if loneliness were one's primary motivation, it might well prove disastrous (just as is so often the case in first marriages). When you have lived with another person for a long time, you become accustomed to all their idiosyncrasies, faults and virtues and so adjusting to someone else could not possibly be easy. Anyone looking for a new partner needs to be aware that we are all unique, and so it is vital not to try to find a 'replacement' for one's former spouse, but rather to remember that "variety is the spice of life". It is never too late, though, to make completely new friendships and to find love – especially when we remember that every 'new' relationship will in reality be the revival of an old one from a previous life.

The fact that it is now the norm for women to have full-time careers is one of the factors at present making residential homes for the elderly and nursing homes increasingly necessary in the West. One of the really sad things about this to my mind is that these tend to be big money spinners for people with the enterprise to buy up large houses and convert them. It breaks my heart to see old people using up their life savings on exorbitant charges, with the profits going not to the workers, who tend to be genuinely caring people and are normally grossly underpaid, but to those who see it purely as good business.

Though residential homes for the elderly solve a problem for many families, they are on the whole far from being an ideal solution. In my experience, most of the residents spend the great part of their time sitting in front of the television, and the diet is often a very unhealthy one. Improvements, however, would only take a little bit of imagination. For instance, I have heard that some residential homes in America now have crèches. What a brilliant idea! Firstly it solves a problem for parents needing care for their small children, and secondly it gives the elderly – many of whom will of course have had the experience of both parenthood and grandparenthood – a very worthwhile and absorbing occupation. I greatly hope that ideas like that will spread rapidly.

One of the saddest things about our society is the loss of a sense of community. (Remember that Margaret Thatcher said that there was no such thing as society?) So I always applaud any efforts to redeem that. In America in recent years, retirement communities have begun to spring up in several areas, which seems to be at least the beginnings of a solution to the growing problem of increasing longevity. I know someone who has moved to such a community in Arizona, which he told me is growing very rapidly and will ultimately consist of two thousand homes. Eighty per cent of these are restricted to people over fifty-five, and the remaining twenty per cent to people over forty-five (or, in the case of couples, where at least one of them has reached the required age). Steve and his wife have settled happily and made good friends, though he is realistic about the cons as well as the pros of running such a huge organization, where people are still dependent on cars even though the place will ultimately (once the shops have been built) be completely self-sufficient.

This resort is restricted to people who are still active and, though nothing is formally organized, there are meeting rooms available for those wishing to form clubs or host other activities. Once people have reached the stage of requiring twenty-four-hour care, this is available not too far away, and hopefully by then they will have made friends who will care enough to visit them regularly and prevent them feeling completely cut off from the community. In the interim, however, Steve says that medical care can be a problem since there is no hospital nearby.

Another of Steve's reservations is the fact that there is no real concern for the environment when the bulldozers plough up the green desert in order to build new homes. He feels too that, whereas his and his wife's motives in moving there were a community spirit and a desire to keep active in retirement, some of the younger ones, who are in, for instance, computing jobs that they can do from home, are motivated more by desire to get away from the city. Though these houses are well insulated and people, when ordering their homes, can opt for the installation of solar panels, this resort has no formal 'green' policy.

Fortunately, however, there is a growing movement world wide of people who desire both the preservation of the planet and to live in a real community. Eco-villages are springing up in many different sorts of places, and they could be the ideal solution for the care of people of all ages. In the ideal society no-one would ever be cast out or shut away with strangers, and in an eco-village it should be possible for the younger inhabitants to care for the older ones as necessary and then to have their turn at being cared for when their time comes.

My husband and I were at one time involved in an eco-hamlet project in Shropshire, but it unfortunately turned into an 'ego-project' and we withdrew when the person running it dismissed our well-chosen architects because he had decided that he wanted to design all the houses himself. A similar project, has, however, been realized on a smaller site, in Stroud in Gloucestershire, and I feel sure that this could be a general way forward for the future.

The last lap often entails moving house, whether or not we have to move into a residential or nursing home. And the move will normally be to a smaller house, which in turn will neces-sitate getting rid of many of our possessions. This can of course help in the process towards non-attachment, but I am finding now in any case that friends of about my age are all seized with desire to start shedding rather than accumulating. Spiritual teachers continually advocate reducing one's luggage, and it would seem a pity not to take the opportunity of doing this during these last years. After all we cannot take any of it with us next time we depart the Earth.

If you want to leave things to your descendants, why not start giving them to them straight away? To quote *The Prophet* once more,

"And is there aught you would withhold?
All you have shall some day be given;
Therefore give now, that the season of giving may be yours
and not your inheritors'."[3]

Your children's need for buying a house might well be greater now than it will be when you are gone. I often receive jokes via email, and one that I have enjoyed particularly concerns a rich man who had accumulated gold all his life. On his deathbed he could not bear the thought of leaving it all, so he put in a special plea to God, who granted him permission to bring just one suitcase with him. This he filled with gold bars, and on arrival at the pearly gates he was told that it was not allowed through. He explained his special case, and so the angel went to check and then came back and said: "Yes, you are allowed one carry-on bag, but I have to check the contents." When the man opened it, the angel exclaimed: "What? You brought paving stones!"

I have tried to expound the advantages of setting out on the spiritual path reasonably early. Leaving it till these later years can be fine, but one thing that seems clear to me is that it does not get any easier. We should not, however, let ourselves be daunted by that, because by the time we get to the last lap, we will normally have learnt that the most worth while things in life have all been acquired through effort, and that it is by overcoming obstacles that we learn and grow. Though I should not, since they have earned it in previous lives, I sometimes envy the people who are close to Sai Baba (living permanently in the ashram and so on). But He is a very hard taskmaster with those who are a long way ahead spiritually. At the ashram I always enjoy the lectures given by the American couple Jack and Louise Hawley, who are devoting their 'last lap' to working for Him. They recount an experience following their first visit to Puttaparthi, when they had booked a holiday in Bali on their way home and were greatly looking forward to relaxing. On their first evening in the hotel, Louise said to her husband: "Won't it be nice to have a lie-in tomorrow morning?" At three o'clock in the morning, however, she was woken by Sai Baba at the foot of the bed saying firmly, "Get up. It's time to meditate"! She prodded Jack saying "Look who's here!" and he awoke just in time to see Baba going out through the door.

As I said, the Hawleys are a very advanced couple! For those of us who are at a lower level, meditation at seven a.m., or even seven p.m., is likely to be acceptable. The important thing is to find and then do what is right for us at our own individual and unique stage in *samsara*. It is never too late for change, and if we are on the last lap and feel that some of our life has been wasted or misused, we can always do something about it .(Remember the workers in the vineyard who were called in at the last hour and were paid the same as those who had been working all day?) There is always help available. The last lap is often the most extensive, and I hope I have convinced you that it can also be the most rewarding. And if we do make the very most of it, death, which we must turn to next, need not make us fearful.

Notes

1   *The Tibetan Book of Living and Dying,* Sogyal Rinpoche, Rider, London, 1992.

2   This quotation comes from the *Spiritual Diary – An Inspirational Thought for Each Day* published by the Self-Realization Fellowship, USA, 1982, ninth reprinting 1996.

3   *The Prophet*, Kahlil Gibran, Mandarin, London, 1991.

EXERCISES

1   Are you already on what is generally regarded as the 'last lap', or feel that it is now imminent? If the latter is the case, are you apprehensive about it? I hope that this chapter will help to alleviate your fears, at least in part. Remember that it is good to keep both the body and the mind active, but at the same time not to overdo it. Having time for oneself is especially important at this stage of life. For one thing, one can tire more easily than younger people. So try not to push yourself and then (a big fault of mine!) get cross with yourself for what you fail to achieve. It is good to have goals,

but remember too that non-acceptance is what keeps pulling us back to Earth.

2   Are you aware that your memory is deteriorating? If so, rather than constantly chiding yourself for it:

    (a) appreciate that it is a perfectly normal part of growing older, and

    (b) make a habit (I'm preaching to myself here!) of writing appointments down in a diary or on a wall calendar and then looking at it regularly.

3   Are any of your faculties (e.g. eyesight, hearing) beginning to fail? If so, rather than complaining about it, see it as an opportunity for developing inner vision or hearing, which can sometimes be even more valuable. Also, look around you: you will always find other people whose physical condition is worse than your own. So remember to be grateful for what you do have!

4   Have you a hobby that you have never had enough time for, or do you fancy developing some completely new interest? Well, now is your opportunity, so make the most of it!

5   Are you in the privileged position of being a grandparent? If so, again – make the most of it! Firstly, grandchildren can bring you untold joys, and secondly they can benefit immensely from your wisdom. Time that their parents may not have to give them can give them memories that they will treasure for the rest of their lives.

6   Are you living with a partner whose role in the house is almost completely different from yours? (This is of course the norm in most, if not all, societies.) Have you thought deeply about the many implications of one or other of you dying before the other? Now might well be the time for a woman to learn to change a plug or deal with the finances, or a man to learn to cook and iron!

CHAPTER TEN

DEATH

Death is like taking off a tight shoe.
Ram Dass

Death is not a deplorable event; it is the journey's end, the owner getting out of the car when the time is up and the goal is reached. It is a consummation, a happy conclusion, or at least it ought to be, if only all are wise enough to treat it as such and be prepared for it.
Sathya Sai Speaks, Vol. VI

I arrived at the hospital ward, the bunch of flowers I had picked hastily in our unkempt garden clutched in one hand, the card on which I had endeavored to express my love and sympathy in the other. It was a visit I genuinely wanted to make yet had also been dreading. Ursula had been so sick now for so long. Each visit to her home and latterly to the residential home had been more painful than the last. It grieved me to see her so thin, so reluctant to consume the food that the workers in the home tried so hard to tempt her with. Often unable to sit up in her chair, she was restless in bed, itching all over, and her doctor had failed to prescribe anything that gave relief from any of her afflictions. A woman of strong faith who had led a full and worthwhile life, at eighty-four, Ursula was now ready and eager to go to her Maker and – like the weary traveler restlessly watching for the sign to appear at the airport gate – was finding it hard to understand the reasons for the delay in her call.

As soon as I heard of Ursula's transfer from the home to the hospital, I knew that I must hurry if I was to say "goodbye". But I dreaded it too. Ursula was a good friend, though not a close one. I knew her family only from the names she would occasionally throw into the conversation, and conversation had been becoming increasingly difficult with her rapidly deteriorating health. She was never afraid to talk of death, but I had to suppress my longing to share <u>all</u> the fruits of my reading on the Afterlife with someone who was such a strong Catholic and therefore reluctant to take on board anything that was not formal Church doctrine. Perhaps I would be too late to say "goodbye". Never mind: that would solve the dilemma of what to say, and at least she would know that I had made the effort.

"I've come to see Ursula W.", I said brightly to the nurse who approached me.

"Oh", she replied gravely. "Just wait a moment while I fetch Sister."

"So I clearly am too late," I thought to myself. "Why does she have to fetch Sister? Why can't she tell me herself?"

"I'm sorry to have to tell you," said Sister with a long face, "that Ursula passed away just a couple of hours ago."

"Oh good!" I exclaimed, no doubt a trifle too jubilantly, and then, in response to the slightly shocked and bewildered look, I added, "Well, she'd been suffering so much for so long; she's much better off now. Please could you put these on the coffin for me?"

"Yes of course," said Sister. "Thank you for coming."

"What is it?" I asked myself as I strolled back to the car, "that makes everyone in this country so afraid of death? So desperate to preserve indefinitely even an already long life like Ursula's that has so clearly become full of nothing but pain?" My thoughts drifted back to the funeral we had witnessed in Ghana fifteen years or so previously. The dancing, the drumming, the singing, the general display of jubilation which, we were told, would carry on for several hours after our departure. Weeping and wailing too, of course, but overall a public acceptance of death as a fact of life. It may be a platitude to say that death is the inevitable sequel to the moment of birth, but platitudes often convey eternal truths. This Africans understand, Indians understand, our own direct ancestors understood. Only we in the modern, 'technologically advanced' West try to run away from it, or even to defeat it. Only the interval of time in between the moment of birth and the moment of death varies from lifetime to lifetime. And that of course depends upon our karma and upon the Plan that we make before we come in.

As a child I was overprotected from the reality of death. When I was five years old, my parents had what they must have genuinely thought to be my interests at heart, but they missed a golden opportunity of introducing me to death naturally and painlessly. We were living at that time in the upstairs flat of Great Aunt Judith's house (Judith Anne Merivale, after whom I was named). Aunt Judith was eighty-five, and she passed on sitting comfortably in her chair in her living room. "How wonderful! How fortunate!," the adult me says now, but back in 1945 the unspoken nuances in my family were quite different. "How terrible! Poor Mummy who found her!" were more the sentiments conveyed, and I and my younger sister and baby brother were kept well out of the way until the funeral was over. As a result I grew up with a completely paranoid fear of death and of one day seeing a dead body. I retained this fear until my mother's death, when I was forty-seven, and a trip to the undertaker's to view the body seemed inescapable.

So for someone already in her seventies, I am in one sense somewhat inexperienced in the matter of death. One of my school friends died when she was only fifty-five. I went to the memorial service in Cambridge where she had been a don, and mourned her loss and celebrated her life with fellow school friends, but distance had prevented me from visiting her when she had been in the last stages of cancer. Nor did I have the opportunity to visit my husband David's sister in law when she was dying. As I am writing this, he has gone to see his eldest brother, who has been diagnosed with cancer. I am hoping there may be time for me to do so as well, but in such cases one never knows what may happen from day to day.

How then can I consider myself qualified to write on the subject of death and dying? Well, we can all have our own thoughts on this most important moment of our lives, and I have for long had many. Also, firstly the memories of countless of my own deaths are all buried deep in my subconscious and a few of them have occasionally resurfaced, and secondly I have witnessed many re-enactments of death both among my own clients and on Roger Woolger workshops.

My interest in the subject of death mainly concerns its spiritual aspects. I have no medical training and little medical knowledge and am consequently not attempting to discuss any of the physical questions. But I recently purchased a book entitled *THE WAY WE DIE* by Leslie Ivan and his wife Maureen Melrose[1], and this book deals very comprehensively with all the physical aspects of death. Also, without making any judgments or taking any particular moral stance, it tackles such thorny issues as the vegetative state and euthanasia. I therefore strongly recommend it to anyone who desires to make a more in-depth study of this whole subject.

"Death is the end", says Western society; "There is no such thing as death," say our more spiritually oriented counterparts. Both are true! What is life but paradox? Death is the end of the physical body, but the physical body is but a shell – an overcoat to be discarded when it is worn out or has served its purpose. The real you – the *atma* – can never die; it is a part of God and therefore indestructible. Sometimes, it is true, we shed these overcoats apparently prematurely, well before they are worn out – at birth or even before, in childhood, in accidents, in sudden illness like my dear school friend Caroline and (much more recently) my friend Rhiannon – but there is always a reason for it. The reason may be obscure to ordinary people like you and me, but it will always be apparent to the more spiritually aware and to guides and helpers on the other side. "He only needed a few more months on Earth to complete his karma," is one explanation I have heard for a cot death. "She did it for that family, to help them to learn to cope with loss," is another possible explanation of child death. "He was murdered because he himself had been guilty of murdering her in a previous life"; and so on and so on.

May 17th, 2009, saw the death of Dr. David Lloyd, Ludlow's local historian, who had for almost twenty-five years been giving Tuesday morning history lectures in our town's Assembly Rooms. My husband and I started attending his lectures regularly soon after we moved here in 2004, and we also often used to meet him in the town center when we were shopping. Our last meeting with him was on May 15th, when we had a long chat about our forthcoming visit to Italy and the coach trip that he was due to lead the following month as part of the annual Ludlow Festival. Since the lecture season was over, my David asked him "So are you relaxing a bit now, David?" at which point I butted in with a joking "David doesn't know the meaning of the word 'relax'!" When, upon our return from Italy, we found a letter returning our check for the coach trip "due to the sudden tragic death of David Lloyd" two days after we had seen him, it was of course a big shock. But I cannot go along with the use of the word "tragic" in such circumstances; I see it as a cliché which people in our society are too prone to using unthinkingly.

If it were a case of a seventeen-year old killed on a motorbike, I would not object to describing the death as "tragic", but David was born in 1935 and had therefore already comfortably passed his "allotted three score years and ten". He had led a very full and rewarding life, and had just finished correcting the proofs of his latest book. Of course I feel immense sympathy for his beloved wife, who found him dead in his armchair when she took him his Sunday afternoon cup of tea, but it surely would have been even worse for her if he had had a long lingering illness. As for David himself, who was an active churchman and always donated the profits from his various enterprises to the Conservation Trust of Ludlow's beautiful St. Laurence's, I cannot imagine that he would have coped well with prolonged illness either. The launch of his new book took place not long after the funeral, and I am sure that he must himself have been present on both occasions. As for the lectures, they have since been ably carried on by a group of other well-qualified people. Although he will continue to be greatly missed for a long time, I should like to make a plea for more thoughtful use of vocabulary. Personally I am convinced that David Lloyd had completed his life's work and was looking forward to new adventures on the other side, so how about describing this as a "sudden joyous death" rather than a "tragic" one?

Dr. David Lloyd's is one story – the story of a highly educated man who lived a life in a comparatively well to do country – while the death of someone who had spent a life in an underprivileged country would of course be quite different. Yet karma applies equally in all cases. "No-one can escape from the cycle of *dharma*, and must pursue it without envy if he be poor, and without self-criticism if he be rich. This age-old and barbaric philosophy maintained the debased Indian victims in the gutter and most of my well-heeled commercial and official Indian acquaintances in comfort, with the Government of India endlessly preaching the betterment of the one and leaving untouched the establishment of the other, and this is why India remains basically a country of the hungry and unhappy." So says James Cameron in *An Indian Summer*[2], first published in 1974. I cannot help wondering whether, were he writing now, this enlightened journalist (who died in 1985 at quite a good age) would have moderated his view somewhat. In any case I look forward to debating the question with him on the other side, for – far from being barbaric – this age-old philosophy is surely both just and logical. Besides, having myself paid twelve visits to India (albeit for shorter periods than Cameron's), while endorsing his use of the word "hungry", I dispute that of "unhappy". No country in the world is without its unhappy inhabitants, but whether India has more than its share I doubt very much. Indeed I would venture to suggest the contrary.

The loss of a child in countries where that is now comparatively rare is what all parents surely see as the "worst possible thing imaginable". Yet to live in a country where this is rare is a great privilege, and only a very few generations back, child mortality was common in Europe. Let's face it: throughout history most people have had to cope with the trauma of the death of a child. And if you accept my assertion that we have all lived many, many lives already, then surely not one of us has escaped such a tragedy. And we have all survived it! When I relived the loss of my older son (then the twin of his now younger sister) in the Elizabethan era, I shed many cathartic tears while writing about it, but I was able to console myself with the knowledge that this very same soul was now my son again. How often have I yearned to console bereaved parents of my acquaintance with my conviction that their child's life was not its only one, and that many children who die subsequently return (either in their same life or in a subsequent one) to the very same parents! This of course tends to be difficult, if not impossible, in our society where belief in reincarnation has been stamped out. However, one hears many touching stories of dying children who do a great deal themselves to console their parents. The German doctor with whom I shared a room on my visit to Puttaparthi in 2002 (another Caroline, but pronounced of course the German way) has witnessed countless deaths and is often called upon to issue death statements. She told me that she finds that the sense of peace which tends to surround a corpse is often accentuated in the case of children, as is a sort of luminosity emanating from the body.

While on the subject of child death, it is perhaps appropriate to touch briefly again upon the thorny question of abortion, and here I can include natural abortion, commonly known as miscarriage. I suffered from the consequences of the latter at sixteen, when my mother lost at five months the youngest sister[3] whose arrival I had been greatly looking forward to, and again when the soul who would have been our first grandchild was miscarried at twelve weeks. How much worse must it have been for the mothers themselves! In my mother's day, to the best of my knowledge, burial ceremonies were unheard of in such cases. A period of grieving is vital after any loss, and funeral ceremonies, which I am glad to say are now common after miscarriages, are a real help for those who have to say "goodbye" and come to terms with their bereavement. Not so, alas, for induced abortions! It is sad that, in these days when contraception is so readily available, abortion is still the most common form of birth control world wide, but facts have to be faced, and so help and advice – whichever way she decides – should be readily available to every potential mother. My brother who is an Anglican vicar has frequently found himself counseling women who have had an abortion as much as twenty years previously, and I feel that more effort should be made to make women contemplating an abortion fully aware of the possible consequences of their action. One must of course always have compassion for the young woman for whom motherhood seems an impossible burden, yet in our society which talks so freely of 'choice', what about the choice of the baby or the father?

However, I am now quite sure that abortion is rarely, if ever, the end of that particular mother-child relationship. Remember my friend Joy, who named all her lost babies and is still waiting for Dominic to return as her grandchild? I once corresponded at some length by email with a woman who, like Sharon, had had an abortion forced on her at an early age. A few years later she recognized her aborted daughter when she returned to her as a

potential step-daughter; (the child came up to her at a swimming
pool before they had even been introduced, and the bonding was
instantaneous). Dr. Michael Newton claims in *A Journey of Souls*[4]
to have evidence that people who abort subsequently adopt that
same soul in a future life. (Why adopt rather than conceive? Well,
I suppose one possible answer is karmic retribution for an act
that was not wholly desirable. As a parent of both natural and
adopted children and the acquaintance of many adoptive
parents, I can testify that adopted children are generally a lot
harder to bring up than natural ones. But that is the main subject
of my next book!)

Part of the aim of this book is to show that there is a good
reason for everything that happens in life, however painful it is.
Mark Ireland, the son of the famous American psychic Dr.
Richard Ireland, suffered the loss of his younger son Brandon in
a mountaineering incident shortly before he was due to go off to
college. His intense grief over this loss started him on a quest
which began with visits to a number of mediums and, once he
had proved Brandon's survival beyond any shadow of doubt, he
wrote a book[5] aimed at helping other parents who have suffered
similar loss. But it did not stop there: now Mark Ireland is
lecturing on the subject of survival, and he is convinced that
Brandon had completed what he needed to do on Earth and that
his own quest and its results are the fruits of his son's Life Plan.

Having said that, however, the very last thing that I would
wish to do is to belittle the immense pain and grief that death can
cause. Even a conviction that the separation is only temporary
does not normally alleviate the pain of physical absence. I know
from personal experience how unbearable even the sudden loss
of a pet dog can seem. Losing a child must be worse still: every
future birthday that comes round will cause one to think about
the age that the child would have reached and wonder to oneself
what he or she might be doing if they were still alive. Yet grief,
though some people experience much more of it than others, is a

vital ingredient of <u>every</u> life. Without it our hearts remain closed and we cannot feel compassion for humanity. Those who deliberately cut themselves off from their feelings may well (as I have said before) fall ill with something like cancer. Alternatively they will be forced to get in touch with their feelings in a future life.

Bereavement counseling is of course very valuable, as my friend Alan confirmed in the previous chapter, and a trained counselor will always encourage anyone they are helping to really be in touch with their feelings. Fortunately the days of shedding tears being seen as 'unmanly' are more or less over! Tears are important because they are very healing, so be thankful if you are someone to whom they come easily.

Sometimes the shock of a death can delay the dawning of its reality, but when physical presence is withdrawn eventual dawning is inevitable and so support and understanding for the bereaved person at that point are vital. It breaks my heart when I hear bereaved people recounting how acquaintances will even cross a road in order to avoid talking to them! <u>Of course</u> it is never an easy topic to broach – and, as I have discussed already, our society tends to shy away from the reality of death – but hardly any of the most worth while things in life are easy.

Personally I find fascinating the human capacity to feel intense grief and intense joy simultaneously. Sofia Tolstoy, whose wonderfully written diaries[6] reveal one of the most difficult lives imaginable, suffered the loss of her youngest and favorite son (affectionately known as 'Vanechka') when he was only seven, and she wrote about him repeatedly throughout all her remaining years. She was an extremely gifted woman, but her husband – great man though he was and ahead of his time in many ways – failed to appreciate her talents. One of these was for music, and the parts of the diaries that move me the most are when she writes almost in the same breath of her grief over the loss of Vanechka and her joy at hearing a truly wonderful piece of music.

Very different from Sofia Tolstoy's loss is that of my friend Marjorie, whose only child, Martin, was tragically killed (and here I am using the word "tragic" advisedly!) in a car accident at the age of twenty. Marjorie and I were at university together, where we made friends through the Catholic Society, but it is only thanks to Facebook (of which I am not in fact a great user) that we got in touch again, quite recently. It was of great interest to me to discover that we had during the long interim developed in similar ways, leaving behind the Church of our upbringing as a result of coming to believe in such things as reincarnation. Marjorie telling me about Martin's death made my heart ache dreadfully, but I was absolutely fascinated when she told me about her subsequent experiences of her son. These are her words: "As for Martin, he was the love of my life, and part of me, and when he died, after a few days he (or some of him) came and lived inside me for eighteen months. His already good sense of humor had been enlarged by death and there were many times when it was very hard not to laugh at his remarks in front of other people. I also spent a lot of sleeping time with him in another dimension. I would always know on waking that we had been together, and sometimes I remembered what we had been doing, and sometimes not. He told me a lot in that time, too, but I was not supposed to pass it on, but I am no good at keeping my mouth shut, so eventually the only way was for him to tell me and then soon after wipe my memory. When I objected to this, other beings who were around said not to worry, it was all there inside my head, but they were just taking steps to stop me blabbing it to all and sundry."

Then Marjorie continues: "In my last dream of being with Martin, I saw him from a little distance, and he was trying to sneak out of the building with a suitcase in each hand, without my seeing him. 'Little blighter', I thought to myself, 'that's his karma in those suitcases and he's off to re-incarnate hoping I'm not going to notice!' He knew as soon as I thought this and turned back with a rueful expression. 'That's all right,' I said, quite happily. 'If you want to go off and reincarnate, that's fine.' And in my dream state, it was. But when I woke and found him gone, then that was bereavement all over again, just as bad as the first time. Five months later (not nine) he was put into my arms as a new born babe – John he is called this time, and he knew me as a baby, and was very like Martin in his ways. But at about age seven or eight his this-time genes began to kick in, so he became less like my son. I am John's godmother, and he is grown up now and lives in Hartlepool, which is a long way north of where I live."

Well, I cannot imagine that experiences such as Marjorie's are at all common, but I would very much hope that bereaved parents might find some consolation in the thought of their child returning to Earth to continue their learning, work out more of their karma and, perhaps, bring happiness to another family. Marjorie also said to me, "I do know, as a bereaved mother, that when your need is great the help does come, in various miraculous ways. It would not be possible to get through it otherwise."

I was interested to note that the timing of Martin's entry into his new body coincided with the results of my research as expounded in Chapter Two, and also that his interlife period this time appears to have been quite short. This agrees with the contention that people who die young tend to return quite quickly.

Sudden death like Martin's can obviously occur at any age, and of course in such cases the primary element for all concerned is likely to be shock. When an accident causes instantaneous death or deaths, those who have left their bodies may not realize it for a while. This is because, as we have seen already, the 'etheric' body looks the same as the physical body, and also the 'astral plane' surrounding the Earth looks the same as the Earth that we know. I perform soul rescue work, and the last time that I did this my spirit went to the area of the March 2011 tsunami in

Japan. Hardly surprisingly, there was total confusion there, and in "the mess" I found it unusually difficult to pick out souls that I could help, but I was as always thankful for the help that was also forthcoming from the other side. Those on the other side whose job it is to help the deceased to cross over require our assistance in making the initial contact, and there is at present an ever increasing need for people on Earth to do this (but that is the subject of yet another book that I have planned!).

When a death is sudden (like David Lloyd's mentioned above) but the person concerned nevertheless dies 'consciously' (something we should all aspire to since it can save a lot of 'time' and anguish on the other side), those left behind can – and in my experience normally do – feel happy about their loved one having been spared prolonged illness, but the shock is likely to make acceptance much harder for anyone left behind. Ellen, who had had heart problems as a child and then had an operation for a new heart valve when she was about fifty, died extremely suddenly when she was sixty-five, which naturally left her partner Peter completely shattered. When someone has been the closest person to you for forty years, it must be like having half of one's body suddenly torn off, but, when Peter and I talked shortly after Ellen's funeral, it was clear that one of the hardest things for him was not even having had time to say "goodbye".

However, a point about this case that is to my mind most interesting is that Peter was not totally unprepared for what happened. Talking to the surgeons at the time of Ellen's operation had made them both aware that she could have died then, and the knowledge that "anything could happen at any time" was reinforced when Peter himself had a heart attack about eleven years later. He told me that, "I probably have always since then had a rough idea of what could go on, and probably somewhere prepared myself for it mentally." What is more, after his heart attack they both went to the hospital to learn how to do CPR and so, thanks to that, when Ellen collapsed Peter was able to do more than he expected. He said, "When this happened to Ellen I didn't even have to stop and think, let alone panic. I just got straight into performing CPR as though I had prepared for it for years - maybe I had?" And I found it most interesting when he added, "the brain is such a powerful processor that it has probably, via background processing, started to sort things out for various possible scenarios."

However, unfortunately in this case, although the emergency services lost no time in responding to Peter's call, he says that his immediate and correct response "made no difference whatsoever, as I do not believe that it was a simple heart attack as it was so instant and final from the first couple of seconds and there was no sign of recovery or life from that moment on." He thinks that, despite the fact that Ellen's heart was eventually restarted and the body was breathing on its own, it was probably a stroke because she made no sound, seemed in no pain and it was so sudden. He explained that, "She made no sound either then or afterwards."

Peter also commented, "I had obviously wondered after my heart attack in 2006 who would go first – sort of an even bet really, thinking about it." Yet another interesting point is that Ellen was apparently always convinced that she would go first, which of course again accords with the thesis of this book. Work and family commitments had made them until 2004 unable to live together all the time, which meant that they were less dependent on each other than many couples – another form of preparation for Peter and another point of confirmation of their Life Plans! He says that, "she knew that I was capable of all of those things [cooking, washing and so on that I had asked him about] and her constant theme was 'make sure that you look after the cat when I've gone'." (He stresses that it was when not IF anything happened to her!) Despite her heart problems (which I did not even hear about until after her death!), Ellen was someone who always led life to the full and her final years were packed full of voluntary activities in service to the community in which the couple lived. So I am personally sure that her example will help Peter through his bereavement, as will the support from his friends, who he says "do go back a long way, even though I have very few and do not make friends easily or often." It is common knowledge among the spiritually minded that deceased partners stay around their loved ones until they either join them on the other side or no longer need them. (Alan in the previous chapter knows for certain that Rosalind is now helping him in his work for the bereaved.) This is not at all the same thing as being "stuck" on the Earth's plane, like the tsunami victims I just mentioned. (I'll say more on that whole topic in a moment!) Peter, while having no firm belief in an Afterlife, reflects that having lived apart from Ellen for many years, "my thoughts were with her from a distance during the week, and of course my thoughts now are pretty similar, so it's not that unusual." My own hope is that (as Alan does with Rosalind) he will soon feel Ellen speaking to him, which I am sure she is trying to do, and that this will help them both with the fact of not having been able to talk together during her last moments.

Although they never talked specifically about funeral arrangements, Peter thinks that Ellen herself had sorted out most of the choices. She had, for instance, "made general comments over time that she was not fond of the local Anglican church, although she would attend carol services and other events held there. She had always said that she wanted 'All things bright and beautiful' at her funeral so was obviously, again, quite sure that I would be there to organize it!" And he told me that Ellen's simple wicker coffin that I admired was "similar to the one she had admired last year at a funeral of her cousin which she attended." Peter found both the minister at the Methodist church (which Ellen had attended during her childhood and youth) and the funeral director very helpful, "as was a friend who plays the organ at many funerals."

So Peter, like Alan and countless numbers of other people

who are widowed "early", has been deprived of the joys of shared retirement. I do not need to say that this is obviously both sad and hard for those left behind, but I will stress yet again that it is part of the Plan that they agreed to before they were born. Alan (another aspect of whose story is in my next book) knows that he and Rosalind planned their abbreviated life together beforehand as the trigger for getting him firmly on to a spiritual path and into what he now sees as his "life's work". My brother-in-law, who was widowed fairly suddenly at seventy-two, when he himself was still in excellent health, has found the ensuing fourteen months extremely lonely as well as difficult from a practical point of view, yet my husband and I have nevertheless been pleasantly surprised at how well he has been coping generally and how he has opened up to the friendship of neighbors in a way that is entirely new for him.

In complete contrast to sudden, or fairly sudden, deaths that are difficult for the bereaved to deal with, are people who linger on long past their apparent 'sell by date', and I believe that the possible reasons for this are never brought into the euthanasia debate. Alan is at present thwarted in his desire to start a completely new life near to his son by the fact of his almost ninety-nine-year old mother living near to him, but as a spiritual person he is wonderfully accepting of his frustration. Equally spiritual is our dear friend Susie, who has for long had numerous ailments that she endures incredibly cheerfully. She told me when she was about eighty that she felt ready, and was rather hoping, to "go soon", yet when I visited her today (23 March 2011), less than a month before her eighty-sixth birthday, she said that she intended to live to a hundred! Her memory has got very much worse during the interim, so is that she has forgotten about her desire to cross to the other side, is it that she is completing her karma, or is it that she is still here as an example to people like myself and the staff in the nursing home who are caring for her so well? I like to think that it is this last reason; I know that care for the elderly and infirm can be a very good way of working off karma.

So one of the main theses of this book is that death by any means – be it abortion, natural or unnatural, early, later or much later – is very definitely not the end. Nor can we say that it does not exist at all, since obviously the physical body does die. On the now rare occasions when I hear the Creed recited in a Catholic church, the phrase "I believe in the resurrection of the body" makes me smile. "Which one shall I choose?" I ask myself bemusedly. "The seductive Indian dancer cut down in her prime by a fall? The crusader who killed and plundered? (I wouldn't want to do that again, but it would perhaps be nice to have such a strong body.) The woman who worked so successfully as a healer but was then condemned to death for it?..."

But now let me be serious. There are many aspects to this inevitable death of the physical body. When I viewed my first corpse (my mother's), the horror and fear that I had been harboring for so long vanished instantly. I found that there was nothing in the least repugnant about the sight of it; it was just a shell. Recognizable, yes (just!), as the body of the woman who had cared for me during the first part of my life, and for whom I and my siblings had more recently endeavored to care, but it was not my mother. She was still there – a palpable presence in that room – but she quite clearly no longer had the slightest interest in that cancer-ridden body.

What to do with these physical shells is now my next question. According to many sources, the etheric body (which is the 'next layer up') takes about three days to detach itself fully from the physical body. That is the reason why resuscitation is never possible after three days. For this reason, according to Anne and Daniel Meurois Givaudan[7], the custom among the Essenes was not to touch the body at all during the three days immediately following the death, and this is also the practice in Tibet. In initiation rites in Ancient Egypt, people would leave their physical bodies for three days[8]. During this period the subtle bodies would hover above the physical body gathering information from higher realms, and the only real danger was of not returning in time.

Quite apart from the question of the welfare of the etheric body, is not the rushing in of undertakers a symptom of our society's desire to hide death away? Is not the home the best place for grieving, and if so, is not the corpse a good focus for that? Sogyal Rinpoche, in his great spiritual classic, *The Tibetan Book of Living and Dying*[9], explains the effectiveness of continuing the reading of the *Bardo Thodol* (erroneously translated as *The Tibetan Book of the Dead*) to the person even for several days after they have first passed over. He also says that prayers for the dead are always useful, but particularly so during the first three weeks following the death. This is because at that point their links with this life are stronger and they are therefore more susceptible to help. The discarnate soul is easy to guide, he says, and the living can consequently direct it towards a good rebirth.

When the mother-in-law of one of my brothers was diagnosed with terminal cancer, my sister-in-law and my brother were determined to nurse her in their own home. Their children, who were quite young at the time, were made fully aware of what was going on and were free to wander in and out of "Granny"'s bedroom both before and after her death. They were sad, of course, but they accepted it, and "Granny" herself greatly appreciated having her loving family so close at hand during those difficult few weeks.

This, to my mind, is the ideal, but obviously it is not always possible. Often hospital is essential at the end, and then the shortage of beds, as well as the feelings of the other patients, will make keeping cadavers around for three days impossible. But we can always have goals, and one goal that I would dearly like to see in Western society is to keep as many dying people as possible out of hospital. Hospices do a wonderful job, as do such agencies as the Macmillan Nurses for cancer patients, but we can keep searching for other solutions besides.

Apart from Sogyal Rinpoche[9], the leading name in the field of death and dying must be that of Elisabeth Kübler-Ross, whose autobiography[10] I recommend most strongly. Rather than going here into her well-known analysis of the various stages of dying and death (ranging from denial to acceptance), I refer you to her book on death and dying[11]; but I would also at this point like to mention another of the most recent deaths in my own experience. My friend Rhiannon, a member, like myself, of the Shrewsbury Sai Baba group, was sixty when she died on 20 September 2007. Only a few weeks beforehand we were visiting her in hospital on account of a broken hip, so the shock was immense when we heard that, instead of going home as she had been expecting, she was being tested for cancer since they thought that the bone had broken too easily. After that the only moves she made were firstly to the cancer ward in the same hospital and secondly to a nearby nursing home, where I myself only had time to visit her once.

So Rhiannon had only a few weeks in which to go through the Kübler-Ross five stages, and, though it was not for me to dig deeply into her innermost thoughts, I certainly did not observe in her either the second stage of these (anger)* or the third (bargaining). On a visit that I made to the hospital shortly after the cancer had been diagnosed, Rhiannon commented to me quite humorously that she had told Baba that she was not yet ready to depart, but, after reaching the point when denial was no longer possible, she barely exhibited even depression (the fourth stage), despite being in a great deal of pain. How easy would it be to spend several weeks in the same hospital ward bed without getting a little bit depressed? Yet our mutual friend Sarah, who had known Rhiannon for longer than I had and was able to visit her more frequently since she lives in the same town, says that she never found her depressed. Now Sarah comments, "I often find myself in spare moments just saying 'Well done, Rhiannon, for the best exit I've ever seen'. Her take-off was just like the space shuttle." I do think that is the difference between the truly spiritually oriented and most other people, particularly in our society. Rhiannon is (how can I say "was" when I know her to be still around?!) a very spiritual person, and Sarah shares my view that it was her faith in Sai Baba, rather than shortage of time, that helped her to reach the fifth stage of acceptance so quickly. As she observes, "Rhiannon was very connected to where she was whisked away to", and that is surely something we could all find to be well worth aiming for.

As I have been saying all along, we have an allotted life span each time we come in, and Rhiannon was aware of that consciously as well as unconsciously, which must have helped her a great deal. It also helped us, her friends, to come to terms with the shock of losing her so quickly and apparently 'prematurely'. Unfortunately the same was clearly not true for Rhiannon's family, whom I met at the funeral, but they did find some consolation in the fact that, after she had been moved to the nursing home, her suffering at the very end was alleviated by a stroke, which was probably the real cause of her death. This we regarded as a deserved gift from Baba and, when I met Rhiannon on a shamanic journey that I made a few days after the funeral, she looked radiantly happy. She had for many years been a keen astrologer, and she told me on a subsequent journey that she was now busy deepening her astrological studies with the aim of helping people to choose the most appropriate moment for their birth.

The question of pain during the last weeks, days or hours is another important one, which frightens many if not most of us. It is of course indelibly linked to karma and so there is nothing to be gained by trying to escape it all together. Rinpoche[8], however, makes the point that anxiety can increase pain, so if we have trained ourselves to be less afraid about death, this will pay off here too. We can also be thankful for modern technology. Even those who try to avoid the use of all allopathic drugs need surely have no qualms about accepting anything that might bring relief from pain on their deathbeds, especially if the pain distracts from God rather than bringing one closer to Him.

However, through my long studies and practice of regression therapy, I have learnt that, when departure from the body is obviously inevitable (for instance if one is being burnt at the stake), the soul will withdraw itself <u>before</u> the actual death – before the pain becomes too excruciating. This is endorsed by the fascinating account of Edgar Cayce not stepping into a lift, which then broke. Edgar Cayce had auric sight, and it was only after the lift had crashed and all its occupants had been killed that he realized that, when the door opened for him, he had noticed that none of the people inside had auras!

However, Roger Woolger reminds his students constantly that the problem is that, though the soul does not at the time feel the pain of, say, the flames or the guillotine, the <u>body</u> remembers it. Imprints from the physical body are stored in the imperishable essence that is us and are then transferred to the new 'overcoat' that we take on for our next incarnation. A client of mine who could not bear to wear anything that fitted tightly around her neck went back to a lifetime in which her father had throttled her. Woolger himself has countless stories of people whose symptoms came from a noose around their neck. Fortunately death by hanging is no longer performed in Britain, but those countries which do still practice execution by any means must be accruing much bad karma for themselves.

Deep Memory Process therapy allows us to experience the pain which our physical bodies escaped at the moment of the actual occurrence. Does this seem unnecessarily barbaric? Not if it spares us innumerable future lives in which the problem or the discomfort will resurface! Hypnotic regression obviously works for many people, but experience has led me to the conviction that the Woolger method of focusing on the pain or sensation is a quicker route to a death trauma, as well as a more effective and powerful tool for dealing with it and finally letting go of it for good. Woolger stresses the fact that traumatic death frequently causes *samskaras* that need dealing with, and I have indeed witnessed countless such releases on his workshops. However, my personal experience of taking people through past deaths in my own practice is that the great majority of these are easy, peaceful, and very often almost painless.

In Chapter Two I wrote about Anne and Daniel Meurois-Givaudan's friend Rebecca, whom they watched preparing to be born. In another of this couple's books[12], they encounter on the astral planes a woman called Elisabeth, who is preparing to die, and they follow her journey right through to the end. I find this book interesting from two points of view. Firstly because of the way in which Elisabeth, a fairly ordinary sort of woman such as one might meet any day, anywhere, reacts to the shock of discovering that she is near the end and then very gradually comes to terms with it; and secondly because of the very useful tips that Anne and Daniel give on helping people to die – the points that one can massage, for instance. Clinging on to life against all obvious logic seems to be one of the deepest of human instincts, and is no doubt important for self-preservation in order to fulfill our blueprint, but once our time is up, it is surely best to recognize it and to accept any help available. My husband had the privilege of being present at his mother's death, and he was filled with admiration for the young nurse, whose role, he said, appeared more like that of a midwife.

Someone I knew called Judy, who had had cancer for a while, also died recently. When another friend of mine approached her husband with some literature about some miraculous American Indian cure for cancer that she had just heard about, he thanked her kindly but replied that his wife was now ready for and looking forward to the end, which was expected to be fairly easy.

Judy was still at home and when, a few days later, my husband and I called on her ourselves with the dog, we all three received the warmest and most joyous of welcomes imaginable. She was eager to make us a cup of tea, and my own eagerness to talk with her about what was happening had to be suppressed owing to a steady stream of other visitors. (Our little town is a friendly one and Judy was a very popular person.) In fact I have rarely seen anyone looking quite so joyful, and the fact that her husband (who was out walking that particular day) was clearly not fighting the inevitable and hanging on to her must clearly have helped her to make a speedy transition. And I found the Quaker funeral – where everyone was free to stand up in turn and recount some of their memories of Judy – an exceptionally moving one.

Sometimes, however, the opposite occurs. If relatives are having difficulty in coming to terms with the loss of a loved one, he or she may linger unduly simply for their sake. I have stressed previously the importance for parents of being able to let go when their children come of age; now at this end of life the tables are turned! Giving the loved one permission to go – and for that words may not even be needed, since soul communication is more powerful – can spare him or her hours, days or possibly weeks of suffering. In fact, clinging on the part of spouses or relatives can even prevent a newly departed soul from moving on beyond the lower astral realms.

Our family experienced that some years ago when my daughter's little spaniel sadly died at the age of only two and half. We, unfortunately, were on holiday in Spain when Rincewynd was suddenly stricken with severe gastro-enteritis, and so dealing with the vet was left to the friend who was kindly looking after him. One afternoon when we were in the apartment in Spain, my husband looked up momentarily from his book and, to his immense surprise, he saw Rincewynd lying on the sofa opposite him. He made a mental note of the time and date

"just in case anything had happened to the dog", but told no-one.
I, unusually, had already felt very uneasy about leaving the dog,
but had remonstrated with myself for "being silly". I felt anxious
all the way home from the airport, and our feelings when my
friend greeted us with the news can easily be imagined by any
dog lover; (this death occurred in the days before cell phones and
email.) The next day, when my husband mentioned his vision to
my friend, he found that the timing coincided very closely with
the moment of the death. Rincewynd had clearly wanted to say
"goodbye" to us. After that my husband saw him twice more:
once in the car as we were getting into it and another time just
outside the house.

When I poured out my woes over the loss to my good friend
John, he commented that we were obviously hanging on to
Rincewynd. He suggested that, since our absence had made a
proper funeral impossible, we organize a little farewell ceremony
and set the dog free. The friend who had been looking after the
dog agreed wholeheartedly, saying that her family had done the
same for her mother and that the effect had been very beneficial.
So we all gathered in a circle, talked about some of our fond
memories of Rincewynd, lit a candle for him, and then sent him
formally on his way. My husband did not see Rincewynd again
after that, and young Alice said the next day that she had no
longer expected to see him running round the corner of the house
to greet her on her return from school. Soon after that too, she felt
ready to start looking for a new puppy (who, I am glad to say,
lived ten years longer than Rincewynd had).

Animals have a most important role to play in many people's
lives. For one thing, the fact that their lives are so much shorter
than most human beings' can give us good experience of the
reality of death as well as teaching in letting go. For another, they
can be a marvelous source of companionship for the elderly and
bereaved. Peter unfortunately does not share Ellen's love of their
cat, and has never wanted a dog either, but when a widowed

neighbor of ours lost her dog, she was completely devastated and I was delighted that age did not prevent her from acquiring another dog not too long after. I always feel very sad when elderly people I know whose dog dies tell me that they are "too old to get another one because it would outlive me". This is the time of life when dog lovers can benefit the most from having one to care for, dog walking services are normally readily available to the infirm, and there are also always rescue services ready to find new homes for bereaved dogs!

Paramahansa Yogananda in his wonderful autobiography[13] has a very telling story about a pet fawn to which he was very attached. This fawn slept in his room and at dawn would toddle over to his bed for a morning caress, and when one day it fell very ill, he saved its life through his prayers. The next night, however, the fawn appeared in Yogananda's dream saying "Please let me go", and so he agreed and then awoke to inform his pupils, who were also extremely fond of it, that it was dying. After a last effort to rise and stumble towards him, the fawn fell dead at Yogananda's feet. He explains: "According to the mass karma which guides and regulates the destinies of animals, the deer's life was over, and it was ready to progress to a higher form. But by my deep attachment, which I later realized was selfish, and by my fervent prayers, I had been able to hold it in the limitations of the animal form from which the soul was struggling for release. The soul of the deer made its plea in a dream because, without my loving permission, it either would not or could not go. As soon as I agreed, it departed."

Suffering often cannot be avoided, and in any case it can give those caring for the dying an excellent opportunity for working off negative karma. The German doctor, Caroline, that I mentioned before, who has much experience of dealing with the dying, still finds this work immensely difficult, but she told me a story of an occasion in her very early days. She was on her way to a particularly unpleasant case of an old down and out man who was an alcoholic. Feeling unable to cope, she prayed ardently for help, and as a result found herself on arrival at the bedside suddenly able to see what she described as "the beautiful" in it. She could not really explain exactly what this "beautiful" was – only that she felt transported to the higher level, and that ever since that moment she has continued to be able to see things from the higher level whenever she has to deal with things that are unpleasant on the mere Earthly level. She also prays for her dying and newly deceased patients and is quite sure that this helps her as well as them.

Funerals, as the Africans know so well, are extremely important for both the living and the deceased. Much reading on the subject, as well as witnessing many deaths in regression, have convinced me that a newly departed soul will normally attend his or her own funeral. My mother died before I had started on my in-depth studies of these matters, but I well remember the party at my brother's house when everyone kept forgetting that she was not there. We all felt her presence just as I had when I had paid her body my respects at the undertakers', and now I appreciate much better the extent to which our intuitive feelings were correct. But even before the party, the highlight of the day for me was when all the younger grandchildren started jubilantly throwing flowers into the grave. Children's instincts are invariably right: they knew that their dear Nana had much cause for celebration.

Funerals are important, but does that mean that they need to be elaborate and expensive? Personally I do not think so, and it always disturbs me to see posh-looking coffins being lowered into graves to molder invisibly. When I was doing my research for this chapter, I called in to our local undertakers' for some information. He (needless to say perhaps!) was surprised at my interest, but eager to furnish me with a booklet on funeral plans[14]. Paying in advance for a funeral is no doubt a good idea for families who are short of money, but to my mind an even

better idea is a cheaper alternative. So, before it had unfortunately closed down, I also called in to the Alternative Funeral
shop in Bishops Castle, a little town in Shropshire near to where
we are now living. The proprietor of the shop makes both simple
cardboard coffins and 'acorns' for ashes, and also very beautiful,
hand-painted coffins, which she told me many people like to buy
and use initially in their homes for storing, for instance, blankets.
But she also told me that on 'green' burial sites it is permissible
to wrap the body in a shroud and not use a coffin at all.

I have a friend who, a few years ago, buried her mother under
her favorite apple tree. Obtaining special permission for this was
quite a complicated process, and it also aroused some contro-
versy in the neighborhood, but fortunately the number of firms
now offering alternatives is steadily increasing. I do of course
appreciate firstly that families sometimes want to spend money
on a funeral as a token of their love for the person who has just
died, and secondly that their grief can be so great that they prefer
to hand over all the organizational details to outsiders, but at the
same time I think it is useful for us all to be aware of what is
available nowadays.

For those who want to be 'alternative', there are numerous
options, ranging from a totally DIY affair to one organized
entirely by an alternative funeral director. A friend of mine who
was, to his great distress, thrown out of a Catholic seminary on
account of his desire to remain a free spirit, has since been very
happy to officiate at green funerals, where trees have been
planted instead of gravestones. The *Natural Death Handbook*[15]
gives a complete list of alternative funeral suppliers in England,
and Kate Gordon in her book *Rites and Ceremonies: A Practical
Guide to Alternative Funerals*[16] gives advice on such things as how
to lay out the body.

On the question of burial versus cremation, it is worth noting
that the Catholic Church has for some years now permitted the
latter. Personally I am fond of graveyards and have never felt the

same atmosphere of peace in a crematorium, but feelings on these matters are very individual. My father-in-law described himself as an atheist and his funeral took place entirely in a crematorium. For myself, being used to requiem masses followed by additional prayers and little ceremonies at the graveside, it all seemed rather abrupt, but my husband's family were all quite happy with it. Such things are a matter of cultural tradition as well as personal taste, and feeding corpses to vultures, which is completely repugnant to me, is logical in a place like Tibet where there are no obvious graveyards available and wood is too scarce and too precious to be used for funeral pyres.

My in-laws were fortunate in that, although he was very ill during the last months of his life, my father-in-law was sent home towards the very end. When my husband went down there with our daughter, his father was already in a coma from which he never awoke. You often hear it said that you can never assume that someone who is unconscious is unaware of what is going on around them, and this makes perfect sense when you reflect that the soul leaves the body during sleep. Many stories are told of people who have near-death or out-of-body experiences during surgery and later astound the surgeon and nurses by repeating to them the words that they had uttered during the operation. There is no way to predict how long a coma will last, and after a few days spent in his parents' home, my husband felt obliged to return to work. So he and Alice both said "goodbye" to his father, who then died while they were on their way to the train station.

Just as astrology indicates that we choose the moment of our birth, so am I now convinced that we also choose our moment of death. My husband, as the youngest of three, was overprotected by his parents, who always endeavored to shelter him from anything unpleasant. He was particularly close to his father, who I am sure would have regarded death as something distasteful from which children should be hidden, and Alice was only twelve at the time. So my father-in-law clearly waited until they had said their "goodbye" and left the house to make his departure! Even though the approximate length of our life tends to be in our blueprint, this is well-known to be adjustable by minutes, hours, days, or even more, according to external circumstances. I have heard it said that the more spiritually advanced have the capacity to bend their astrological specifications, and Sogyal Rinpoche also says that good spiritual practice can prolong life or avert an untimely death.

In the case of my mother's death, it is equally obvious to me that she chose the precise moment very carefully. Her cancer struck when she was only seventy-four and had been enjoying nine years of widowhood; (and I mean enjoying! Life with my father can never have been easy). She did not feel ready to go and was looking forward to the arrival of a new grandchild. She was an extremely private person and, though we six siblings discussed her impending death amongst ourselves, we were completely unable to get her to do so. She avoided using the word 'cancer', and only made it clear by hints and innuendoes that she knew her 'end' to be nigh. Her last four days were spent in a nursing home. She was rarely alone, yet she died during the only five minutes when my sister who is a qualified nurse had left the room to summon all the rest of us by telephone! A private person in life, my mother chose to remain private in death too. But Rinpoche[9] also says that it is often better for the dying person not to have their nearest and dearest present, as this helps them to achieve non-attachment.

A priest friend of mine, who died in 2007, was a hospital chaplain for many years. He told me that in his experience people invariably knew when they are dying, whether or not a doctor or their relatives told them. This confirms the view that it is always desirable, if possible, to talk about impending death with the person concerned.

Following my own experience with my mother, I feel very strongly with Elisabeth Kübler-Ross that talking about impending death openly helps all concerned to come to terms with it. And so it is sad when unwillingness, dementia or Alzheimer's makes this impossible. When my husband's sister in law was dying of cancer, he was unfortunately unable to visit her, and he is consequently now very glad of the opportunity to go and visit his eldest brother and, since they come from a family that normally tended to avoid talking about delicate subjects, he was delighted when he found a willingness to discuss the present situation. David comments too that words are not always necessary. He remembers well a visit he made with his father to his dying brother. His father's parting words to his brother were "See you again soon", whereas they both knew quite well that this would not be possible.

I believe that my mother's difficulty in talking about her cancer stemmed at least partly from her intense fear of death; and the experience of Caroline, the German doctor, is that such fear is more or less universal. My mother was a very saintly person who had been a devout Catholic all her life, and one could therefore say that her fear was quite illogical, but how often do our minds act logically when confronted with new situations? I have known many good Christians who shared this intense fear of death. (As Alan says from his experience in bereavement counseling, "often religion doesn't help"!) Hence my regret that the Churches, despite being ostensibly concerned with the Afterlife, offer no education at all on the subject. I am consequently attempting to provide a little of this education in my next and final chapter.

Help, however, is always available on the other side, and no incumbent departure ever goes unnoticed 'over there'. My husband knew which morning his mother was going to go because, when he woke up, he saw his father (who had died a couple of years previously) standing at the foot of our bed. This made David realize immediately that he had come to collect his mother, and he and his brother then hastened to the nursing home, where she tallied for only a few further hours. Often dying people are seen very clearly to be communicating with loved ones on the other side, and angelic presences are frequently felt or even seen. Experts on this subject tell me that nobody is ever left to die alone.

According to both Buddhist and Hindu philosophy, it is our last thought that will determine the nature of our next life. Obviously the way in which we lead our lives is likely to have much bearing on our last moment. Though death-bed repentance is of course always possible, and any priest would no doubt tell us that it is a frequent occurrence, good habits are sure to be helpful. Sai Baba says: "No-one can escape death. But the goal of life must be to think of God at the time of death or to have sacred thoughts only. There is a proverb in Telugu, which says the type of death one meets with is the proof of the virtuosity of man. How the last few moments of the mortal life are spent are the only proof of real devotion". Final departure from the body – just like everything else in life – is a very individual matter. While a Buddhist is likely to appreciate having the *Bardo Thodol* read to him or her, a Catholic will prefer to receive the 'Last Rites' (now known as the Sacrament of the Sick) and communion from a priest. Rinpoche[9] quotes the Dalai Lama as saying that one should not read the *Bardo Thodol* to someone who would have been anti-Buddhist during their life. Many people would like to have some of their favorite music played, while others might prefer total silence.

Just as I was starting this chapter, I received news of a most moving death in Geneva. Ali, an elderly retired doctor, was for a number of years spiritual advisor to the Geneva Sai Baba group, and he attended Thursday bhajan meetings and study groups unfailingly. When I received an email informing me of the time of his funeral, I was slightly surprised since I had not heard that he was ill. Before I had had time to send my condolences to Zara his wife, I received a telephone call from a mutual friend who had already been in touch with her and heard exactly what had happened. It appears that Ali had just led the recitation of the 'aums' with which the Baba group meetings always commence, and was about to start giving a talk on a spiritual subject, when he suddenly collapsed. One of the other members of the group who was present was a heart specialist, but he failed to resuscitate him. The group then remained with the body for several hours, chanting bhajans continuously. Zara felt very happy (or at least as happy as any new widow could possibly feel) because it was quite clear to her that Ali had had the death he wanted, and I feel sure too that he must have now merged with Sai Baba.

The question of death – or, to use what is to my mind a preferable term, departure from the body – has innumerable different aspects, and I have not even attempted to exhaust them. I hope, however, that these, rather personal, reflections may sow the odd seed of thought in some of you. I would like to end with a further quotation from the great Yogananda[12]. Following his account of the death of his beloved fawn, he says "All sorrow left me; I realized anew that God wants His children to love everything as a part of Him, and not to feel delusively that death ends all. The ignorant man sees only the insurmountable wall of death, hiding, seemingly forever, his cherished friends. But the man of unattachment, he who loves others as expressions of the Lord, understands that at death the dear ones have only returned for a breathing space of joy in Him".

So now at last it is time for the most exciting bit: what can or might come next!

Notes

1   *The Way we Die*, Leslie Ivan with contributions by Maureen Melrose, Pari Publishing, Italy, 2007

2   *An Indian Summer*, James Cameron, Penguin, London, 1987.

3   I found out many years later, on a family constellation workshop, run by one of my fellow Woolger graduates, firstly that this miscarried baby was in fact a girl, and

secondly that she has now reincarnated as my darling granddaughter, Delilah.

4   *A Journey of Souls*, Dr. Michael Newton, Llewellyn Worldwide, USA, 1995.

5   *SOUL SHIFT - Finding Where the Dead Go*, Mark Ireland, North Atlantic Books, USA, 2008.

6   *The Diaries of Sofia Tolstoy*, Alma Books Ltd., England, 2009.

7   *The Way of the Essenes – Christ's Hidden Life Remembered*, Anne and Daniel Meurois-Givaudan, Destiny Books, Vermont, 1993.

8   See *Winged Pharaoh,* Joan Grant, Ariel Press, Ohio, 1985.

9   *The Tibetan Book of Living and Dying,* Sogyal Rinpoche, Rider, London, 1992.

10 *The Wheel of Life – A Memoir of Living and Dying*, Elisabeth Kübler-Ross, Bantam Press, London, 1997.

11 *On Death and Dying,* Elisabeth Kübler-Ross, Routledge, London, 1995.

12 *Chronique d'un Départ – Afin de guider ceux qui nous quittent*, Anne and Daniel Meurois-Givaudan, Editions Amrita, France, 1993.

13 *Autobiography of a Yogi,* Paramahansa Yogananda, The Philosophical Library, New York, 1997.

14 *Solutions to Future Funeral Costs – A choice of plans with inflation-proof guarantees*, Help the Aged, 2002.

15 *The New Natural Death Handbook,* edited by Nicholas Albery, Gil Elliot and Joseph Elliot of the Natural Death Centre, Rider, London, 1997.

16 *Rites and Ceremonies – A Practical Guide to Alternative Funerals,* Kate Gordon, Constable, London, 1999.
    *On this point my friend Alan comments that the stages are not necessarily linear: "Someone can often go back to the anger stage, for instance, time and time again."

EXERCISES

1   Are you afraid of dying? Don't worry – you are in no way unusual! Many people, however, have had their fears totally alleviated by a Near Death Experience and so I strongly recommend reading one or more of the many books on this subject. Another way of helping to overcome one's fear is practice, and I was encouraged to do this on a workshop entitled *Death, Dying and the Beyond*, led by the English shaman Simon Buxton. You can use a drumming tape or CD, lie down and visualize yourself floating easily out of your body. Prior to doing this exercise myself for the first time, I had read a great deal about Near Death Experiences and, having always as a child had a great fear of rides at fairgrounds, I dreaded the thought of being "whooshed through a tunnel"! So for me it was a pleasant surprise to find myself being met not by a scary tunnel, but by a boat into which I could step and be rowed gently away by a loving figure.

2   Have you made any plans for your funeral? Since you will be the most important person attending it, it is a very good idea to make sure that it will be done exactly as you would like it! For me the choice of music is the most important thing, and my children have already been given clear instructions on the subject, but others may well have quite different priorities. So I strongly suggest writing it all down and making sure that your nearest and dearest know exactly where to find what you have written.

3   Are you grieving the loss of someone very dear to you? Don't worry how long ago it was; it is perfectly natural for the pain to continue seemingly for ever. But realizing that no-one is ever really lost can be extremely helpful. Have you tried talking to the person concerned? If you find this difficult, have you thought of consulting a medium? A message can never be guaranteed, but many people find consolation that

way. I can also strongly recommend a session of Deep Memory Process therapy as an excellent way of meeting with a loved one in what we call the 'Bardo'. You might well be told the reason why the person had died when they did and/or what their present job is in spirit. And once communication has been established, you should hopefully be able to continue it.

CHAPTER ELEVEN

THE AFTERLIFE

We will be seen on this stage of life again and again, until we become such good actors that we can play our parts perfectly, according to the Divine Will. Then our stage manager will say "You need go no more out. You have done my Will....."
Paramahansa Yogananda

The previous chapters of this book have been filled with examples from real life. However, since I am not a clairvoyant medium, this is obviously much less easy when writing about the Afterlife. The tale that follows is therefore fictitious, but the scenarios it describes are all borne out by the experience and/or research of clairvoyants, regression therapists, writers on near-death experiences, and those (such as Peter Richelieu[1]) who report on actual encounters with spirits.

I have attempted to put together into this story the essence of several years' research in the field and, rather than giving vast numbers of references, I am appending a bibliography, which is not even intended to be comprehensive. These are simply books that I can recommend from personal experience; there must be many more. The thing that has struck me most in all of my reading on the afterlife, and also in my personal experience of performing regressions to in between lives, is the large number of common features in the accounts given. That is my only claim to 'authority'! We are all individuals and, just as each lifetime is unique, so can there be no general rules for post-death experience, but there seem nevertheless to be common trends. My tale is not aimed at winning either the Man Booker Prize or one for realism, but I hope nevertheless that you will enjoy it.

* * *

Charles had for some time suspected that his wife Jennifer was having an affair with Roland, whose rival company had in the last several years exceeded his own in profits. One hot summer's day he took Jennifer by surprise by coming home from work over an hour early. His fury when he walked through the front door and found her almost naked in the arms of Roland was indescribable. Without pausing for a second's reflection, he leapt on Roland from behind, tearing him off his wife like a lion who had not eaten for a week, and then punching him relentlessly. But Roland was the stronger of the two even when his anger had not been aroused. With all the force he could muster, he kicked Charles in the crotch, hurling him against the ornamental banister. Alas for Charles, this banister which he prized so much was decorated with wrought iron spikes, one of which pierced his back as he fell, digging so deeply into his flesh that he was killed instantly.

"Revenge! I want revenge!" screamed Charles, and, without pausing even to notice that he had died, sped after the terrified Roland, who fled from the house without so much as a backward glance at his beloved Jennifer. Roland leapt into his car; Charles leapt in beside him, beating Roland's head with his fists and then grabbing hold of the steering wheel when he started up the engine. Roland drove home in a stupor, oblivious both to Charles' yelling and to the heavy blows he was receiving. Puzzled and frustrated, and without pausing to reflect on the dangers of opening the door of a car that was traveling at fifty miles an hour, Charles shot out and dashed home to vent his rage on Jennifer. Flying past the gory corpse without noticing it, he found her in the kitchen cowering next to the telephone, obviously too distraught to pay him any attention. He never-theless gave her a big piece of his mind and, when this had failed to produce any reaction, he decided to go straight to the police station.

The entrance hall of Hampstead police station was full of officers emerging from a meeting, and Charles was mildly surprised that not a single one of them questioned his barging through them. Undeterred, however, he screamed out his story: "They can both go to prison. That's what they deserve, the bloody bastards! Roland Crump is a criminal. He's not only stolen my wife, he's also kicked me in the crotch. Can't you see, you idiots? I'm seriously wounded. You must catch him quick and put him in prison. And you can get Jennifer too while you're about it. She's a crafty old bitch doing things behind my back with my worst enemy..."

The police ignoring him as well increased Charles' fury still further. When he had got beyond words, he lashed out at them all with his fists before, in desperation, setting off to Manchester to see Sophie, his daughter. At Euston station he boarded the first train without bothering to purchase a ticket, but before the train had got very far, he heard a young couple fighting in the corridor. "I'll get my own back on you for that!" screamed the young woman as she lashed out at her partner. "Ah yes, revenge! Revenge – that's what we need," muttered Charles, to himself this time, and the next thing he knew he was inside the young woman's belly. Six months later a baby was born in a Manchester maternity hospital, and so the cycle began all over again.

Charles had never loved Jennifer. He thought he loved her of course. She was his "prize possession" – the "belle of the ball" in Hampstead circles, who only needed to smile flirtatiously at a man to have him fall at her feet. Wealthy businessmen, bankers, stock brokers...all had been held in her thrall, and it was only Charles' exceptional good looks, combined with his exaggerated claims about his company's potential, that had enabled him to persuade her to take him as her husband. When Sophie was born, five years after the marriage, both parents regarded her as an inconvenience to their social life, and their resolve not to make the same mistake again was never broken.

Jennifer got bored with Charles very quickly after the wedding, but, though she resented being treated as a possession, she enjoyed the comfort of their Hampstead home and the many gifts that Charles regularly showered upon her. She enjoyed a series of clandestine affairs too, but Roland was the first man that she had really loved. They had both been seriously contemplating divorce, but Roland's wife had some strange power over him which made it very difficult for him to broach the subject.

When Jennifer realized that her husband was dead and her lover had fled, she was panic stricken. She knew she should phone the police, but how could she? They would blame her and, if she denied any part in the accident, they would obviously search for another suspect. She simply could not bear the thought of her beloved Roland being incriminated. So she sat, frozen, by the telephone for over three hours. But she and Charles were due at a dinner party that evening and had been offered a lift by some neighbors. So, after the doorbell had rung loudly three times, Jennifer realized that she had no choice. She opened the front door and promptly fainted. The events that followed can easily be guessed at: police, doctor, Sophie summoned from Manchester, a trial that dragged on for weeks…but never once was Roland's name mentioned. Though devastated that her phone calls to his work number were never answered, Jennifer remained loyal to Roland to the end. The fact that the fatal injury had been caused by a foot in the crotch meant that there were no fingerprints, and the lovers had somehow managed to keep their relationship a secret from everyone but Charles. At the trial Jennifer was the only suspect, but she of course pleaded innocent and the evidence against her was insufficient. Abandoned by her friends and too proud to ask for help from her daughter, Jennifer was forced to sell her beloved jewelry piece by piece in order to live; then the house, and she eventually died many years later in abject poverty.

Though she had never had any sort of spiritual life, Jennifer had been brought up with vague Christian ideas of Heaven and Hell, and these were reinforced by Sophie, who upon her marriage had become a Catholic. Too absorbed in her hedonistic lifestyle to pay heed to Sophie's admonitions, the concept of 'eternal damnation' had nevertheless rubbed off sufficiently on Jennifer to convince her, as she gradually lost everything, that that was what she had condemned herself to. She blamed herself for Charles' death, she blamed herself for Roland abandoning her, she blamed herself for Sophie not being a supportive daughter like those of so many of her acquaintances. So, when she finally left her body (quite easily, at the height of a bout of pneumonia), she found herself, just as she had anticipated, in 'Hell'. And what did her Hell consist of? The only physical difference that she noticed when she 'woke up' was that she no longer had pneumonia. But she was still living alone in a cold grey house, and her mental torture was increased by the thought that this was now for ever – that, being dead, she no longer had the ultimate escape of death to look forward to.

Roland, on the other hand, died some years before Jennifer. Riddled by guilt over Charles' death and by the fear of some day being found out, he threw himself back into his work with fervor. His fear of what his wife would say if he were tried for murder was greater even than his pining for Jennifer, and making vast profits for his company helped him to push both these issues right down to the bottom of his consciousness. It is hardly surprising that he in due course dropped dead over his computer from a heart attack. His last thought, however, as the chest pain seized him, was "Oh, Jennifer, I do so love you!"

And this little thought of love was Roland's salvation. Straight away he found himself in the hovel of a home in which Jennifer was now living. She was asleep – he worked so late into the night these days – but suddenly her mouth opened and she cried out "Roland, Roland!" When his embrace failed to wake her, he returned frustrated to his office, where he was amazed to observe a replica of himself slumped over the computer. He prodded the body, but it did not stir. He said to himself "This body looks like mine, and this is definitely my computer, which no-one else ever uses, but this body looks dead. How can that be? How can I possibly have two identical bodies, one dead and one alive? It doesn't make any sense!"

Something then made the puzzled Roland look up, and what should he see but an enormous bright light. Almost involuntarily, he found himself being pulled through a sort of tunnel towards it. On emerging from this tunnel, he found himself in the most beautiful landscape he had ever seen. Gently rolling hills, trees and flowers in abundance, were all bathed in a wonderful bluey-grey luminosity, although the sun was nowhere to be seen. In the distance he noticed a group of people and, wondering who they were, he instantly found himself standing right in front of them. Several of the faces seemed familiar, but the ones that stood out most he recognized immediately as those of his parents, who had both died several years previously. This puzzled him still further, but their radiant smiles and obvious joy at seeing him prompted the question "Am I dead too, then?"

"Yes," replied his mother laughing. "You worked yourself into the grave and had a heart attack."

"But your physical body isn't in its grave yet," added his father. "Do you fancy going to the funeral?"

"Funeral?…I don't understand. It's true I saw a body that looked like mine slumped over the computer, but I've still got a perfectly good body. Look!"

"That's your emotional body," replied his mother. "They do look exactly the same as the physical body, which is why often, when people die suddenly, they don't realize that they're dead. But there are people on this side whose job it is to help in such cases. You remember old Uncle Fergus? He's been doing that sort of work for years now. (Years in Earth time, that is. We don't really have such a thing as time up here.) He would have been here to greet you as well, only he's just had to dash off to the scene of a car accident."

"Some people don't even give themselves time to find out that they're dead," continued his father. "Charles, for instance, whom you accidentally killed, clung on so tightly to his etheric body and his desire for revenge, that he got sucked straight back into a new incarnation."

"Charles! Please don't talk to me about Charles. I'll never get him off my conscience. I deserve to be severely punished for what I did…Anyway, what's an etheric body?"

"The etheric body is the one you take on last before you enter a new physical body in preparation for another incarnation. It's the exact double of the physical body, with all the organs and so on, and because you put it on last, it's the first one that you shed when you die. It is now about three days in Earth time since you died, and so your etheric body has finished detaching itself from your physical body and is at present floating around in your office. But it will soon disintegrate."

"Oh. So now do I get to keep this 'emotional body'? I must say, come to think about it, that it has a lot to be said for it. It may look the same as that old one, but it's a lot more flexible!"

"Not only is it more flexible and pain free," replied Roland's mother, "but also you'll find that you can change it at will. At the moment you feel comfortable being Roland aged fifty-four because that's what you've recently been used to, but when you've been here a while you may decide you'd rather go back to how you looked when you were, say, thirty. And of course you might want straight away to change out of that formal suit and wear some clothes that feel more comfortable."

At that point Roland suddenly noticed that both his parents were dressed quite differently from when he had last seen them on Earth. They were wearing gorgeously colored, flowing robes, with bright girdles round their waists; they had jewels in their hair and their feet were bare."

"Change my clothes!" exclaimed Roland. "Are there clothes stores around here, then?"

"No, we don't need stores," laughed his mother. "All you need to do is just think about what you'd like on, and then you'll find yourself wearing it."

"I can't believe that!"

"Well, try."

"OK." Roland remembered the T-shirt that Jennifer had liked so much on the fateful occasion of their last encounter, the trousers that he had chosen so carefully to tone with it, and suddenly his pin stripes and stiff-necked shirt were gone.

"You look much more relaxed like that," said his father. "No wonder Jennifer liked the garb you chose especially for her!"

"How did you know?" gasped Roland.

"You'll soon re-remember," said his mother, "which is how Plato described learning, that we don't need language to talk with up here. We all communicate telepathically."

"What! So you could read my mind just now when I was thinking about the clothes Jennifer liked?"

"Never mind," said his father. "You'll soon get used to it again. But now would you like to go for your Life Review before it's time for the funeral, which I'm sure you won't want to miss? Julia's only just found out that you're dead, but she'll soon be busy preparing things on a grand scale."

"Life Review? That sounds terrifying! My life was a total disaster."

"We all make disasters of some of our lives," said Roland's mother consolingly. "That's how we learn. Your karma with Charles is complete now; there's only Jennifer to whom you still owe a debt."

"What do you mean, my karma's complete?"

"Do you remember that lifetime in Egypt when Charles killed you and then ran off with Jennifer? We were your parents then too. Of course, it would have been better if you hadn't killed Charles – he could eventually have found some other way of paying his debt to you – but you were acting in self-defense; you hadn't actually intended him to die."

"True, but I shouldn't have run off like that and abandoned Jennifer."

"Sure, it was a bit cowardly," said his mother, "but you'll know better next time round. In the meantime you could attend some classes on overcoming cowardice."

"Classes?"

"Oh yes," said his father, "there are schools at all levels here. After a bit you'll be able to teach people who are less evolved than you are, as well as learning from those who are more evolved. But now I think it really is time for your Life Review. Look, here's a handsome wolf come to take you there!"

Roland had had a fascination with wolves all his life. As a child he had always headed for the wolves' den first whenever his parents had taken him to the zoo. For their honeymoon he had taken Julia to Canada and, to her horror, had penetrated high into the Rockies hoping to spy a wolf. So now when the wolf signaled to him telepathically to follow, he trotted off behind it quite happily.

For a while the wolf led Roland up hill and down dale, but to his amazement his feet and legs did not get in the least bit tired. He was enthralled by all that he saw and sensed around him: pretty little cottages with gardens full of roses, geraniums, hollyhocks, foxgloves, some of hues he had never seen on Earth; many flowers to which he could not give a name – he who prided himself on his knowledge of flowers; woods with trees quite unlike any he had seen before; birds, foxes, badgers, deer... "We're at present on the second plane of the astral realms," explained the wolf telepathically. "After your Life Review and then the funeral, you'll probably want to stay here for a while before moving on to a higher plane."

"So what's the first plane like?" asked Roland.

"Oh, that's an exact replica of Earth. That's why people who land there first often take quite a while to realize that they're dead. Ghosts are often people who just go on hanging around the Earth until someone's managed to explain to them that they're no longer in a physical body and need to move on. Another type of ghost is simply an imprint. In places where there have been violent scenes such as a battle, the memory of it goes on playing over and over like a video, and people on Earth with a certain sensitivity can tap into it. You might occasionally want to go back to the lowest astral plane just for fun. Say you fancied a meal out or something. But it's better here really; you can find more variety here."

"A meal out? You mean there are even restaurants?"

"Oh yes! Of course our emotional bodies don't actually need food, but old habits die hard. You businessmen tend to get attached to things like *steak-au-poivre* and Beaujolais, so you don't have to give them up immediately. You can pay a visit to your preferred haunts whenever you want, and order your old favorites – you were always very partial to French fries and ratatouille, weren't you? Even on this, slightly higher, plane, people still go in for things like little tea parties. But look! Now we're coming near to one of the Halls of Learning."

And a more impressive building Roland had never seen. Its white marble glowed with a luminosity such as can never be espied on Earth, and above its Grecian-type pillars were the most exquisitely carved frescoes. He could have just stood gazing at them for hours, but the wolf was leading him inside to one of the far corners. "I'll say 'goodbye' now for the time being. But we'll meet again. I was your totem animal the last time that you were an American Indian. Remember?" A vague memory of a lifetime as a shaman passed through Roland's mind, but was immediately supplanted by the sight of three powerful beings of light, who emanated the most wonderful feeling of love imaginable.

"So you've come for your Life Review?" one of them asked gently.

"What a wasted life it's been!" replied Roland, "just chasing money to try to compensate for not being able to be with the woman I loved; neglecting my family in a vain attempt to escape from Julia's nagging..."

"Well, just sit back in this comfortable seat here and watch your film," said another of the beings of light. "And as you do so, try to notice the good points. The occasions when you sacrificed yourself for others, for instance. Charles' death was an unfortunate mistake, and it would have been good to have given yourself up, but you were sorely provoked. The court would probably have realized that."

"But you've now learnt the lesson that cowardice doesn't pay," said the third being. "By the time of your next incarnation you'll have moved on from there and be more ready again for a lifetime of service. Like the time when you were such an excellent American Indian shaman."

"Oh, I do hope so!" exclaimed Roland. "I'd love to be of service to Jennifer. And my children of course. Even Charles!"

"All that will come in time. Now here's your film starting. Look at that delightful little boy Roland. Look how helpful he is to his mother..."

Tears started to roll down Roland's cheeks as he watched the moving scenes from his childhood. Their flow increased as the story moved on through adolescent troubles, heartbreaks, the huge error of his marriage to Julia (who he thought at the time was the only woman who would have him)...

"You've re-remembered how to weep," said the second powerful being. "That's immense progress already!"

"But what a waste of potential!" sobbed Roland. "If only I'd carried on thinking always of others in the way that I used to think of my mother. I had a good brain too, didn't I?"

"A very good brain. That's why your business was so

successful," said the second being.

"That's why Charles was so jealous of me! It never really had very much to do with Jennifer, because he's never loved her."

"Charles is busy working out his karma back on Earth now. It'll probably take him a few more lifetimes yet, but don't worry about him for the time being. You can, however, be of help to Jennifer. Would you like to serve her as a guide once you've had a while to explore around here and get used to how things work again on these higher planes?"

"That sounds a <u>wonderful</u> idea! But can you explain to me about the different planes? I seem to have forgotten nearly everything."

"Don't worry. It'll all come back soon. I think the best thing for you would be if, after the funeral is over, Green Feather gave you a bit of a guided tour. Green Feather was your wife when you were that shaman. She was one of your guides when you were a child, before things started to go awry. She's thrilled to have you back here again! You'll recognize her; you're members of the same soul family. She actually lives on the mental planes now, so she's having to tone down her vibrations to enable you to see her, but she'll be here in just a moment."

Green Feather embraced Roland, and a host of memories of times when they had been together came flooding back to him. She was dressed in a pretty green robe, which showed off her nut-brown skin and her dark hair and eyes to perfection. "I've come to escort you to your funeral," she said. "You may find it a bit distressing, but once it's over you can let go of Roland's life and enjoy a tour of the realms to which you at present have a passport."

"A passport?"

"You don't need to take that too literally! What I mean is that we progress gradually when we first get back here. The vibrations of Earth are much lower than ours, so someone like you who has only just left them can't be ready straight away for the realms which have the highest vibrations. You remember from your Sunday School days how Jesus said that 'in my Father's house there are many mansions'? Well, you'll find yourself most comfortable among people like me who are old friends, and among those who have reached more or less the same level of evolution as you have. You might want to build a house for yourself and Jennifer on one of the higher planes of the astral realms, but eventually you'll both need to move on to the mental realms, where people don't need houses to live in any more. As you go back to school and then university to carry on learning, your vibrations will become higher and higher, so that you'll find yourself able to face more and more light. If I'd come to you from the mental realms in my normal state, you wouldn't have even been able to see me."

"A house for Jennifer and me sounds wonderful, but I wouldn't be any good at building."

"You don't need to be. In this world we build with thought forms. All you'll need to do is to think of the type of house you'd like and then it will appear. And when Jennifer eventually joins you, she'll be able to make any changes she wants. But your funeral's just starting…"

The funeral was certainly not the sort of occasion Roland would ever like to have to attend again, but he appreciated that it was right for him to be there. Julia's tears were clearly (to him at least) a sham, but seeing his son and daughter genuinely upset was a revelation to him. He had given them so little time in recent years, yet here they were at the elaborate meal afterwards reminiscing with each other and with other relatives about the wonderful things he had done for them when they were little. Suddenly Roland realized just how much he loved them, and so it was hard tearing himself away, but once all the guests had gone, he remembered that Green Feather would be waiting for him.

"Come on, Sitting Bull, you can leave the Earth's plane now.

There's work to do!"

"Sitting Bull?! I'm Roland…Wait a minute…" Roland thought for a moment, then he noticed his skin color change and a handsome American Indian headdress appear on his head.

"You're right to want to dress just as you did when you were my husband. Now we can call on that difficult son of ours, Grey Cloud, and he will recognize you more easily. He's been stuck on the second plane for a while now. It's time he moved on. He was Scottish in his last life and never got over his failures in golf. Now he's having a whale of time because where he is the ball goes in with every single hit!"

"Doesn't that get a bit boring?"

"It does indeed, which is one of the many reasons people find that they want to move on, but Grey Cloud is being slow to get bored. Also, although he was never an alcoholic, he used to enjoy his tot of whisky each evening and is finding it difficult to give that up. It's what the Hindus call the *kamarupa,* you know. Our 'desire body'. The Creator gave it to us as a servant, but so often we let it become our master. While we're still caught in the thrall of the *kamarupa* we can create thought forms of tots of whisky, cups of tea – even strawberries and ice-cream! – and enjoy them on the astral plane just as much as we did on Earth. Grey Cloud has yet to learn that while the *kamarupa* is still enmeshed in his being, it enslaves his mind and body, preventing him from attaining eternal peace."

"And can you teach him that?"

"I keep dropping gentle hints, but in time he will get bored anyway. You see, your Higher Self always ensures your reawakening when the time is right. When he's ready, you could come and lead him on to one of the higher planes that I'm about to re-introduce you to."

They found Grey Cloud so intent on his golf that, after proudly showing them his perfect shot, he seemed to have little interest in pursuing a conversation with them. So, reminding

Roland of the interest he had had in history before work had started to dominate his life, Green Feather took him up to the third astral plane to see some museums. These were so enthralling that Roland did not want to be torn away until Green Feather suggested going to a concert. "Concerts too!" he exclaimed. "I haven't been to a concert for longer than I can remember." So Green Feather gave him a choice and he chose Tchaikovsky, Jennifer's favorite; ("Well, she is such an incurable romantic!"). The standard of the performance far exceeded anything that Roland had ever heard on Earth, and as they wandered on through these higher planes, he became more and more dazzled by the beauty of the buildings, the variety of the trees, fruit, flowers and other plants, and the vibrancy of the colors. Eventually he asked "When's nightfall? I feel as though we've been going for days, not hours. How come I'm not tired?"

"There's no night in these realms," Green Feather laughed, "and no need for sleep either. It's only physical bodies that get tired. Which is just as well, because we have so much to learn here, and when we're ready we have to work as well!"

Green Feather then went on to explain to Roland about some of the different work opportunities that would in due course be open to him, all of which he thought sounded rather exciting, and then she attempted a description of the still higher realms to which he did not yet have a 'passport'. She talked of the work of artists, philosophers, scientists and so on, who carried on with the work that they had been doing on Earth; of *Devas*, who had an important role in the overseeing of developments on Earth that pertain to nature, as well as being wonderful musicians. She talked of the 'second death', which happens when you are ready to progress to the mental realms. "But don't worry about it," she said. "Shedding the emotional body is not painful in the way that shedding the physical body can be."

So Roland was never either unhappy or bored during the period in which Jennifer was finishing her life on Earth. After a bit of a 'holiday' renewing acquaintance with those souls on the higher astral plane to which he belonged, exploring the sights on some of the others, and learning a little bit more about the mental realms, to which he knew he would progress in time, he firstly decided which classes he wanted to attend and secondly tried his hand at a few different jobs. Eventually he decided, as the beings of light had suggested, on the rather difficult task of serving as a guide to Jennifer. That way at least he could be with her a lot of the time, and also begin to prepare himself for paying the large karmic debt that he had incurred to her.

Sophie, Charles and Jennifer's daughter, had, as can well be imagined, anything but a happy childhood. Carted off from pillar to post when her parents wanted her out of the way for whatever reason, and left with any one of a long list of rather unsatisfactory babysitters when they went off socializing in the evenings, her biggest lack besides love while she grew up was security. She had, however, something of her mother's looks, so as an adolescent she was never short of boyfriends. Her parents made no attempt to push her into higher education, and at the age of twenty she met a man a few years older than her who was a fanatical Catholic. Captivated both by her elegant figure and by her obvious need for someone to look after her, Sean soon started taking Sophie along to his parish church, because he would not consider marrying anyone who did not share his Faith. She rapidly found that the Church with its rules and dogma gave her the security she had been seeking all her life, and so she was a very easy convert. Charles and Jennifer, relieved to see her in the hands of a slightly older man with good prospects, were only too happy to pay for a lavish church wedding.

Sophie had three children – Matthew, Arthur and Lucy – and she bent over backwards to give them everything that her own parents had so dismally failed to give her. "But most of important of all," she said to them, "is the Faith. That's what my parents were unable to give me, but now I can thank the Lord for giving it to me through Daddy." Mass every Sunday of course went without saying, but in addition they were dragged to confession at least fortnightly, to weekday mass in the holidays, and to Benediction every Sunday evening. Once they had got into their late teens, all three rebelled. Matthew, who was the best academically, became first a successful scientist and then a complete atheist; Arthur left school early, got into drugs and rapidly became the despair of his parents, while little Lucy, who had always aspired vainly to be a ballet dancer, ran off with first one and then a whole series of 'undesirable' boyfriends.

Arthur was the first to die. At eighteen he found himself forced to admit to being gay, but he dared not tell his parents. After progressing from soft drugs to hard, and at the same time working his way through a series of both jobs and partners, he eventually settled with someone that he really loved, referring to him on the rare occasions that he met his parents simply as his "flat mate". Arthur had never been very much of a bookworm, but Peter, his partner, worked as a librarian and never took anything stronger than cannabis. Determined to get Arthur off the hard stuff, he took him to a clinic, and he also gradually introduced him to literature.

Arthur was making really good progress and had actually held down a new job for four months, when the blow struck: he found that he had contracted AIDS. Peter was as devastated as Arthur himself, but the devastation started them off together on a spiritual search. Peter brought home book after book from the library, and as soon as they had both read *The Tibetan Book of Living and Dying*[2], they decided to go along to their local Buddhist Centre.

The sicker he got, the more ardently did Arthur pursue his studies. He soon realized that he felt a strong affinity with Tibetan Buddhism, and the monk who became his great friend and counselor explained to him that he had probably had many previous lives as a Buddhist. This monk encouraged Arthur in his desire to help other drug addicts and AIDS victims. Arthur gave up his job (which was becoming too physically taxing for him anyway) and, when his strength permitted, threw himself into founding a new AIDS Help Centre. He was surprised at how quickly he came to terms with the thought of his own death, but gradually he became aware of his Life Plan – that he had actually chosen this difficult and painful path not only to pay off a lot of karma, but also so as to be able to shine as an example. He became loved and admired by all who met him at the Centre, and he was able to give real help to a great number of them.

Arthur died very peacefully after a few years, with Peter by his side and his Buddhist monk friend reading to him from the *Bardo Thodol*[3], and when his soul left his wasted body he went straight to the most beautiful hospital imaginable. Surrounded by the most caring nurses and doctors, who healed mainly with color, Arthur's emotional body soon recovered from the harm that the drugs and the AIDS had done to it, and then he rose forthwith to the sixth astral plane, for he was actually quite an evolved soul. There, during his Life Review, he was led to an understanding of the causes of his homosexuality. Firstly, prior to his incarnation as Arthur, he had had a rapid succession of feminine lives, which had made him forget what it was like to have a male body; and secondly his difficult relationship with Sophie, who never understood him at all, had given him a problem in expressing his masculinity. But he realized that this, like the drug addiction that he had so successfully overcome, and the AIDS that he had weathered so courageously, were all useful lessons.

After a little while spent integrating these lessons and absorbing them into his Higher Self, and joining in discussions with scientists who were busy creating blueprints for new discoveries on Earth – Arthur had himself been a prominent scientist in one of his recent feminine incarnations – he moved on to the seventh astral plane. This he found to be the home of many highly evolved *Devas* and also of souls who had been hermits on Earth. Still extraordinarily beautiful, it had no buildings, and was an ideal place for solitude. Arthur became enveloped in a feeling of bliss that he could never have imagined to be possible, and before long he was approached by a wonderful being, who explained to him that he was now ready to progress to the mental realms.

"You will find the second death quite simple," said this radiant being. "All you need do is to fall asleep (similar to the way in which you used to fall asleep on Earth), and when you wake up you will find yourself clothed only in your mental body. Your emotional body will slowly disintegrate, and you will be welcomed by old friends in the same way as you were when you left your physical body." This is indeed exactly what happened, but there are no words available in the English language with which to describe the wonders that Arthur woke up to. He had for long been a great lover of Beethoven and, whereas on the sixth astral plane Arthur had been accustomed to watching the most superb performances of symphonies, piano concertos and quartets, here he found that the moment the thought "Quartet Opus 132" came into his head, this magical work was suddenly being played all around him although no string players were visible. "This really is Heaven!" he exclaimed to himself, but meanwhile, back on Earth...

Sophie and her husband were completely distraught by Arthur's death, but they in no way blamed themselves for it. "We did everything for that child," Sophie moaned. "Brought him up in the Faith, and what did it come to? First drugs, then AIDS, then Buddhism. What have I done to deserve this?" At the funeral, which Arthur's fellow workers at the Help Centre had insisted on organizing, she was amazed at the numbers present and at the good words said about her son, but that did nothing to console her. She went home again and had mass after mass said for him, praying all the while that he had been condemned not to Hell but to Purgatory ("in which case there would at least be hope for him eventually"!).

Matthew, the successful scientist, despised his younger brother, and would not even have bothered to attend the funeral had Sophie, his father, <u>and</u> his wife Madeleine not insisted. He too simply could not understand how such a 'ne-er-do-well' could have attracted such numbers and such eulogies. As for poor Lucy, though she had always felt quite close to Arthur, she was too absorbed in her own problems to give much time to mourning him. Her last boyfriend had cleared off leaving her pregnant, without even giving her a contact number or address, and she had not had the courage to tell her parents about the baby. At the funeral, however, her condition was painfully obvious, and it gave rise to the most almighty row with her parents. "You must never come home with <u>that</u>!" screamed her mother, pointing a finger at the poor girl's belly. "I could never look any of our fellow parishioners in the face again."

Lucy had already decided to keep the baby. After all it was <u>hers</u>, something to treasure, and it would also entitle her to housing benefit. So little Rosalind grew up with no father, no grandparents, but a doting mother who, thanks to her best friend having got involved in such things as crystal healing, spent the money that her parents dutifully continued to send her each birthday and Christmas on self-help workshops. Rosalind was a truly delightful child, Lucy's pride and joy, but soon after her sixth birthday she suddenly contracted meningitis. Within less than a week she was dead, leaving Lucy inconsolable.

Little Rosalind woke up in the astral realms delighted that her headache had gone. The first thing she said was "Where's Mummy? She's going to be really pleased now that I'm feeling so much better!" A kindly lady took her by the hand and said gently "I'll take you to see your Mummy, but you mustn't be upset to see her crying. She's unhappy now because she thinks you've left her, but when she goes to sleep at night she'll be able to join you up here and you'll have a great time together. I'll look after you during the day and show you all sorts of exciting things, and Mummy will look after you when it's nighttime on Earth. That'll be quite a good arrangement, don't you think? And we'll also find a nice man to be a Daddy to you – someone who was your Daddy in a lifetime you had on Earth before you were Rosalind."

And so Rosalind adapted quickly to life on the astral planes, enjoying many of the things of which she had been deprived during her last life. "Can I go swimming?" she asked one day as she and her adoptive mother were wandering by a river. "I always wanted to have swimming lessons, but Mummy said they were too expensive."

"Of course you can," her new mother replied. "Just jump in! You won't have any problem." Fearless, and not stopping to bother her head about not having a bathing costume, Rosalind leapt into the inviting river. She splashed about joyfully for a while and then, to her amazement, found that she could do an excellent breast stroke. On climbing back on to the bank, she exclaimed "I'm not wet! How can that be?"

"Lots of things are different here," her adoptive mother laughed. "You'll be able to explain to Lucy all about it next time you see her! Now, remember how you always wanted a pet? Would you like to go and choose one now?"

Rosalind's delight with her new puppy was equaled only when her father made her a bicycle. "Can I stay here for ever and ever?" she asked one day. "I didn't know that Heaven would be quite as good as this!" But the answer from her adoptive parents was that she had yet to see the very best things, that that time would come eventually, but that she had to be patient. "Because, you see, it'll soon be time for you to go back to Earth. No-one can stay six for ever. You need to grow up, but it will better for you to do that on Earth. You served an important purpose in your life as Rosalind, giving Lucy six years of joy and then helping her to learn to let go, but now you need to start over again and have a much longer life. You need to reach maturity on Earth. But don't worry: we're going to find you a nice family with two parents to care for you, <u>and</u> some grandparents who'll be proud of you…"

Unfortunately for Lucy, she never remembered when she woke up all the interesting things that she had been doing with Rosalind. Of course she was sometimes aware of dreams about her daughter, but these always accentuated her grief when she woke up and realized that Rosalind was still dead. She was a brave soul, however, and her daughter's death had moved her parents to some sort of reconciliation. Though Sophie disapproved violently of Lucy's New-Age friends and prayed earnestly for her daughter's return to the Faith, she persuaded her husband to give her an allowance for some study, and with this Lucy decided to train in reflexology and aromatherapy. On one of her courses she formed a liaison with a new man (the first since Rosalind's father), but he alas turned out to be bi-polar. Lucy then set herself the task of healing him, but all her efforts were vain. One evening she got home to find that he had poisoned himself.

Lucy could not believe her eyes. "God!" she screamed. "If you exist, where the Hell are you? First you take away my Rosalind, my beautiful rose, and now this happens. For Heaven's sake HELP ME!" Lucy lay on the bed too upset for tears, too distraught to think what she should do. "Why, oh why do I have to be all alone?" she howled, but in reply she heard a gentle voice say "You're not alone. I am always with you." She looked up and there, to her astonishment, in the far corner of the room, was a tiny orange-robed figure. He had a massive shock of Afro hair, and his eyes…Oh, his eyes! Lucy knew that she would never forget them. Another second and he was gone, but Lucy was left with an extraordinary feeling of peace. Suddenly she knew deep inside that everything was going to be all right. Calmly she got up from the bed and phoned a doctor. Calmly she made all the funeral arrangements. The friends that she met over the next few days marveled at how well she was coping.

About three weeks later Lucy happened to walk past a shop near Baker Street tube station in London, when suddenly she noticed a large portrait in its window. She could not believe her eyes. There was a picture of the orange-robed man who had appeared in her room on the night of her partner's suicide! Quickly she went inside the shop and began to talk. "Yours isn't the first story like that we've heard," said the assistant. "Sai Baba makes Himself known to those who are ready for Him. You'd better read some of these books. In fact, are you free this evening by any chance? You could come along with me to a meeting…"

And so began Lucy's path to Liberation. The Baba group that she joined gave her much support through her studies, and in due course she built up a successful healing practice. Even her parents were impressed with the results that she was having, and Sophie managed not to voice her horror when their generous birthday check was promptly spent on a trip to India. As time went on Lucy did so well getting clients that her trips to India ceased to be dependent upon the generosity of her parents. Her seventh visit to Puttaparthi was at the time of the festival of Shivaratri, when 'Swami' (as she now affectionately called Him) brought up lingams from inside His body, and to her complete astonishment, she actually saw one emerge, following a long night of meditation and chanting. The reason for her surprise was that she knew that Baba said that those who saw the lingam emerge would not need to be reborn on Earth, and she did not feel herself worthy of such a privilege.

"Why not?" asked the smiling Swami, when Lucy peacefully left her physical body some thirty-five years later. "You have followed My teachings. You have been of service to others. You have had as many lives on Earth as there are leaves on that tree in Regents' Park that you so loved to meditate under. My mission is to bring all My children back home. Welcome! Now you can join Arthur and Roland in helping your grandmother."

Lucy's death occurred, however, some time after her mother Sophie's. And Sophie, despite the disappointment in her own children, did throughout the second half of her life obtain some joy from little Jenny, her only grandchild. Jenny was Matthew and Madeleine's daughter. She had been named for her grandmother because Matthew, despite the scandal and despite deploring her descent into poverty, always maintained something of a soft spot for her. (He was the only member of the family who sent her Christmas presents, and these, though Jennifer's pride would never permit her to confess it to Matthew, sometimes saved her from near starvation.) For the busy, successful Matthew and his materialistic wife Madeleine, a doting grandmother was a very useful baby sitter, and so Jenny was not only taken frequently to mass on a Sunday, she was also enrolled in catechism classes. These she enjoyed, and even after the family moved to a bigger house right outside Sophie's parish, Jenny kept up some of the friendships she had formed there.

Jenny was bright, and she fulfilled Matthew's expectations by obtaining a place at Bristol University. While studying there, her rebellion against her parents (which is a natural part of development for any undergraduate!) took the form of voting Labour and joining the Justice and Peace group at the Catholic Chaplaincy. (Though Sophie and Sean, to whom Jenny dutifully wrote letters occasionally, did not know quite what to make of the former, they were delighted that "the child is attending mass every Sunday"!) On graduating, Jenny went off to do Voluntary Service Overseas in Africa, and for some years after that she tried a number of different jobs and a number of different churches, but the firm foundation of her early years in Sophie's parish always brought her back to Catholicism, though never back to the Conservatism of her family.

Jenny never found relations with her parents easy, but she continued to visit her grandparents whenever she was in Manchester, always endeavoring to avoid religious arguments.

For, though she deplored their narrow-mindedness and anti-ecumenism, she felt that they were not to blame since their views were simply a feature of that generation. When her grandfather died quite suddenly, she was a great support to Sophie. Sophie also received a lot of support from her parish priest and many of her fellow parishioners, and she weathered her few years of widowhood courageously. Her death when it came was not too difficult, confident as she was about going to a well-earned eternal rest.

The first thing that Sophie saw on entering the astral realms (having of course just made her last confession and received the sacrament of the sick) was St. Peter. He was dressed rather as she had expected, was holding an immense golden key, and was flanked on either side by an angel. She nodded to him reverentially as she walked past and sensed that he nodded back to her. She then took a place in a row of pews that she saw in front of her, immediately recognizing Mrs. Jones, who had always argued vehemently against the introduction into their parish of communion under both kinds, and who had died only weeks before her. "It's all right, Sophie. We're not expected to take the wine here, only the host. Oh, and you'll be glad to see too that there are no married priests in Paradise. Nor are there any eucharistic ministers or women readers!"

"Paradise? Is this really Paradise?" asked Sophie, heaving a sigh of relief at having apparently avoided Purgatory.

"Of course it is. Look at all those angels with harps. They've just been giving a concert. I expect there'll soon be another one if you just hang on a bit."

So Sophie hung on. She hung on through the next angelic concert and the one after that. She hung on while the priest who had received her into the Church all those years ago preached another of his lengthy sermons. She hung on while Mrs. Jones and Mrs. Davidson did the flowers on the altar just as they had always done in Manchester. It was all a bit monotonous, but then

Sophie's life on Earth had never known much excitement.

Roland in the meantime had already for some little while been paying regular visits to Jennifer in her self-made Hell, but he was having immense difficulty in getting through to her. She was too absorbed in her misery to be able to see or even hear him, and when she did get an inkling of his presence, she immediately dismissed it as wishful thinking. Arthur, however, now a *Bodhisattva*, resolved to rescue his grandmother before returning to Earth to help others there. In the mental realms he received special training in rescuing people from the Hell realms. He had not of course known Roland in their last incarnation, but they were in the same soul group, and so when they met, Roland recognized him immediately and was very grateful for the offer of assistance. They were then soon joined by Lucy, who was thrilled to see her dear brother again and to be able to introduce him to Sai Baba.

Rescuing Jennifer was not an easy task by any means, but when Arthur and Lucy eventually succeeded in convincing her that Roland actually <u>was</u> in her miserable hovel of a house, standing right in front of her, and that what she was seeing was not the figment of a desperate imagination, she collapsed into his outstretched arms and clung to him like a limpet. She feared that, if she loosened her grasp, he would disappear into oblivion. When, however, she was finally convinced that Roland was not melting away, her upward journey was comparatively plain sailing.

Jennifer nevertheless took a while really to believe in the 'miracle'. "Shouldn't I be going to Purgatory next?" she asked the knowledgeable Arthur, as the four of them were wandering past the most beautiful lake imaginable. "Sophie always used to talk about Purgatory as being the place that everyone went to first unless they were saints. That was, if they weren't wicked enough for Hell."

"Don't you think you already had your Purgatory down there

in Hell?" Arthur replied with a big smile.

"Well, what about the Last Judgment then? If there really is a God, surely He won't think that I'm worthy of Heaven?"

Roland's arm tightened around her waist. "There is a God," he assured her, "but He never passes judgment on us. He is all Love. The only person who will ever judge you up here is you yourself." And so began Jennifer's real learning.

Apart from Lucy, Jenny, and his wife Madeleine, Matthew was the last to die. A convinced atheist to the very end, he simply melted, just as he had expected, into nothingness. Madeleine, who mourned her husband's loss greatly even though she had been prepared for it, began to hope that maybe he had been wrong, that maybe she would one day see him again. So, although she had never been taught to pray, she made an attempt to pray for Matthew. Morning and evening she said silently "Oh God, if you exist, please take care of my dear Matthew, and please bring us back together again." These prayers were all stored in the credit side of her karmic bank account as well as giving real help to Matthew. When she died too, a couple of years later, she did not find Matthew, but she found a few old friends on the second astral plane, and there she was able to go back to quite a good social life in very pleasant surroundings.

With Jennifer thoroughly enjoying life in the lovely house that Roland had built for the two of them, and her learning well under way, the *Bodhisattva* Arthur returned to Earth into a Buddhist family. There, as soon as he was old enough, he began to pray regularly for all those souls who had died in ignorance of their immortality. Some of these prayers were directed, together with the prayers of Jenny for her atheistic father, by evolved beings in quite high realms towards the lost Matthew. So when Jennifer asked after her favorite grandson, she was told that she could join forces with the help that was already available for him. With Roland, she attended some classes on waking people up and, since she had by now learnt all about travel and how to adjust one's vibrations to those on a lower level, the two of them, joined now by Lucy, together all thought "Matthew". Then, lo and behold, they found themselves standing beside his sleeping emotional body. It took quite a few prods, but Matthew's astonishment when he woke up and saw the three of them can easily be imagined. They talked and talked and, once Matthew had been introduced to the astral planes and been through His Life Review, they decided that their next task could be to tackle Sophie.

This again was anything but easy, for the last people that Sophie expected to meet in Paradise were her atheistic son, her 'New Age' daughter, and her unfortunate mother (who had surely been "condemned to Hell for all eternity"!). Nor had she ever met Roland. Once over the shock, however, she agreed to go with them all on a "bit of a tour", because she had begun to think that eternity in Paradise was getting to be a bit tedious. Their first port of call was a church round the corner in the next street. Sophie was amazed when she looked at the notice board outside it – "St. Anselm's Presbyterian Church". "How can there be Presbyterians so close to my own congregation here in Paradise?" she asked in bewilderment. A bewilderment that only increased as they moved on straight past the hymn singing to a Buddhist temple. Inside that they saw maroon-clad monks prostrated in front of a gigantic statue of the Buddha, but rather than letting her linger, they all dragged Sophie on to look at a little Methodist chapel. Finally Sophie could bear it no longer. "I DON'T UNDERSTAND!" she exclaimed, bursting into tears. "Where am I? And where's Jesus? I haven't seen him since I got here!"

"The Master Jesus," explained her mother gently, "lives on a very high plane indeed. People who are still at this level wouldn't be able to withstand his brightness."

"What do you mean – "this level"? Isn't this Paradise? It couldn't be Purgatory because I've seen so many angels, and it certainly isn't Hell because the Devil isn't here."

"Don't worry about the Devil!" said Roland. "The only demons anyone ever has to contend with are human negativity. Up here we're working hard to conquer all that."

"But you will see Jesus in due course," said Jennifer consolingly. "So will all those Presbyterians and Methodists. But the trouble is that at the moment they're all so busy thinking that they're right and everyone else is wrong, that they're the only people in Paradise, that they aren't ready for Jesus' bright light. Like you, ever since they died they've been making thought forms of what they expected to find in Paradise – angels and harps and so on – and they're firmly convinced that it's all real. Even those Buddhist monks we passed think that that big statue of theirs is really the Buddha. They aren't so evolved as your dear son Arthur, but they'll learn too eventually."

"My dear son Arthur – the bane of my life!"

And so began Sophie's learning, which leaves us only with Jenny. Jenny having tried her hand at a number of jobs, finally trained as a social worker. She never married or had a family, but she led a very full and worth while life. She found fulfillment both in her work and also in her Church activities, particularly the Justice and Peace movement, through which she made many good friends. When she died at quite an advanced age, these same friends said many prayers for her and, like her uncle Arthur, she was thus helped to move quite quickly to one of the higher astral planes. Here she soon renewed acquaintance with her grandparents as well as with the great-grandmother for whom she had been named, and Roland. Like them, she gradually became eager to progress to the mental realms, but this she did not do before first toning down her dazzling appearance and visiting her parents. She found that they were having a good time, living in expensive-looking houses, but that they were not together. Each was living happily with a different partner, but they always greeted one another cordially when they met at parties. Jenny realized that her father in particular would in due course have quite valuable work to perform on a higher plane in the scientific field, but she also realized that neither of them was quite ready yet to be persuaded to leave their current lifestyle. She said a quick "Hullo" to each of them, but neither was particularly interested in having much conversation with her, so she returned to her friends on a higher level.

* * *

My tale, as I said, is fictitious, but I have tried to make it fairly comprehensive. One omission is the case of spirits who attach themselves to others, thus remaining Earthbound when the other reincarnates, but this phenomenon has been discussed in earlier chapters. (My teacher, Dr. Roger Woolger has on occasion released whole armies from people who in previous lives had been their commanding generals and still felt responsible for their deaths centuries later!) An alternative scenario for Charles would have been to attach himself to Roland and remain discarnate (and also Earthbound) for much longer. Two things that I hope I have made clear are firstly the fact that death brings no immediate change to our personality, and secondly that we not only should not, but CANNOT judge others. A "down and out" appearance can sometimes mask quite an evolved soul; and vice versa.

In September 1999 my husband and I spent a memorable weekend with the Ananda Community near Assisi. Founded by Swami Kriyananda, the Ananda communities give courses based on the teachings of Paramahansa Yogananda, of whom Swami Kriyananda was a student. It is for me impossible to imagine any place on Earth more suitable for such a Center than the beautiful countryside surrounding Assisi. On the weekend of our visit we were blessed with warm weather, but we also experienced two massive thunderstorms. Walking the eight hundred meters from the house in which we slept to Il Rifugio, the main house, for breakfast on the last morning, I was enthralled by a sky which bore no resemblance to anything I had previously witnessed in my entire life. The torrential rain had fortunately just ceased and the beautiful, gentle mountains, set in St. Francis' much loved woods, and field upon field of fading sunflowers, were plainly visible, if less bright than they had been in the sunshine of the previous day. To our right the sky was a sea of thick grey cloud, but to the left was an amazing Three-D scene consisting firstly of tiny patches of bright blue sky in the background. In front of that, in the middle ground, were clumps of thick, thick cotton wool clouds, each with a silver lining and, in front of them again, in the foreground, were thin wisps of grey cloud. These wisps were being driven at tremendous speed across the whole picture by the wind which had been blowing relentlessly for a solid twenty-four hours. I found it quite difficult to concentrate on walking carefully along the main road as I watched the silver-lined cotton wool clumps disappear and reappear behind the grey wisps. As I watched one particular clump, its lining grew gradually brighter, so that I was forced from time to time momentarily to avert my gaze. I was at the same time very much aware of the solid grey on my right and praying that we would not again get drenched as we had the night before. Being accustomed to English autumns, it did not occur to me that the sun would make its presence felt at all that day. Suddenly, however, in a moment when my eyes were glued to my chosen patch of silver lining, this again grew dazzlingly. Then, as though in a deliberate desire to surprise the world, there burst forth from the cotton wool a bright yellow ball and I, totally unprepared, beheld the sun in its full glory and had of course to avert my eyes instantly.

In some of our incarnations we walk only in the bank of grey cloud which on that day was covering Assisi's mountains to my right, unaware of anything that could be going on on the left. After death at the end of such a lifetime we might remain in the grey before returning to Earth, or we might, with help from other souls (incarnate and/or discarnate) become aware of the silver lining and the God who is its cause. The grey clouds are 'Maya' – the illusion which we have all created for ourselves that Earth is where we belong. In some incarnations we ourselves <u>are</u> the wisps of grey that have no resistance to the wind. The wind is the force of evil – human negativity – which can all too easily gain control and direct the wisps wheresoever it wants. In other incarnations, however, we are the thick banks of cotton wool cloud, more stable, blown too, certainly, but much, much more slowly, and quite often aware of our own silver lining. In many lives we might incarnate and live for a while in the bank of dark grey and then get pushed – often by a traumatic event or a sudden flash of 'divine inspiration' – over to the left where the blue is visible in patches. Or it could be the reverse. The more evolved we become, the more we free ourselves from our karmic debts, the less difficult will it be to escape, at least at times, from the Maya of the dark grey and fix our eyes on the blue, even if the silver is too dazzling for us. Blue is the color of peace and harmony and is therefore a wonderful world in which to live. Jesus at the moment of his Transfiguration gave two of his apostles a tiny glimpse of the source of his silver lining. Krishna as a child was accused of eating soil and, when requested by his foster mother to open his mouth so that she could see whether this was true, revealed to this awed beholder a vision of the universe. A very similar story is told of Sai Baba of Shirdi, the previous incarnation of the present-day Indian avatar Sathya Sai Baba. The latter explains that in coming to Earth He had to take on an ordinary human form because with our present limitations we would be unable to cope with anything else. But Sathya Sai Baba has from time to time over the years given to some of His devotees little tiny glimpses of His true self.

If we work hard during each sojourn that we have on Earth to focus on the blue sky (however small the patches may be), bringing through service to our fellows the peace and harmony that is everyone's right, fewer and fewer and shorter and shorter will become the periods in which we are immersed in the grey. Gradually will our awareness of the silver linings that are to be found, not only around the clumps of cotton wool but even behind the banks of grey, increase, and gradually, as our eyes become more accustomed to the brightness, we will be less dazzled and thus able to focus our gaze for longer. Eventually not only will we be able to look straight at the sun, but we will realize that we also ARE that sun. Then, and only then, on returning to the high level which is our True Home, will we be given the choice either to stay there permanently, or once again to clothe ourselves in physical bodies with the sole purpose of returning to Earth to guide, like Yogananda and the other Masters, those left behind along the path back home. In the meantime, may the Lord bless us all on a 'bon voyage'!

Notes

1 *Journey of a Soul*, Peter Richelieu, Thorsons, London, 1996.
2 *The Bardo Thodol* is known erroneously in English as *The Tibetan Book of the Dead*, and is translated by Evans-Wentz
3 *The Tibetan Book of Living and Dying*, Sogyal Rinpoche, Rider, London, 1992.

EXERCISES

1 You are probably already a believer in something other than the material world, or you would not have got to the end of this book. Are you, however, clear in your own mind about where you are heading for? If not, I recommend some more reading, and there is a bibliography appended.
2 All the Masters say that how we die and carry on after death depends upon how we have lived our life. So a periodic review is always a good idea. In fact spiritual teachers normally recommend doing this daily. Offering oneself and

one's actions to God first thing in the morning and last thing before going to sleep only takes a moment and is an excellent habit to get into.

3   If you have not yet read Sogyal Rinpoche's *The Tibetan Book of Living and Dying*, DO SO. You do not need to be a Buddhist for it to be relevant.

BIBLIOGRAPHY

Death, Transition and the Spirit Realms: Insights from Past Life Therapy and Tibetan Buddhism, *a paper by Roger J. Woolger, Ph.D., 1998, Woolger Training International, P.O. Box 8187, Silver Spring, Maryland 20910, USA.*

Life in The World Unseen, A Detailed Description of the Afterlife given to Medium Anthony Borgia from Monsignor Hugh Benson, *Two Worlds Publishing Co. Ltd.. London, 1997.*

Récits d'un Voyageur de l'Astral, Terre d'Emeraude, Les Neuf Marches *and* Chronique d'un Départ, *Anne and Daniel Meurois-Givaudan,* Editions Amrita, France.

BETWEEN DEATH AND LIFE: Conversations with a Spirit, Dolores Cannon, Gateway Books, Bath, 1996.

LIGHT BEYOND THE DARKNESS – The Healing of a Suicide Across the Threshold of Death by Doré Deverell, published by Temple Lodge, London.

Divine Intervention by Hazel Courteney, Cima Books, London, 1999.

Testimony of Light by Helen Greaves, C.W. Daniel, Saffron Walden, 1985. (First published in 1969.)

Life After Life and *The Light Beyond* by Dr. Raymond Moody (Bantam but currently out of print).

REUNIONS – Visionary Encounters with Departed Loved Ones, Dr. Raymond Moody, Ivy Books, New York.

THE TRUTH IN THE LIGHT – An Investigation of over Three Hundred Near-Death Experiences by Peter and Elizabeth Fenwick, Headline.

HEADING TOWARD OMEGA – In Search of the Meaning of a Near-Death Experience, Kenneth Ring, William Morrow.

LESSONS FROM THE LIGHT – What can we learn from Near-Death Experiences?, Kenneth Ring, Perseus Books.

Embraced by the Light, Betty Eadie, Thorsons, London

Saved by the Light and *At Peace in the Light*, Dannion Brinkley, Piatkus, London

Closer to the Light and *Transformed by the Light*, Dr. Melvyn Morse with Paul Perry Piatkus, London.

ORDERED TO RETURN – My Life After Dying, George G. Ritchie, Hampton Roads, Charlotesville VA, 1998.

The After Death Experience, Ian Wilson, Corgi.

DEATH'S DOOR – True Stories of Near-Death Experiences, Jean Ritchie, Michael O'Mara Books Ltd., London, 1994.

Life After Death and the World Beyond, Jenny Randles and Peter Hough, Piatkus, London.

Eternal Ties – The Reality Behind Relationships, Graham Bernard, Destiny Books, Vermont, 1990.

Journey of Souls, Dr. Michael Newton, Lllewellyn, Minnesota, 1995.

Life Between Life, Dr. Joel Whitton and Joe Fisher, Grafton, London, 1987.

THE STORY OF EDGAR CAYCE – There is a River, Thomas Sugrue, ARE Press, Virginia, 1997.

Many Mansions, Gina Cerminara, Signet, New York, 1978.

Holiday in Heaven by Aron Abrahamsen, Aron and Doris Abrahamsen, Ozark Mountain Publishing, Inc., USA.

The Country Beyond, Jane Sherwood, C. W. Daniel, Essex, 1991.

Children's Past Lives, Carol Bowman, Element, Dorset, 1998.

Deja Who?, Judy Hall, Findhorn Press, Scotland, 1998.

SOULS UNITED – The Power of Divine Connection, Ann Merivale, Llewellyn, 2009.

TWIN SOULS – A Guide to finding your True Spiritual Partner by Patricia Joudry and Maurie D. Pressman (Element Books).

Twin Souls and Soulmates, Channelled from St. Germain through Azena Ramanda and Claire Heartsong (Triad, Australia).

An Artist's Life After Death by Kenneth Butler Evans (Ken Evans Prints, Devon).

The Wheel of Life by Elisabeth Kubler-Ross (Bantam Press).

Dead Happy by Lance G. Trendall (Lance Trendall Publishing).

A Child of Eternity by Adriana Rocha and Kristi Jorde (Piatkus).

The Soul and its Mechanism by Alice Bailey (Lucis Press Ltd., London).

COMING HOME – The Experience of Enlightenment in Sacred Traditions by Lex Hixon (Larson Publications).

VOICES FROM HEAVEN – Communion with Another World by Stephen O'Brien (Aquarian Press).

Astral Travel for Beginners by Richard Webster, Llewellyn.

From One World to Another by Rita Rogers, Pan Macmillan, London.

6th Books, investigates the paranormal, supernatural, explainable or unexplainable. Titles cover everything included within parapsychology: how to, lifestyles, beliefs, myths, theories and memoir.